SEX, DEATH & OYSTERS

SEX, DEATH

&

OYSTERS

A HALF-SHELL LOVER'S WORLD TOUR

ROBB WALSH

COUNTERPOINT

BERKELEY

Library of Congress Cataloging-in-Publication Data

Walsh, Robb, 1952-
Sex, death, & oysters : a half-shell lover's world tour / Robb Walsh.
p. cm.
ISBN-13: 978-1-58243-457-5
ISBN-10: 1-58243-457-3
1. Cookery (Oysters) 2. Oysters—United States. I. Title. II. Title: Sex, death, and oysters.

TX754.O98W35 2009
641.6'94—dc22

2008035704

Cover design by Kimberly Glyder
Interior design by Megan Cooney
Printed in the United States of America

COUNTERPOINT
2117 Fourth Street
Suite D
Berkeley, CA 94710

www.counterpointpress.com

Distributed by Publishers Group West

10 9 8 7 6 5 4 3 2 1

For my little pearl, Ava Maeve Walsh

CONTENTS

SEX, DEATH & OYSTERS

ONE

The Texas Shell Game

GALVESTON BAY WAS CALM, the sky was blue, and the water temperature hovered at sixty degrees—perfect oyster weather. I stood on the deck of the *Trpanj*, a typical Texas oyster lug. Wide across the middle with a huge foredeck, it looked like a barge with an upturned nose. The captain steered from a wheel set up front where he could see the dredge, a five-foot metal-rake-and-net contraption that he dragged across the bottom of the shallow bay.

With a belch of exhaust and a roar like a tractor trailer entering the highway, a powerful diesel motor spun a spool of cable that hauled up the dredge full of oysters and debris. The dredge swung on its chain, and two Mexican deckhands balanced it on a metal frame welded to the side of the deck before tipping its contents onto a worktable. The deckhands sorted the "keepers" out of the gray jumble. Then they shoved the empty shells and undersized oysters back overboard and dropped the dredge again.

The *Trpanj* is owned by oysterman Misho Ivic and named after his home village in Croatia. Misho's son Michael had agreed to take me out on the oyster boat and show me how the dredging business worked. I studied a map of the Galveston Bay oyster reefs from the bow. There are four categories in Galveston Bay, Michael explained, pointing to them on the map.

The "prohibited" reefs are close to shore. They are closed to oystering due to the wastewater runoff they get from suburban lawns, cow pastures, and other possible sources of contamination. "Conditional" areas are open to fishing most of the time, but the game wardens rule them off-limits after heavy rains because of the runoff. "Open" oyster reefs are the public reefs that are open throughout the season. And "leased" areas are private oyster reefs.

Michael grabbed a dripping oyster from the pile of keepers on the deck, pried off the top shell and handed it to me. Shocked by its sudden exposure to the air, the oyster's delicate lips contracted almost imperceptibly. I tilted it back and slurped the wet flesh into my mouth, chewing slowly. The flavor was salty, a little metallic, and surprisingly sweet.

Eating raw oysters is at once perverse and spiritual. A freshly shucked oyster enters your mouth while it is still alive and dies while giving you pleasure. As I savored the wonderfully slick texture, delicate briny flavor, and marine aroma, it was easy to see how oysters came to be associated with the tenderest portion of the female anatomy.

But since oysters from the waters of Galveston Bay carry a common bacteria that kills a few people every year, I also found myself contemplating my mortality as I swallowed. It's quite an exciting thing to put in your mouth, a meek and vulnerable living being brimming with bold seafood flavors, vivid sexual fantasies—and the threat of death.

For the last twenty years, oysters have been making a comeback on the American food scene. And as a food writer living in one of the nation's largest oyster-producing states, I was keen on learning more about them. With my camera and notebook constantly in hand, I asked a lot of questions.

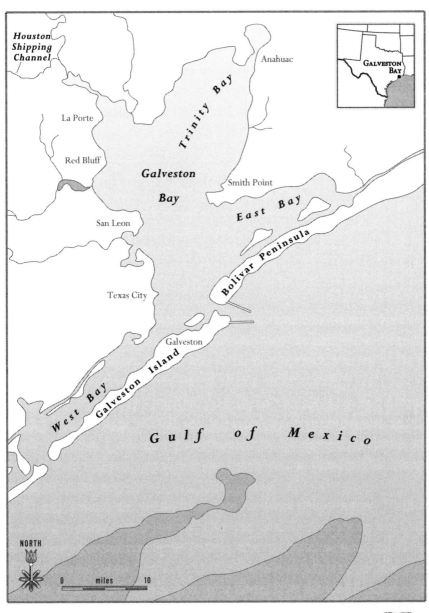

Houston
Shipping
Channel

Anahuac

GALVESTON
BAY

La Porte

Trinity Bay

Red Bluff

Galveston

Smith Point

Bay

East Bay

San Leon

Bolivar Peninsula

Texas City

Galveston

West Bay *Galveston Island*

G u l f   o f   M e x i c o

NORTH

0   miles   10

Galveston Bay, Texas

Ivic and the oystermen on the *Trpanj* regarded me as an earnest idiot. As would the oystermen I interviewed in New York, California, Washington State, England, France, and the rest of the oyster-producing world.

The tried-and-true formula for writing about oysters is to go find colorful oystermen and copy down their stories. You go out on a boat or visit an oyster farm and eat some quivering mollusks on the spot, rave about your intense perception of *terroir* (or "merroir," as the marine version of this poetic sense of place is sometimes known). And then you quote the oysterman on the important facts to know about oysters.

I attempted to employ this formula myself. But it didn't work out. In the five years it's taken me to write this book, I asked too many questions. I never lost my passion for oysters. But I did lose my innocence. I learned that terroir, or merroir, or whatever you call it, is a very flexible concept—and that most of what oystermen have to say about oysters is malarkey.

I was eager and clueless when I climbed aboard the *Trpanj* in December of 2003 to write my first article about oysters for the *Houston Press*, a weekly owned by the *Village Voice* chain. I called my feature "Sex, Death & Oysters," just the sort of racy title an alternative weekly editor loves. I wrote about the oysters' reputation as an aphrodisiac, and did a little investigative work on why tainted Texas oysters seemed to be killing people. It was mainly a good excuse to go for a ride on an oyster boat and eat a lot of oysters.

I thought pollution would be a good angle. The waters of Galveston Bay that I could see were a frightening shade of mud brown. To our southwest, a line of rusty oil tankers were steaming in from the Gulf of Mexico, proceeding north through the Bay and up the shipping lane toward the Houston Ship Channel. Lots of toxins are found in the sediment out in the Gulf of Mexico. Surely there were some environmental hazards to expose in Galveston Bay.

But I never did find any. The murkiness, or "turbidity," as scientists call it, came from suspended sediments and plankton. "The Adriatic is beautiful blue," Croatian-born Misho Ivic told me, "but there's nothing living in it. It's sterile. Galveston Bay looks muddy because the water is full of food. Good for the oysters, good for the crabs."

I didn't trust him, of course. East Coast and West Coast oystermen say that the waters of the Gulf of Mexico are filthy. And maybe they are. But oysters live in brackish water in freshwater estuaries, not in the Gulf of Mexico. And the scientists I interviewed said that Galveston Bay was in pretty good shape.

"We always fight the perception that the bay is polluted, but the reality is that the water quality overall is good," Scott Jones, water and sediment quality coordinator for the Galveston Bay Estuary Program, told me. He said dissolved oxygen levels have gone up markedly in the last thirty years thanks to a cleanup of wastewater treatment plants mandated by the Clean Water Act of 1972.

Misho Ivic and a marine biologist named Dr. Sammy Ray put pollution into a historical perspective for me by comparing Galveston Bay to Chesapeake Bay. Chesapeake Bay produced millions of bushels of oysters in the 1800s, before it was polluted. It now produces about 1 percent of its historic peak. Conservationists in Maryland and Virginia are making progress and the oyster harvests are increasing, but since the surrounding wetlands were long ago destroyed, the long-term prospects are limited.

In 1900, Galveston Bay and a couple of other small bays in Texas produced a record 3.5 million pounds of oyster meat. But modern harvests regularly exceed that. In 2003, the largest harvest of oysters ever

recorded was taken—6.8 million pounds, nearly double what was produced at the turn of the century.

New York Harbor and Chesapeake Bay lost their oysters due to
industrial pollution. Galveston Bay is at its historic peak production.
In 2003, Misho Ivic's oyster company alone outproduced the entire
Chesapeake Bay.

The *Trpanj* turned in endless circles as it dredged the bottom. The average depth of the bay is only around eight feet. When we were heading
due north, I saw dozens of oyster boats to the east. They were dredging
the massive oyster reef in the middle of the bay that's open to fishing by
anyone with a license.

The oysters were plentiful, and spirits were high. But things turned
suddenly somber when a Texas Parks and Wildlife patrol boat pulled
up alongside and two uniformed game wardens jumped aboard. Game
Warden Bobby Kana came forward wearing wraparound sunglasses and
a tough-guy frown.

The Texas Parks and Wildlife Department polices the oyster-fishing
business. Everybody knows the rules. But the unprecedented number of
oyster boats working Galveston Bay that season put tremendous pressure
on the system. Nerves were frayed, and there was tension between the
locals and boats from other waters. The out-of-state boats are licensed to
work on the 22,760 acres of public oyster reefs. On the *Trpanj*, we were
working one of Misho's leases.

There are 2,371 acres of private oyster leases in Texas. Leaseholders
pay the state an annual fee for the exclusive rights to an underwater plot
that had no existing oysters. The lessor must create his own oyster reef by

dumping "cultch." Pottery shards, mussel shells, and suspended branches have all been used as cultch over the centuries, but in Texas, cultch means empty oyster shells. Oyster companies with shucking operations, such as Misho's Oyster Company, generate tons and tons of them. By dumping the empty shells, they create new oyster reefs.

"Captain, do you have a permit to be on this lease?" Warden Kana asked. We were fishing on one of Misho's Oyster Company's leases, and the game wardens recognized Misho's boat. But Ivic didn't have the right paperwork, and some of the buoys that should have marked the lease were missing. Kana produced a strange, square, C-shaped contraption and started using it to measure the oysters in the pile on deck. I introduced myself and asked him what was going on.

"It's Misho's boat and Misho's oyster lease, right?" I asked the game warden.

"Yeah, but the permit hasn't been filed," the officer explained. "And the lease is not properly marked."

"Are the oysters the right size?" I asked.

"Most of them are okay," he said. He held up an offender that slipped through the measuring device. If the game warden determines that more than 10 percent of the catch is undersized, they will order the oysters to be dumped overboard. "Two-and-a-half-inch oysters are very popular for oysters on the half shell," Kana told me. "But anything under three inches is illegal in Texas."

Because of the violations regarding the lease, the game warden ordered all of the *Trpanj*'s oysters dumped overboard anyway and fined the boat $250.

"You must be having a busy day," I observed, looking out over the Bay. "I've heard that there are 430 oyster boats working Galveston Bay this year."

"That's about right," the warden confirmed. In Louisiana, oyster-men were having trouble finding oysters, so they brought their boats to Galveston Bay, where everybody was limiting out.

Everyone involved agrees that the Texas oyster fishery is sadly mis-managed. Texas oysters are the sweetest in January and February, when the water is coldest. But there aren't many oysters left on the pub-lic reefs by then. When the season opens on November first, there's a four-hundred-boat free-for-all, and the Texas oyster reefs are quickly scraped bare.

The problem is, the game wardens at the Texas Parks and Wildlife Department aren't in a position to come up with a better oyster manage-ment plan. Their job is to enforce the law. "Texas oystermen are coming to us and asking us to help them save the oyster reefs," said the depart-ment's Lance Robinson. "But there is nothing we can do."

And so far, no state, federal, or local government entity, no fisher-men's association or marketing group, has come up with a policy to man-age the Texas oyster fishery.

I also asked Dr. Ray about the long-term prospects of the wild oys-ters in Galveston Bay. Oyster reefs locate themselves where freshwater and saltwater meet. Oysters themselves can tolerate fairly high salinity, Dr. Ray explained; in fact, high salinity is desirable during the mating season. But oyster predators—mainly oyster drills, starfish, and a micro-organism called dermo—live in saltwater. So you need a steady supply of freshwater to keep the salinity down and the pests away.

We're dependent on the survival of our coastal wetlands for a steady supply of freshwater. "If you want to save the oysters in Galveston Bay," Dr. Ray said, "people in Houston need to stop building in the flood plain."

❖

After my ride on the *Trpanj*, I came back frequently to buy oysters fresh off the boat. Hanging around on the docks, I watched the boats come in and unload their oysters. And I saw a steady stream of tractor trailers loaded with Galveston Bay oysters headed out for Florida and Maryland, among other places.

Places that were famous for their oysters one hundred years ago, like Chincoteague Bay, Maryland, and Blue Point, Long Island, aren't the centers of oyster production anymore. But people still clamor to buy oysters with famous names, so oystermen engage in a "shell game," if you'll pardon the pun.

Texas oysters make great stunt doubles. They're sold as "Blue Points" in many oyster bars across the country. They're also served in Washington, D.C., and Maryland oyster bars, where people assume they're eating Chesapeake Bay oysters. It's the public that's deceiving itself, the oystermen will tell you.

I once asked the waiter at a Houston chain restaurant called Willie G's where the oysters came from. Hilariously, he told me the oysters I was eating were Blue Points from Long Island. I asked him to bring me the bag tag.

By federal law, oysters must be packaged with a tag stating their place of origin and date of harvest. This allows health authorities to trace the origin of the oysters in case they cause any illnesses. Oyster bars aren't required to show the tag to customers, but if they refuse, it's usually because they're trying to put one over on you.

While the waiter went to get the tag, I slurped down an oyster and studied the bottom inside of the empty shell as if I were divining some hidden information. I bet my tablemate five bucks the oysters came from Galveston Bay. That was some easy money.

Check out the statistics on commercial oyster landings and you can probably win a few wagers yourself.

Oyster Production
(National Marine Fisheries Service)

The commercial landings data for oysters are supplied to the NMFS by state authorities. The totals include commercial fishing and aquaculture sources for shucked oysters as well as half-shell oysters.

Annual totals for 2003 (pounds of oyster meat)

By Region:

1. Gulf Coast	27 million
2. Pacific Coast	11.5 million
3. East Coast	2.8 million

Top Ten Oyster Producing States:

1. Louisiana	13,608,565
2. Washington	9,391,479
3. Texas	6,813,469
4. Mississippi	4,042,136
5. Florida	1,752,848
6. California	1,216,965
7. Oregon	823,121
8. Alabama	815,530
9. New Jersey	713,928
10. New York	466,117

❖

In March 2004 I drove down to Gilhooley's Raw Bar, an oyster bar in the village of San Leon, to interview Misho Ivic and Dr. Sammy Ray again to wrap up the "Sex, Death & Oysters" article.

"Raw" describes the San Leon oyster shack in more ways than one. The building is made entirely of salvaged materials. When it rains, the roof leaks. The parking lot is paved with oyster shells, and there are usually a few Harleys parked in front. There's a sign on the door that says NO CHILDREN, and one above the bar that says SHOW US YOUR TITS.

I sat down at the table where Ivic and Ray were already seated and ordered a dozen on the half shell. They came on a beer tray under a jumble of ice cubes. On top of the oysters sat a red-and-white paper container like the ones used for French fries. This one contained a half sleeve of Saltines, a lemon cut into wedges, and a clear plastic cup full of cocktail sauce. Tabasco sauce and an assortment of other Louisiana pepper sauces were arrayed on the table.

I asked Dr. Ray what made the winter oysters taste so good and if there was any truth to the "never eat oysters in a month without an R" wisdom. That's when I got my first tutorial in the life cycle of the oyster. It was the most useful information about oysters I'd ever been given.

When water temperatures get colder at the end of the summer, oysters begin storing a carbohydrate compound called glycogen, Dr. Ray explained. To humans, glycogen tastes like sugar. As the water gets colder, more glycogen accumulates, and the oysters get plumper and taste sweeter. Gulf oysters are at their absolute peak at the coldest part of the winter.

With the onset of warmer water temperatures in April, oysters begin to convert glycogen to gonad (reproductive material). As the summer approaches and temperature rises, the oyster progressively loses its sweetness, becoming more and more "fishy" tasting. It's not an unpleasant flavor—in fact many oyster lovers like it—but it isn't sweet.

In early summer, when the oyster is spawning, it becomes slimy and produces a white milky substance that almost no one wants to eat.

When they spawn, Gulf oysters secrete sperm and eggs into the water. These combine to produce millions upon millions of larvae. Most of the tiny swimming larvae are consumed by predators or fall to the ocean floor and die. Those that find a hard surface to attach to (like an empty oyster shell) become oyster spat. (Spawning oysters were once said to "spit" their larvae into the water, hence the name spat.)

In late summer, after spawning, oysters lose much of their body weight and nearly all of their flavor. They appear deflated and flat. When the water begins to cool again, the cycle starts over.

Summer is also the time of year when bacteria are a problem. Winter, when oysters taste best, is when they are safest to eat. The "months without an R" saying came from Northern Europe. But the seasons are different in the Gulf of Mexico.

When I set out to write this book, I knew I'd be eating oysters by the thousands. Since I didn't want to die in the process, I called Gary Heideman of the Seafood and Aquatic Life Group at the Texas Department of State Health Services and asked him how to eat lots of raw oysters and survive.

"Even though *Vibrio vulnificus*, the potentially deadly bacteria found in Gulf oysters, has no effect on most healthy people, there is always some risk," Heideman told me. "But you can improve your odds."

When the water temperature at the point of collection is below sixty-five degrees, little or no *Vibrio vulnificus* is detectable, he said. In Galveston Bay, the water temperature stays below sixty-five degrees from about Christmas through Easter. (After talking to Heideman, I started checking the exact temperature in the marine section of the weather report.)

I eat raw Gulf oysters in the winter when the cold water makes them sweet and the bacteria is scarce. In the fall and spring, I eat raw oysters from colder water and cooked Gulf oysters. In the summer, when a raw oyster is most likely to harbor harmful bacteria and has little flavor or substance left anyway, I stop eating oysters altogether.

I used to make an exception for sterile oysters called triploids from Northern waters. But thanks to global warming, another harmful bacteria, *Vibrio parahaemolyticus*, appears to be moving farther northward. Raw shellfish consumed in the warm summer months have sickened people in Washington State and even as far north as Alaska.

The people who are the most adamant about summer oysters being perfectly safe tend to be the people who make money selling them, like oyster farmers and oyster bar owners. The risks really aren't that great, but neither are the rewards. Summer oysters, like winter tomatoes, are out-of-season foods. I have quit eating oysters in the summer, no matter where they come from. You can make up your own mind.

> *"It is unseasonable and unwholesome in all months that have not an R in their name to eat an oyster."*
> —Samuel Butler, 1599

I sure wish the shuckers at Gilhooley's would stop piling chlorine-flavored ice cubes on top of the oysters, I told Ivic and Dr. Ray. I brushed the ice cubes to the side and selected a medium-sized victim. I ate it without any condiments and savored the sweetness.

Dr. Ray had one fact he wanted me to be clear about. "*Vibrio vulnificus*, the bacteria that's killing people, has nothing to do with pollution." It's a point that journalists all over the country have repeatedly gotten wrong, he said.

The idea that pollution is the cause of oyster-borne illnesses is deeply rooted in the collective consciousness—with good reason.

Oysters contaminated by sewage have caused numerous typhoid epidemics over the years. The worst was in 1924, when 1500 people were sickened and 150 died in Chicago, New York, and Washington, D.C. In 1925, the surgeon general responded to the public uproar over contaminated oysters by creating the National Shellfish Sanitation Program, which in turn gave birth to the Interstate Shellfish Sanitation Conference. The ISSC oversees the system of tagging bags of oysters to identify where they come from in order to quickly respond to oyster-borne illnesses.

But *Vibrio vulnificus*, which was first identified in the 1970s, is a different sort of problem. Bag tags won't help, because *Vibrio vulnificus* is everywhere. It's a naturally occurring bacteria that multiplies in warm seawater. So in the hottest part of the summer, the amount of *Vibrio* in the water is extremely high. And if oysters harvested in the summer aren't properly refrigerated, the bacteria level in them can climb even higher. It's not peculiar to oysters, either. You can contract a *Vibrio vulnificus* infection while swimming at the beach with an open sore.

The thing is, very few people are susceptible to *Vibrio vulnificus*, and most of the ones who are will experience only a mild stomach disorder after eating oysters with a high *Vibrio* content. But it can be lethal for "at-risk groups," including people with severe liver damage, diabetes, or other diseases.

Antacid users have recently been added to the at-risk groups. A team of researchers at Mississippi State University built a model of the human stomach and introduced oysters containing *Vibrio vulnificus* to try to understand what happens to the bacteria in the human gut. They found that while stomach acids usually were enough to kill much of the bacteria, some common medications changed the equation radically. When the researchers added antacids to the model stomach, the bacteria quickly grew to a level ten times higher than without antacids.

Some oyster experts are predicting that the problems caused by summer oysters will soon be resolved, not by the FDA or the oystermen, but by the insurance industry. "The handwriting is on the wall," Lance Robinson, of Texas Parks and Wildlife, told me. At the most recent meeting of the ISSC in Texas, oystermen were warned that insurance companies may stop writing liability policies for restaurants that serve raw oysters in the summer.

"He's right," Misho Ivic agreed. "Some kind of law is going to be passed that allows only post-harvest treated oysters to be sold in the summer. I am building a facility to freeze oysters for summer sales right now."

I won't be eating any of Misho's frozen oysters. Post-harvest treated oysters are the Gulf oyster industry's favorite new product, a half-shell oyster that is safe to eat all year round. I have sampled them all, the frozen, pressurized, and heat-treated varieties, and I can say with some authority—they all suck. Dead oysters just don't taste the same.

I would rather wait until the winter and eat big fat oysters like the ones sitting on the table at Gilhooley's. "How did you like the oysters?" Misho asked as I finished off the last of them. The oysters were absolutely succulent, big and fat, with a flavor that was both salty and very sweet. "I picked them out myself," he said. Gilhooley's is Misho's favorite hangout, so they get his choicest oysters.

I was still savoring the flavor as I drove home. And I kept turning the story over in my head: a record oyster harvest a few miles from the Houston Ship Channel, of all places. And hardly anyone seemed to know a thing about it. Newspaperman that I am, I wondered if there were more oyster stories out there waiting to be discovered.

That's how I got hooked.

TEXAS OYSTER STEW

"I like my oyster stew to be mostly oysters with a little milk, not a bowl of milk with a couple oysters," says Dr. Sammy Ray. Here's his recipe.

   16 fluid ounces (1 pint) shucked oysters and their liquor
   ½ teaspoon sea salt
   ½ teaspoon pepper
   Dash of cayenne pepper
   ½ cup milk or half-and-half
   2 tablespoons butter, cut into pieces
   Soda crackers
   Tabasco sauce

Pour the oysters, including all of the liquid, into a large soup pot, and add about ½ cup of water. Season with salt, pepper, and cayenne. Bring nearly to a boil and turn down to a simmer. Cook until the oyster gills curl. Add the milk and heat over medium until hot, but do not allow to boil. Stir in the butter. Serve in a soup bowl with an extra pat of butter on top. Crumble soda crackers into the bowl while you eat and add Tabasco sauce to taste.

Makes one big bowl.

TEQUILA OYSTER SHOOTER

Turning an oyster cocktail into a bar shot is as easy as pouring a shot of tequila. This tangy cocktail tastes best ice cold. For best results, stash your tequila bottle in the freezer overnight before you make an oyster shooter.

   1 freshly shucked oyster, cold
   1 tablespoon hot sauce

Pinch of horseradish
Squeeze of lime
1 ounce chilled Herradura Silver tequila
Dash of tomato juice

Shuck the oyster into a double shot glass or small juice glass. Season with the hot sauce, horseradish, and lime juice. Add the cold tequila. Add a little tomato juice if desired and slurp immediately.

Serves one.

FRIED OYSTER NACHOS

This is a favorite appetizer all over the state of Texas. Oyster nachos were invented by Austin chef David Garrido; the recipe first appeared in the 1995 cookbook we co-authored, *Nuevo Tex-Mex*.

Peanut oil, for frying
12 fresh raw oysters
Buttermilk, for dredging
Flour, for dredging
12 large tortilla chips (round shape preferred)
½ cup salsa

Pour oil in a small skillet to a depth of one inch and heat to 375° F. Put the buttermilk and flour into two shallow bowls. Soak the oysters in buttermilk, then dip them in flour. Fry each oyster for 45 seconds to one minute, or until lightly brown. Transfer the oysters to paper towels to drain. Put a teaspoonful of salsa on each chip, then a fried oyster. Serve immediately.

Makes twelve nachos.

TWO

Going At It Forks and Tongs

Shortly after my oyster-boat excursion in Galveston Bay, I attended a holiday party in the Montrose, a hipster neighborhood in central Houston, where I ended up in a discussion with two women, both relative newcomers to Space City. One woman was from San Francisco; the other was from Cleveland. They were complaining about the less-than-pristine beaches of nearby Galveston Island and the disgusting waters of the Gulf of Mexico.

"How could anybody swim in the oil blobs and Styrofoam floating in that ugly brown water," the one from San Francisco asked. I smiled and shook my head amiably. Personally, I swim in that water every summer, and I have marinated my children in it for most of their lives. But if Galveston was too unsightly for the newcomers' beach-going tastes, well then, "bless their hearts," as we say in Texas.

I didn't bother pointing out to Miss San Francisco that only blubbery seals and surfers in wetsuits are insulated enough to venture into the icy waters of the Pacific around San Francisco. Nor did I bother reminding

Miss Cleveland that the Cuyahoga River is legendary among pollution watchers for its tendency to burst into flames.

"And who would eat oysters that come out of that water?" the San Franciscan continued. Suddenly, I felt my jaw muscles tighten and my stomach contract. Newly informed about Texas oysters, I had a strange need to defend them.

"I would," I volunteered. "But actually the oysters don't come from the Gulf, they come from Galveston Bay. In fact, it's one of the most productive oyster reefs in America at the moment. And the oysters are fabulous this year."

"Where is Galveston Bay?" the San Franciscan wanted to know.

"It's between Kemah on the west and Anahuac on the east," I attempted to explain, but she had no idea where I was talking about. "You know where the ships enter the Houston Ship Channel?" I continued helpfully.

"Oh, gross," remarked a vegetarian woman who was listening in on the edge of the conversation. "So you think all those chemicals spewing out of the oil tankers give the oysters a special flavor?" Cornered now by skeptics, I felt my adrenaline begin to flow.

I still had the Texas Parks and Wildlife oyster map in my car. I considered going out to get it.

"What I resent is that I can't get good oysters in Houston because they have so many cheap ones here," the Californian said. "Gulf oysters are big and tough. I don't want to chew on an oyster. I would never eat an oyster any bigger than this," she said, making a silver-dollar-sized circle with her fingers. "I like Kumamoto oysters."

"How much do they cost?" I asked her.

"I think the last time I had them, it was like $12 for six . . . "

"I like cultivated oysters too," I admitted. "They're delicious. But six little-bitty oysters for $12? You live in the last place in America where you can get a dozen oysters for a couple of bucks—and you want to import $24-a-dozen cultivated oysters from California?"

"That's right," she said.

"You're an oyster snob," I shrugged.

"Okay," she said. "I have no problem with that."

I tried to put things in a cultural perspective. "You know, there were once oyster houses all over the country—Chicago, New England, Chesapeake Bay—but those places are all gone. The native oysters are all fished out in most of the United States.

"The Gulf Coast is the last place in America with wild oysters. It's the only place where you can still sit down in an old-fashioned oyster saloon and eat oysters for pennies apiece. The end of the golden era of American oyster culture is happening right here in front of our eyes. And you still have a chance to see it," I ranted, perhaps a little too dramatically.

The women backed away from me and struck up other conversations.

We were skimming across the calm murky green water of Big Bayou, a long, skinny inlet of St. Vincent Sound in the westernmost part of Apalachicola Bay. One of the employees of the Thirteen Mile Oyster Company had been kind enough to run a few of us out in a motorboat to meet up with some oyster tongers.

After ranting about the Gulf Coast being the last place you could still witness the "golden era" of oysters, it occurred to me that maybe I ought to go check out some of these famous Gulf Coast oyster locales myself. So I signed up for a "field trip" to Apalachicola sponsored by the Southern Foodways Alliance, a group of food writers, chefs, and regular folks who like to eat Southern food. Part of the field trip was an oyster-tonging excursion.

We slowed down and coasted while we watched a tonger named Charlie Green as he stood on the rail of his flat, gray oyster boat with a pair of oyster tongs in his gloved hands.

The tongs looked like a pair of long sticks that crossed at the waterline. Charlie jerked on the handles like he was trimming a hedge under the water. His wife Mary sat in front of a culling board that was covered with muddy oysters and empty shells. She was breaking up clusters of oysters with an iron claw, sorting out the keepers and shoving the undersize oysters and debris overboard with a short-handled rake.

We pulled up alongside them, and the Greens invited me to jump on board and try my luck. But I had handled enough oyster tongs to know that snipping oysters off the reef and dragging them to the surface with a pair of twelve-foot sticks was a lot harder than it looked. I left the backbreaking work to Charlie, but I did accept an extra-large oyster that Mary shucked for me. It must have been four inches long, but I slurped it down in one gulp.

Tonging is the only method of oyster harvesting permitted by the State of Florida on the public oyster reefs of Apalachicola Bay. The state attempted to limit private oyster leases to tonging as well, but the oyster lease owners won a court challenge that allowed them to continue harvesting with mechanical dredges pulled by diesel-powered oyster lugs. In Texas and Louisiana, where tongs have long been extinct, oystermen will tell you that tonging in the modern era is akin to leaving the tractor in the barn and plowing with a mule.

But in the opinion of conservationists, tonging is easier on the oyster reefs. The fishery is divided among hundreds of small boat operators who harvest a few bags a day. Dredging breaks up the clusters of oysters, destroying quite a few in the process. Tongers rarely kill an oyster. The slow progress of the operation also slows down the rate of harvest so that more oysters come to market in the peak season. The regulation limit-

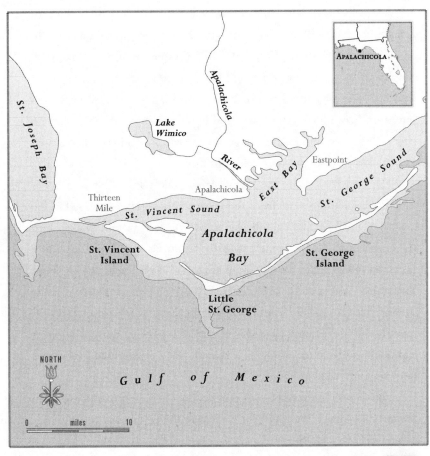

Apalachicola Bay, Florida

ing the fishery to tonging makes sense on many levels, but in the end, it wasn't environmental concerns that caused it to be enacted—it was the Apalachicola oystermen themselves who petitioned the state to hang on to their traditions.

Apalachicola is an isolated enclave where the old Gulf oyster culture remains unchanged. After our visit with the tongers, we all sat down to an oyster feast at Tommy Ward's 13 Mile Oyster Company. Along with the raw oysters, Tommy Ward and his gang were serving some of the best barbecued oysters I've ever had. One variety was painted with a butter-and-scallion mixture, and the other was topped with jalapeño slices. Both were put inside a huge barbecue trailer and smoke-roasted over hickory coals until they were opaque.

The registration for the SFA's "Apalachicola Field Trip," as it was called, was held in the lobby of the Gibson Inn, a grand old hotel in the center of town. A big smile broke across my face when I walked into the hotel bar to get my name badge. It was in this barroom that I'd first tasted an Apalachicola oyster eighteen years earlier. Having heard about the famous oysters of Apalachicola Bay, I'd decided to take a detour while driving with my family from our home in Texas to my parents' retirement home in Florida. I turned south off of I-10 around five, thinking I had plenty of time to get there by dinner. But I grossly underestimated how long a drive it really is.

The Gibson Inn was the only thing open when we finally got to town around nine-thirty. We asked for a table in the restaurant, but the lady behind the bar said, "Sorry, the kitchen is closed."

My then-wife was none too happy. The kids were hungry. My daughter Katie was two-and-a-half, and her sister Julia was eight months old. We didn't have any baby food.

"How about some oysters?" I asked the bartender. "Could we just get some oysters?" The bartender checked with the kitchen and agreed that we could have all the oysters on the half shell we wanted. So we sat down in the empty barroom and had Apalachicola oysters for dinner.

Feeding an eight-month-old baby mushed-up raw oysters is probably not something a pediatrician would recommend. But little Julia liked them just fine. And she loves oysters to this day.

The SFA field trip gave me an opportunity to reacquaint myself with the big, creamy Florida oysters. They're so popular in the Sunshine State that it's become hard to find them anywhere else. As rare as they are, I was shocked to find that a dozen oysters were selling for $3.99 at the Wheelhouse Oyster Bar at the Scipio Creek marina. The price didn't get much higher than $5 a dozen anywhere else in town either.

Apalachicola is the premier "oyster appellation" of the Gulf Coast. No doubt the beauty of the bay and the romance of the tongers adds something to the bivalve's mystique. But the flavor of the Apalachicola oyster is also unique. I think it is the mildest, milkiest *C. virginica* oyster in America. When it's salty, it's like chewing a mouthful of chowder.

Comparing the flavor of oysters of the Gulf with those of New England, M. F. K. Fisher wrote in *Consider the Oyster* that Southern oysters are "languid and soft-tasting to the tongue."

"They are, you might say, more like the Southern ladies than the brisk New Englanders," Fisher wrote. "They are delicate and listless . . . "

Elsewhere in the book Fisher wrote, "On the Mexican Gulf, they are definitely better cooked, although skilled gourmets have insisted otherwise to me, and one man from Corpus Christi once put his gun on the table while he stated quietly that anybody who said Texas blue points weren't the best anywhere was more than one kind of insulting liar."

My sympathies are with the gunslinger. The idea that bland Gulf oysters are better for cooking than eating on the half shell has become a part of American gastronomical dogma. But it's not that simple. Oysters are seasonal.

Oyster Names

Oyster nomenclature is confusing. Place names, common names, market names, and species names are all used interchangeably in oyster bars and seafood stores. Here are the five species of oysters you most often encounter in North American oyster bars.

Latin Name: *Crassostrea virginica (C. virginica)*

Common Names:
Eastern oyster, Atlantic oyster, Gulf
    oyster (U.S.)
American oyster, Blue Point (France,
    British Isles)

Places of Origin:
Malpeque (Prince Edward Island, Canada)
Wellfleet (Massachusetts)
Blue Point (Long Island)
Chesapeake Bay (Virginia, Maryland)
Chincoteague Bay (Virginia, Maryland)
Apalachicola Bay (Florida)
Grand Isle (Louisiana)
Galveston Bay (Texas)

This is the great American oyster, the species that occurs naturally from Canada down the East Coast to New York and Chesapeake Bay and all the way across the Gulf.

Latin Name: *Crassostrea gigas (C. gigas)*

Common Names:
Pacific oyster, Japanese oyster (U.S.)
Creuse (France)
Cupped oyster, rock oyster (Great Britain,
    Ireland)

Places of Origin:
Hood Canal (Washington)
Tomales Bay (California)
Marennes (France)
Arcachon (France)

Introduced to the Pacific Coast of the United States from Asia in the early 1900s, *C. gigas* is the most common farm-raised oyster in the Pacific Northwest and France.

Latin Name: *Crassostrea sikamea (C. sikamea)*

Common Name: Kumamoto

Places of Origin:
Kumamoto (Japan)
Pearl Point (Washington)
Humboldt Bay (California)
Hog Island (California)

This oversized thimble of an oyster is farm raised in the Pacific Northwest. It has a deep bottom shell and a fluted lip. Introduced to Washington from the Kumamoto prefecture in southern Japan in 1947.

Latin Name: *Ostrea conchaphila (O. conchaphila)*
   or Ostrea lurida (O. lurida)

Early taxonomists thought *O. conchaphila* and *O. lurida* were two different species, but in the 1990s, scientists agreed they were identical and combined the two names.

Common Names: Olympia oyster, Oly, tiny Pacific oyster

Places of Origin:
Olympic Peninsula (Washington)
Shoalwater Bay (Willapa Bay, Washington)

About the size of a fifty-cent piece, the tiny Olympia is the indigenous oyster of the Pacific Northwest. Like the European flat, it is a member of the genus *Ostrea*. The fishery collapsed in the late 1800s, but the Olympia oyster has been revived in recent years thanks to the efforts of dedicated oystermen and environmentalists.

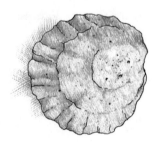

Latin Name: *Ostreae edulis* (O. edulis)

Common Names:
European oysters, flat oysters,
   Belons, (U.S.)
Plates, Belons (France)
Natives (British Isles and Ireland)

Places of Origin:
Cancale (France)
Colchester, Whitstable (Great Britain)
Clarenbridge, Tralee Bay, Strangford Lough (Ireland)

This is the oyster of the Roman orgy and the French Renaissance.
The shallow, round, shell resembles a small dinner plate, hence
the name. The flavor is the boldest in the oyster world with
strong marine components, and an intense mineral aftertaste.
After centuries of overfishing and the ravages of oyster diseases,
O. edulis is on the verge of disappearing.

A thousand miles north of Apalachicola on Canada's Prince Edward
Island, oystermen in small boats tong for wild oysters in Malpeque Bay
just like they do in Florida. Only the seasons are reversed. In December,
when Apalachicola oysters are just getting fat and sweet, the Malpeque
season closes.

The life cycle of oysters grown in cold water is a little different. Like
Gulf oysters, Canadian oysters store glycogen, getting fatter as the water
gets colder—but only up to a point.

By late December, cold water temperatures and lack of sunlight result in a scarcity of the micro-algae and organic materials that oysters
feed on. Lacking food, the oysters begin to lose weight and shrivel up
in their shells. At water temperatures below forty-one degrees, oysters
cease to feed at all and go into "hibernation." Malpeque Bay and many
other Northern oyster habitats freeze over in the winter. When the water
temperature rises in the spring, the oysters begin to store glycogen and
fatten up again. The Malpeque season reopens in May, just about the time
the Apalachicola season is ending.

Put an Apalachicola oyster and a Malpeque oyster side by side and it's
hard to believe they come from the same species. Malpeques have thin,
elongated shells. Apalachicola oysters have thick round shells. Malpeques
have a firm texture. Apalachicolas are fat and soft. They are opposite ends

of the *C. virginica* spectrum. Their differences are due to the enormous disparity in their habitats.

Malpeque Bay on Prince Edward Island is an oyster icebox. The surface water temperature in August averages around sixty degrees. At these temperatures, an oyster can take five years or more to reach maturity. A three-inch Malpeque oyster may be six or seven years old.

Apalachicola Bay, on the other hand, is an oyster hothouse. The surface water temperature in summer averages close to ninety degrees. In winter, the water temperature never reaches forty-one degrees, so they keep getting sweeter all winter. The relatively small bay is fed by the enormous Apalachicola River, which heaps plankton onto the reefs faster than the oysters can digest it. As a result, an oyster in Apalachicola Bay balloons to a size of three inches in as little as eighteen months.

These quick-growing oysters taste creamy and mild, with little or no iodine and mineral flavors. If the wind is blowing from the east when the oysters are harvested, saltwater pours in from St. George Sound and gets trapped in the bay, raising the salinity and giving the oysters a wonderfully briny flavor. If the wind blows from the west, the freshwater dominates the flavor and the oysters taste "too fresh," as they say in Apalachicola.

All of the oyster-growing regions between Malpeque Bay and Apalachicola Bay lie between these two extremes. And their oysters all hit their peak at a slightly different time.

A lot of people insist that expensive Northern oysters taste better than Gulf oysters. One night not long after the holiday party in Montrose, I asked the lady from Cleveland to join me and a fellow Texas oyster lover named John Bebout in a comparative oyster tasting.

We started in the funky turquoise and navy blue dining room of Joyce's Oyster Resort, where we polished off three dozen luscious Gulf oysters and a bottle of Sauvignon blanc. The oysters at Joyce's were almost all below the legal limit of three inches. How is that possible?

When the Texas game wardens who enforce oyster regulations board a boat, they check the size of the oysters being taken. If more than 10 percent of the catch is undersized, they throw the entire catch overboard. If less than ten percent of the catch is undersized, the catch is okay. So, obviously, a significant number of undersized oysters make it into the system.

In Texas, oyster-shucking operations and raw bars have a symbiotic relationship. The big money is in shucked oysters, and the customers who buy them like them big. When you batter and fry oysters, you have to base your cooking time on the average-sized oyster, which means the small ones get overcooked and tough. Meanwhile, the average raw-bar customer is grossed out by oysters that are too big. So the shucking houses set their smallest oysters aside for the restaurants that serve raw oysters.

After our Gulf Coast half shells, we headed over to McCormick & Schmick's, where we were shown to a white-linen-covered table in the dining room. "We're just here to eat oysters," we told the waiter.

"We have Houston's best oysters," the waiter said.

They had twelve varieties of cultivated oysters available—none of them from Houston. We got two dozen comprising three each of eight different oysters and a bottle of lemon-tart French Muscadet.

We sampled tiny Kumamotos, salty "Imperial Eagles," irregular Fanny Bay oysters, little Hama Hama oysters, and several others from British Columbia and Washington State. They were all saltier than Gulf oysters, and the flavors were more concentrated, but they weren't sweeter. It was very difficult to tell some of them apart.

"The difference between some of these is pretty subtle," I observed.

"With an accent on the *b* in subtle," Bebout quipped.

"So what's the verdict?" I asked my companions. A dozen tiny oysters at McCormick & Schmick had cost us $21.65. A dozen Gulf oysters at Joyce's were $6.95.

"I think there are gourmet oyster eaters, and then there are oyster eaters," said Bebout.

"I have to admit, quantity does count," the lady from Cleveland said. "It's one thing to eat oysters as a delicacy, but it's another thing to chow down on them." The price, the atmosphere of the restaurants that served them, and the whole oyster-eating experience made it clear that the Gulf oysters and Pacific oysters came from separate worlds.

But the differences between America's oyster cultures were far deeper than we understood. It's a good thing we tried the Pacific oysters when we did, because they are no longer sold in Houston. Shortly after our comparative tasting, a political battle erupted and Pacific oysters were outlawed in Texas.

In April 2003, the state of California enacted a ban on Gulf oysters harvested from April through October. Numerous deaths in the state had been attributed to *Vibrio vulnificus* in summer oysters from the Gulf. The ban may have been motivated by public health concerns, but it also gave a boost to Pacific oyster sales.

In 2005, hurricanes Katrina and Rita helped shift the country even more toward West Coast oysters. Before the hurricanes, the Gulf states of Texas, Louisiana, Mississippi, Alabama, and Florida produced the vast majority of the nation's oysters. After the hurricanes, Washington State took over the title as the nation's top oyster-producing state.

Then the tables were turned. Stricter interpretation of a peculiar Texas statute outlawed the most popular varieties of West Coast oysters from the state's oyster bars.

In the spring of 2005, I attended an educational seminar put on by the Texas Parks and Wildlife Department. State officials explained the "prohibited species" regulations to seafood dealers and restaurant owners.

For many years, a law on the books had prohibited possession of live Pacific *(C. gigas)* oysters in Texas. The intention was to prevent a rogue oyster grower from planting the Pacific species in Texas waters and thus endangering the native *(C. virginica)* oysters. Pacific oysters can quickly take over an oyster reef, and they are also suspected of passing a disease called MSX to the *C. virginica* species, so the law makes sense.

But last year, that law was expanded to include all non-native oyster species (such as Kumamoto and Olympia oysters), and its enforcement was extended to include seafood dealers and restaurants. The idea that somebody was going to dump oysters that sell for $2 apiece into Galveston Bay seemed silly to me. And why would such a ban affect seafood restaurants in Dallas and El Paso, hundreds of miles from the water? But when I voiced my skepticism at the seminar, another concern was raised.

"California banned our oysters!" someone in the room shouted. Suddenly, I understood what was going on.

Gulf oystermen are cynical about California's ban because it targets only Gulf oysters. A related bacteria, *vibrio parahaemolyticus,* in Washington State oysters, was responsible for 116 reported cases of illness the summer before.

According to the *Journal of the American Medical Association*, in August of 1997, the largest outbreak of *Vibrio parahaemolyticus* infections in North America was traced to summertime consumption of raw oysters harvested from California and the Pacific Northwest. In that outbreak, 209 people fell ill and one died.

The fact is, regardless of where they're harvested, oysters are less flavorful and more dangerous in the heat of summer. But by eliminating only the cheap Gulf Coast oysters from the market, Gulf oystermen felt California was providing an economic concession for local oystermen under the guise of protecting the public health.

Texas authorities denied that the prohibited species law and its new enforcement parameters had any economic or retaliatory motivation. But a waiter at a Houston restaurant summed up the prevailing wisdom: "California banned Gulf oysters in the summer, so Texas banned Pacific oysters to get even."

National restaurant chains such as Portland-based McCormick & Schmick's and Minneapolis-based Oceanaire Seafood Room have had to change their oyster-bar menus in Texas. These restaurants serve Pacific oysters in other locations across the country. Now they can serve only *C. virginicas* in Texas.

Provincialism is intrinsic to the oyster business—it's tied into the whole terroir/merroir concept. And then there's the never-ending spiral of fishermen's enmities. Traditionally, the oystermen of France hated the oystermen of Great Britain. The oystermen of England hated the oystermen of Ireland. And the oystermen of Whitstable hated the oystermen of Colchester. During the Revolutionary War, the oystermen of New Jersey were willing to join either side—as long as the oystermen of New York were on the other.

So it's not terribly surprising that Gulf oyster fishermen and Northern oyster farmers are at each other's throats today.

American oyster bars tend to line up with one side or the other. When you eat Gulf oysters in New Orleans, the shuckers make fun of those tiny $3 oysters up north. And when you eat oysters in New York, the shuckers tell you that Gulf oysters are flavorless and likely to kill you. Your taste in oysters is bound to be influenced by where you live and your social station.

Or, to paraphrase Brillat-Savarin, "Tell me what kind of oysters you eat, and I will tell you who you are."

THREE

Sin City's Wall of Fame

I LOCKED THE DOOR and lit the candles. My girlfriend, Kelly, slipped into something slinky. It was Valentine's Day, and the two of us were in New Orleans to celebrate the lovers' holiday—and to see if oysters really were an aphrodisiac.

Nero believed they induced both lust and gluttony and served them at all his Roman orgies. In Victorian England, they were considered naughty. In the 1700s, New York's oyster cellars were found by looking for the red lights outside. Inside, patrons enjoyed oysters, alcoholic beverages, and the company of prostitutes in curtained booths.

But New York's oyster cellars are long gone, and a good Roman orgy is hard to find. The best places left to enjoy the sinful side of the oyster these days are probably Paris and New Orleans. And New Orleans is a lot closer to my house.

Old-fashioned oyster saloons are a cause for nostalgia in much of the country. But in New Orleans, the proud tradition of blue-collar oyster slurping goes on uninterrupted. Except for hurricane years, Louisiana has long been the number-one oyster-producing state in the country, averaging around fifty million oysters a year.

I made four trips to New Orleans in the course of my oyster research. First, I went with my two teenage daughters to eat in the famous old Creole restaurants of the Crescent City and learn about legendary cooked-oyster creations (more on that PG-rated trip after we finish with lust and gluttony). Along with Valentine's Day, there was another trip after Christmas in 2004. And I went back after the hurricanes of 2005 to check on the oyster reefs as well as the oyster bars (more on that in Chapter Ten).

For our Valentine's Day aphrodisiac experiment, Kelly and I spent a long weekend in the Big Easy. On the appointed night, we shared two dozen raw oysters and a dozen grilled oysters at Drago's in Metairie, then went back to our hotel room and conducted our undercover work. Research has never been more satisfying.

So, are oysters an aphrodisiac?

In 1989, the Food and Drug Administration issued a report that said the powers of most so-called aphrodisiacs were based in folklore, not fact. The scientists' explanation of why oysters are considered an aphrodisiac was particularly interesting.

"Sometimes the reason for an item's legendary reputation is obvious . . . Many ancient peoples believed in the so-called 'law of similarity,' reasoning that an object resembling genitalia may possess sexual powers. Ginseng, rhinoceros horn, and oysters are three classical examples." But according to the report, oysters were unique among reputed aphrodisiacs in that there might actually be some scientific basis for their claim.

"Oysters are particularly esteemed as sex aids, possibly gaining their reputation at a time when their contribution of zinc to the nutritionally deficient diets of the day could improve overall health and so lead to an increased sex drive," the report stated.

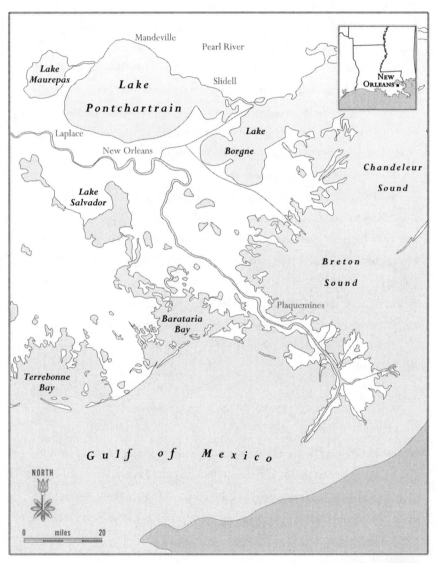

Mandeville

Pearl River

Lake
Maurepas

Lake
Pontchartrain

Slidell

NEW
ORLEANS

Laplace

New Orleans

Lake
Borgne

Chandeleur

Sound

Lake
Salvador

Breton

Sound

Plaquemines

Barataria
Bay

Terrebonne
Bay

Gulf   of   Mexico

NORTH

0   miles   20

New Orleans, Louisiana

The report writers also observed that it's difficult to test aphrodisiacs because of the placebo effect. "The mind is the most potent aphrodisiac there is," said John Renner, founder of the Consumer Health Information Research Institute. "It's very difficult to evaluate something someone is taking because if you tell them it's an aphrodisiac, the hope of a certain response might actually lead to an additional sexual reaction."

In short, if you believe that oysters are an aphrodisiac, they are very likely to have that effect. The FDA laments that there has been a shortage of studies. We were only too happy to do our part.

So what did our experiment prove?

Kelly won't let me provide any graphic details, but my friend John T. Edge likes to point out that not long after that oyster experiment, Kelly and I got married and had a child. So I will simply report that the result of our test confirmed that oysters can be an aphrodisiac, especially on Valentine's Day in a New Orleans hotel room with a voluptuous blond like Kelly. Additional experiments will obviously be required. Perhaps you can independently confirm our results with some experiments of your own.

Having explored the connection between oysters and lust, I took on the sin of gluttony.

My official Acme Oyster House shucker, Russell Magee, shoved another pair of oysters onto the marble bar in front of me. Beside me was a stack of empty shells we were using to keep count. After this one, I would be at an even three dozen. I was sucking them down as fast as Russell could shuck them.

To make it onto Acme's Wall of Fame I had to eat fifteen dozen—180 oysters. According to Acme's Web site, the time limit was four hours. But when I got there, they told me it had been shortened to two hours. That changed my strategy a bit. I thought I would be able to eat some and then go for a walk. But I also discovered that the rules of engagement prohibited me from leaving the building. I couldn't leave Russell's sight, even when I went to the bathroom.

It was December 30, 2004. The temperature in New Orleans was near freezing, and the water temperature in the shallows of the Gulf of Mexico was in the low fifties. Thanks to the cold water, oysters from Plaquemines Parish were at their height of flavor and sweetness.

When my daughter Julia and I walked into the bar, I slipped Russell a twenty and announced I was going for the Wall of Fame.

The tip made him more supportive than his fellow shucker, Bill Cager. Before we started, Cager attempted to talk me out of my attempt by telling me about the last two guys who went for the Wall of Fame.

"The guy sitting in that stool puked after thirteen dozen," he said, pointing to the stool beside me that was occupied by my daughter Julia. "The other guy was six oysters away from fifteen dozen," he said. He had been sitting in the very stool I now occupied, Cager told me with a smile. "But he couldn't do it."

The cautionary tale didn't scare me much. I wasn't really worried about trying to win a contest or set a record. In fact, I find competitive eating and all that high-speed hot dog swallowing disgusting. My Wall of Fame quest had nothing in common with those sideshows. Mine was a high-minded experiment and part of a larger oyster-eating inquiry.

It was the end of my first year of oyster research. I had already embarked on the mission of eating oysters all over the world in order to compare their flavors. And now I was sacrificing my body in order to understand some remarkable facts I had gleaned from reading about oysters in history.

Two thousand years ago, the Roman emperors put away a dozen dozen oysters at a time, and a thousand years ago, Henry IV ate three hundred as an appetizer. I wondered how this was possible. Did people have larger stomachs back then? In order to put the issue in perspective, I wanted to see how many oysters I could eat.

Brillat-Savarin once tried a similar experiment:

Thirty-two Dozen and Counting

"In 1798 I was at Versailles as a commissioner of the Directory, and had fairly frequent dealings with the Monsieur Laperte, who was secretary to the tribunal of the department; he was extremely fond of oysters, and used to complain of never having eaten enough of them, or, as he put it, 'had his bellyful of them.' I decided to provide him with that satisfaction, and to that end invited him to dinner.

He came; I kept him company as far as the third dozen, after which I let him go on alone. He went up to thirty-two dozen, taking more than an hour over the task, for the servant was not very skillful at opening them. Meanwhile, I was inactive, and as that is a distressing condition to be in at the table, I stopped my guest when he was still in full career. 'My dear fellow,' I said, 'it is not your fate to eat your bellyful of oyster today; let us have dinner.'

We dined: and he acquitted himself with the vigour and appetite of a man who had been fasting."

—*Jean-Anthelme Brillat-Savarin,*
The Physiology of Taste

I have always assumed that we eat fewer oysters today because they are scarcer and more expensive than they were in ancient times. So what would happen if money were no object? How would the oyster appetite of an average American (say, me, for instance) compare to that of an ancient Roman, if all else were equal? I considered it an important scientific question.

Kelly, who had become my fiancée on Christmas day of 2004, thought I was making lame rationalizations. She figured eating fifteen dozen oysters was an act of unspeakable gluttony no matter why you did it. She and my nineteen-year-old daughter Katie decided to check out the after-Christmas sales on Magazine Street rather than encourage me.

I knew after I ate three dozen that I wasn't going to go all the way. I tried to break the news gently to my seventeen-year-old daughter Julia, who was kind enough to accompany me. I wanted to find out how many oysters it took to fill me up, I told her, not how many it took to make me puke.

She said she was fine with that, though I could see the disappointment in her eyes. Russell passed me some more oysters, but I ate them at a slower pace. Since Russell was now shucking faster than I was eating, I ordered a dozen for Julia. That made her face light up.

Somewhere around my sixth dozen, a couple sat down next to me at the oyster bar. Max and Jane Jakubowski were from London, and they were curious as to why I had seventy-two oyster shells stacked in piles of three along the bar. So I explained my attempt to make the Wall of Fame. They told me they ate lunch at the Acme Oyster House every day during their vacation. For more than a decade, they have been coming to New Orleans to celebrate the New Year and eat oysters. They choose this time of year because the oysters are at their peak.

I told them that a sampler plate of six oysters at Bibendum Oyster Bar in London had cost me $32, so I completely understood what they were doing here. Eat ten dozen and you save yourself the cost of the airfare, I joked.

While I was talking to the Jakubowskis, I breezed through a dozen without thinking about it. After they left, Russell tested my resolve by putting a couple of giant six- and eight-inch oysters out for me to eat. They were at least twice as big as the average oyster.

"C'mon Russell, quit with the sea monsters," I whined, holding up one of the offending brutes. He giggled. I took a break to count the empties and see where I was. I had eaten nearly eleven dozen in an hour, and I had truly enjoyed them. (Good thing I skipped breakfast.) Russell wanted me to keep going. But I told him to hold off for a while. I would take it easy and see if I had more room when there were fifteen minutes left to the time limit.

Since I couldn't go outside and take a walk, I got off my barstool and wandered around the restaurant. I asked the manager where I could find the Wall of Fame where my name would appear if I ate the whole fifteen dozen. She told me the wall was temporarily down while the restaurant underwent some repairs, but that it would reappear soon.

Looking around, I noticed metal rods holding up ancient wooden beams in the middle of the restaurant. The Acme Oyster House is in such an advanced state of decrepitude, I hadn't even noticed it was under repair. But then again, the place is so dark and the tables crowded so close together, you have to be pretty determined to take a tour of the place.

The oyster bar at the Acme Oyster House is just inside the front door, and my knowledge of the place didn't extend far beyond it. The liquor bar and the front dining room are visible from the marble oyster bar, but it wasn't until I took my walk that I realized there was a larger dining room in the rear. I took several laps around the big dining room, hoping to make some room.

After half an hour of wandering around, I sat back down at the bar and quickly ate another dozen. That made twelve. I managed to slowly down a couple more oysters every few minutes until I had made it to thirteen dozen. But I was losing steam. "Dad, keep going, you can do it," Julia said, poking me from the adjacent stool at the oyster bar. Russell thought it would be a real funny time to lay out a few more sea monsters.

"I know I can't eat two dozen of these," I said, holding up an oyster the size of a quail.

"That's no fair!" my daughter said. She sounded like she was going to cry. Russell buckled at the threat of feminine tears, and replaced the huge oysters with a couple of dainty ones. Now I had no excuse.

There were two dozen oysters lined up on the bar with eight minutes left on the clock. I took a deep breath and sucked them down without regard to the swelling feeling in my stomach.

"After you eat a lot of oysters, it feels like when you go swimming in the ocean and saltwater goes up your nose," my oldest daughter Katie once observed. That's a pretty apt description of the way I felt as I finished the last few.

Julia cheered. Russell shook my hand and congratulated me, and the manager gave me a mesh bag with a bright red Acme Oyster House T-shirt and matching gimme cap inside. Then they handed me the bill. Julia had eaten four dozen oysters herself in the course of her duties as my cheerleader. The total for nineteen dozen oysters at $6.99 a dozen with $12.95 tax came to $145.76. I kept the receipt so I could deduct it from my taxes as a research expense. Imagine explaining that one to an IRS auditor.

After I paid up, Julia and I walked back to our bed-and-breakfast in the Marigny district across Elysian Fields from the French Quarter, a distance of three or four miles. The weather had turned sunny and cool, and it was a nice walk. Julia asked if I felt stuffed. I told her I didn't feel full, like when you eat too much Thanksgiving dinner. It was more of a sloshy feeling, like I drank too much water.

I took an afternoon nap and woke up feeling fine. That night, all four of us went to Drago's in Metaire for dinner. I couldn't face oysters on the half shell, but I ate a couple of their fabulous grilled oysters with garlic butter for an appetizer.

I don't think the Acme Oyster House ever did put the Wall of Fame back up after hurricane Katrina, but they erected a virtual Wall of Fame on their Web site (www.acmeoyster.com). At this writing, the Leader of the House is Boyd Bulot at forty-two-and-a-half dozen. And my name appears near the end of the Fifteen Dozen Club list. You could look it up.

The first of my four oyster research trips to New Orleans didn't have anything to do with raw oysters, but we managed to eat quite a few anyway. Our real mission was to sample the city's famous cooked-oyster dishes at the restaurants that made them famous and bring home some recipes.

It was the week between Christmas 2003 and New Year's 2004, and my daughters and I were house-sitting the Magazine Street apartment of my friend and fellow food writer Pableaux Johnson while we did the cooked-oyster tour of New Orleans.

New Orleans is literally made out of oysters. Some of the oldest buildings in the city are made of a Native American version of concrete called "tabby." The oyster shell was used for both the lime and the aggregate. Oyster-shell piles were once burned along the coast to provide the lime for cement. Oyster-shell-aggregate concrete was used to pave roads up until the 1960s.

Ancient middens suggest that natives of the Gulf Coast ate oysters 5,000 years ago. The Spanish began charting oyster reefs along the Gulf Coast in the 1500s. When La Salle claimed Louisiana for Louis XIV in 1682, he told the oyster-loving king that, among other reasons, the French should claim this part of America because of the abundance of excellent seafood.

In early New Orleans, oysters were sold on street corners by roving vendors. In 1805, the Louisiana *Gazette* reported that these oyster peddlers had become a nuisance. The aggressive vendors went from street corner to street corner blowing conch-shell horns from morning until night to draw attention to their wares.

By the early 1800s, oyster sellers and other fishmongers began to sell their catch from stalls in the French Market. While the culture of oysters began to disappear on the Atlantic and Pacific Coasts in the early part of the twentieth century, it continued to thrive in New Orleans.

One of the most important contributions of nineteenth-century New Orleans to culinary history was oysters Rockefeller, the most famous cooked-oyster dish in the world. Antoine's is the place where it was invented, but getting a table there is quite complicated.

Antoine's opened in 1840 and claims to be the oldest family-run restaurant in the country. They have some old-fashioned traditions. For example, if you walk into Antoine's and ask for a table, or if you make a reservation over the phone without mentioning the name of your waiter, they seat you in a special section reserved for tourists.

In order to get a table in the sanctum sanctorum, the legendary main dining room, you have to ask for your waiter's section when you make the reservation. So what do you do if your family hasn't been in New Orleans for eight generations and you don't have a waiter? You borrow somebody else's.

I called a woman I met at the Words & Music Festival who worked in the mayor's office and asked her for the name of her family's waiter at Antoine's. She shared it reluctantly, so I better not give it out here. But odds are, you wouldn't want it anyway. The food at Antoine's was awful.

We were excited to be there, and we were blown away by the memorabilia and photos of celebrities who have dined there that hung on the walls of the old dining room—Franklin Roosevelt, Calvin Coolidge, Herbert Hoover, Al Jolson, and Pope John Paul II, to name a few.

I explained to my daughters that oysters Rockefeller was created in 1899 by Jules Alciatore, son of Antoine Alciatore, the founder of the restaurant. It was named after the richest man in the country, John D. Rockefeller, because the dish was so rich. The family has kept the recipe a secret, passing it from generation to generation. But they have always maintained that the sauce doesn't contain any spinach.

When our order of *Huitres en coquille a la Rockefeller*, as it is actually called at Antoine's, finally arrived, majestically balanced on a bed of rock salt, we oohed and aahed over it. After the girls tasted it, I asked them if they thought the bright green vegetable used in the sauce was parsley, watercress, or something else.

Katie and Julia said they didn't know or care because, whatever it was, it tasted terrible. I had to agree. I had eaten so many other wonderful versions of oysters Rockefeller made with such ingredients as spinach, Parmesan, and Pernod, that I was disappointed by the original. And I'm guessing most people who have come to love imitation oysters Rockefeller would agree.

The original Rockefeller sauce is bright green and bland, while the imitations resemble the Italian *ostriche alla Fiorentina*, in which oysters are served with pureed spinach, minced bacon, and a béchamel seasoned with exotic spices.

The other dishes we were served at Antoine's included dull crabmeat in a cream sauce, an awful lobster Newburg, and an overdone fish with crabmeat on top. The restaurant should be declared a national monument, but the kitchen is desperately in need of help.

We had a much better time at Arnaud's, where we went for the jazz brunch. It was a delightful experience from beginning to end. The restaurant's famous creation, oysters Bienville, wasn't on the brunch menu.

But when I asked about it, the manager kindly agreed to send out an assortment of all five of their cooked oyster dishes.

First and foremost was oysters Bienville, my favorite baked-oyster dish. It's made with half-shell oysters topped with a rich seafood paste—a puree of shrimp, mushrooms, green onions, herbs, and zesty seasonings—and baked in the oven.

Italian-tasting oysters Kathryn featured oysters baked under a puree of artichoke hearts, garlic, fresh Parmigiano-Reggiano, and extra-virgin olive oil. Oysters Suzette, topped with bacon, pimento, green onion, and bell pepper, would have been a hit under other circumstances, but it paled in comparison.

Oysters Ohan was topped with a savory stew of cooked eggplant and spicy andouille sausage. And lastly, there was Arnaud's oysters Rockefeller, made with fresh spinach, bacon, and a touch of Pernod, which tasted much better than the original version at Antoine's.

Along with the best baked-oyster dish in town, Arnaud's also serves oysters on the half shell. So, of course, we got a dozen of those too.

A jazz trio performed during brunch, and at one point they began to circulate from table to table. In a surprising tribute to *American Idol*, the musicians encouraged patrons to stand up and sing a song when the band arrived at their table. My daughter Julia, who was performing with her school choir at the time, stood up and belted out one of my favorites, "The Way You Look Tonight." We all left with smiles on our faces.

The next day we met the talented writer and quintessential New Orleanian Lolis Eric Elie at Galatoire's, our last stop on the classic Creole restaurant tour. The restaurant was outstanding, as always. My daughter Katie thinks the fried eggplant with powdered sugar and Tabasco sauce served at Galatoire's is among the best dishes in the city. The restaurant's signature oyster dish, oysters en brochette, was not very memorable. I like their oyster and artichoke soup much better.

Five dollars goes a long way in a New Orleans oyster bar. Katie, Julia, and I had eaten nearly a dozen oysters apiece while standing at the front counter at Cassamento's, waiting for a table. The girls were looking at me strangely, since we ordered only a dozen on the half shell for $7.50 and we had eaten way more than $15 worth of oysters so far.

I was embarrassed to expose my avarice, but I explained to the girls in a whisper that I had slipped the shucker a $5 bill. The tip you give an oyster shucker is one of the best investments you will ever make.

I first discovered this important fact a few days earlier, when we sat down at the oyster bar at Dickie Brennan's ornate new restaurant in the French Quarter. The shucker was getting a head start on the dinner rush by opening oysters in advance, arranging them on trays, and then stacking up the trays. When we ordered a dozen, he grabbed a tray and handed it to us.

The oysters he was shucking were wet and gleaming. The ones on the tray had dried out and gotten opaque and sticky. So I shoved the tray back along with a $5 bill and asked the man behind the oyster bar if we could please have a freshly shucked dozen.

He had been working in silence before, but now he began to banter. We got our freshly shucked dozen along with a few jokes and lots of oyster-eating advice. (Shucking and jiving is a time-honored tradition in New Orleans.) And the oysters didn't stop at twelve. They just kept coming.

Cassamento's half-shell oysters are outstanding. It's the only oyster bar I know of in New Orleans that keeps its oysters in a refrigerated storage box, not on ice. This means the oysters never sit in a pool of water losing their salinity, and they're always at an ideal temperature.

Katie and Julia mixed ketchup and horseradish sauce in little bowls to dunk their oysters in, but I like mine naked. So did the French author Alexandre Dumas, who remarked that there is something pathetic about oysters, and eating them is the only way to pay them tribute. They do seem vulnerable, lying there all nude and glistening.

"Where are these oysters from, Daddy?" my daughter Katie wanted to know. I'd described the pedigree of every oyster we'd eaten on the trip thus far, and she expected the same for these.

"Are these Plaquemines oysters?" I asked our shucker, Leon.

"Yessir, I believe that's right," the shucker said.

All the best Louisiana oysters I ate that winter came from Plaquemines, a parish on the east bank of the Mississippi River.

Cassamento's was constructed mid-century in the art nouveau style, and it's a favorite of Uptown locals. There are ornate designs in the yellow-and-white tile walls, which make the dining rooms look like the inside of a fancy lemon wedding cake. But the tile pattern on the floor and on the newly added front counter doesn't match the original design. The result is a gleaming tile interior in a jumble of patterns and styles.

We sat down in the front dining room and looked at the menu. Julia got an order of fried oysters, and Katie and I split an oyster loaf, which is essentially a fried oyster sandwich on toasted white bread.

Cassamento's fried oysters were among the best I have ever eaten. That's because they start with fresh plump oysters and then fry them in pure lard.

I wondered how many oysters Leon would have shucked if we didn't sit down at a table. I said I was pretty sure he would have kept going as long as we kept eating. But my daughters didn't want to put it to the test. They were embarrassed to realize that their greedy father had been bribing the shuckers to get more oysters than we paid for.

Lust, gluttony, and avarice. That made three out of seven on the hit parade of the deadly sins.

My fourth research trip to New Orleans was conducted in the spring of 2007. I wanted to return to some of my favorite oyster haunts, like the Acme, to make sure they hadn't changed. And I wanted to check out the way Felix's and Mosca's had been refurbished after hurricane Katrina.

Felix's is certainly clean and shiny, maybe a little too much so. The oyster poor boy was still pretty wonderful though, and the freshly shucked oysters were also excellent. I got a long lecture from the manager about how banning summer oysters would put Felix's out of business.

I was especially eager to eat some oysters at the new Mosca's, but I needed some tablemates to share the family-style platters. I recruited chef John Currence and food writer Brooks Hamaker to come with me. The gooey casserole of bread crumbs, garlic butter, and oysters known as oysters Mosca was every bit as good as I heard it was.

When M. F. K. Fisher said that oysters from the Mexican Gulf taste best cooked, she was right—more than half the time. Gulf oysters are spectacular on the half shell during the cold winter months. But the rest of the year, when they're short on sweetness, you really are better off cooking them.

Luckily, we have all of these classic Creole recipes to work with. And since it's easy to buy shucked oysters by the pint in most seafood stores along the Gulf, cooking them is actually easier than eating them raw.

OYSTERS ROCKEFELLER

When President Franklin Roosevelt sampled oysters Rockefeller on a visit to New Orleans, his host, Mayor Robert Maestri, leaned over and asked Roosevelt, "How ya like dem ersters, Mr. President?" Thanks to the visiting press, the Mayor's Ninth Ward accent was mocked in every newspaper in the country and the phrase "dem ersters" was immortalized.

The original recipe has never been released by Antoine's. Here is a close approximation. Some people think the original was made with parsley; others insist it was made with watercress. Herbsaint is a New Orleans anise liqueur that tastes like Pernod.

    48 oysters in their shells
    1 pound butter
    1 rib celery, finely chopped
    2 bunches scallions, finely chopped
    1 bunch parsley, finely chopped
    3 tablespoons Worcestershire sauce
    1 teaspoon Tabasco
    ½ to ¾ cup Herbsaint or Pernod
    1 ¼ cups seasoned bread crumbs
    Rock salt

Shuck the oysters and discard the top shells. Drain the oyster meat, reserving the oysters in one bowl and the oyster liquor in another. Scrub out the bottom shells and allow to dry.

Melt the butter in a large skillet and add the celery, scallions, and parsley. Sauté for five minutes, then add the Worcestershire and Tabasco. Reduce heat to medium and cook for ten minutes. Add the Herbsaint or Pernod and bread crumbs; cook for five minutes more. Remove the pan from the heat and transfer the mixture to a bowl. Chill in the refrigerator for one hour.

Puree the vegetable mixture in a food processor while cold to distribute the butter evenly.

Preheat oven broiler. Line eight ovenproof plates with a layer of rock salt about one inch deep (moisten the salt very slightly). Set scrubbed oyster shells in the rock salt, making sure they are level. Place one oyster meat and a little of the reserved oyster liquor in each shell. Spoon an equal amount of the prepared vegetable mixture over each oyster and spread to the rim of the shell.

Broil approximately five minutes or until the edges of the oysters have curled and the topping is bubbling. Serve each diner six hot oysters.

Makes eight servings.

OYSTERS ROCKEFELLER 2

Here's a version of "dem ersters" made with spinach that most people like better than the original.

> 36 fresh oysters on the half shell
> 6 tablespoons butter
> 6 tablespoons finely minced fresh spinach leaves
> 3 tablespoons finely minced onion
> 3 tablespoons finely minced parsley
> 5 tablespoons bread crumbs
> Tabasco sauce to taste
> ½ teaspoon Herbsaint or Pernod
> ½ teaspoon sea salt
> Rock salt
> Lemon wedges for garnish

Shuck the oysters and discard the top shells. Drain the oyster meat, reserving the oysters in one bowl and the oyster liquor in another. Scrub out the bottom shells and allow to dry.

In a large saucepan, melt the butter. Add the spinach, onion, parsley, bread crumbs, Tabasco sauce, Herbsaint, and sea salt. Cook, stirring constantly, for fifteen minutes and then remove from heat and allow to cool. Puree the spinach mixture in a food processor. The mixture may be made ahead of time and refrigerated until ready to use.

Preheat oven broiler. Line an ovenproof plate or platter with a layer of rock salt about one inch deep (moisten the salt very slightly). Set scrubbed oyster shells in the rock salt, making sure they are level. Place one oyster meat and a little of the reserved oyster liquor in each shell. Spoon an equal amount of the prepared spinach mixture over each oyster and spread to the rim of the shell.

Broil approximately five minutes or until the edges of the oysters have curled and the topping is bubbling. Serve each diner six hot oysters.

Makes six servings.

OYSTERS BIENVILLE

In the 1920s, a Frenchman named Arnaud Cazeneuve opened Arnaud's Restaurant in the French Quarter. Arnaud's is the birthplace of the city's second-favorite baked-oyster dish, oysters Bienville. The dish was named after the birthplace of Jean-Baptiste Le Moyne, Sieur de Bienville, the second colonial governor of Louisiana.

    2 dozen oysters on the half shell, drained
    1 tablespoon olive oil

⅔ cup finely chopped mushrooms
1 teaspoon ground white pepper
4 tablespoons unsalted butter
1 ½ teaspoons finely minced garlic
1 tablespoon finely chopped shallots
½ pound boiled shrimp, shelled, cleaned, and finely diced
1 tablespoon flour
½ cup brandy
1 teaspoon sea salt
½ teaspoon cayenne
½ cup heavy cream
6 tablespoons grated Romano cheese
4 tablespoons dry bread crumbs
¼ cup finely minced parsley
4 pans rock salt

Shuck the oysters and discard the top shells. Drain the oyster meat, reserving the oysters in one bowl and the oyster liquor in another. Scrub out the bottom shells and allow to dry.

In a large, heavy saucepan over medium heat, heat the oil and sauté the mushrooms for five minutes or until slightly tender, adding the white pepper while cooking. Remove the mushrooms from the pan and set aside.

In the same pan, melt the butter and add the garlic and shallots; sauté for five minutes or until soft. Add the diced shrimp and cook for one minute or until heated through. Sprinkle in the flour and cook for two minutes, stirring constantly to coat the shrimp. Add the reserved mushrooms and the brandy, stirring to incorporate. Stir in the salt, cayenne, and heavy cream, cooking until smooth. Add the Romano cheese, dry bread crumbs, and parsley. If the mixture is too thick, add a small amount of milk.

Remove from heat, allow to cool, then refrigerate for about one and a half hours. Half an hour before you plan to bake the oysters, place the pans of rock salt in a preheated 500° F oven.

Put oysters on shells, placing six in each pan of rock salt. Spoon one heaping tablespoon of sauce over each oyster. Bake for fifteen to eighteen minutes until well browned. Serve each diner six hot oysters.

Makes four servings.

OYSTER AND ARTICHOKE SOUP

Oysters and artichokes are an old combination, but Chef Warren LeRuth gets credit for making oyster and artichoke soup popular in New Orleans. In his fabled career, LeRuth worked at Galatoire's and many other New Orleans institutions before opening his own restaurant. His soup didn't contain cream, but many people add it anyway.

    4 large artichokes
    Juice of 1 lemon
    Stick of butter
    ½ cup chopped onion
    ½ cup chopped celery
    2 tablespoons flour
    1 cup oyster liquor or clam broth
    ¼ cup chopped parsley
    ¼ cup chopped green onions
    ½ teaspoon dried oregano
    ½ teaspoon dried thyme
    1 quart fresh oysters, shucked
    1 pint heavy cream (optional)

Cook the artichokes in boiling water with lemon juice until tender, about forty minutes. Drain, reserving one cup of the cooking liquid. Allow the artichokes to cool. Separate the artichoke leaves and use a teaspoon to scrape the meat off the leaves into a small bowl. Cut the hearts into a half-inch dice.

Melt the butter in a soup pot over medium heat. Sauté the onion and celery until tender, about ten minutes. Add the flour and cook for one minute, stirring constantly to prevent scorching. Pour in a little of the oyster liquor and stir to incorporate, adding the rest of the liquid a little at a time. Add the reserved artichoke cooking liquid. Cook for about fifteen minutes, reducing the heat to low when the mixture boils. Add the artichokes to the soup and continue to simmer for ten minutes.

Just before serving, add the parsley, green onions, herbs, and oysters to the soup and let simmer just until the edges of the oysters curl, about three minutes. Stir in the cream if desired and cook until heated through, but do not boil. Serve immediately.

Makes six servings.

FOUR

Irish Eye-sters

Seated on a bench by the fireplace at Moran's on the Weir, quite possibly the best oyster bar in the world, I stared into the flickering peat fire with a pint of Guinness in my hand and the taste of a Dunbulcaun Bay oyster in my mouth. Moran's "eye-sters," as they are known in the local brogue, are the best in Ireland.

R. W. Apple Jr. of the *New York Times* called this two-hundred-year-old thatched-roof "oyster cottage" one of the most memorable seafood restaurants he had ever visited. "The oysters are quite simply the best that one fanatic—a man who has eaten Olympias in Seattle, Chincoteagues in Baltimore, Sydney rock oysters, Belons and Blue Points, Colchesters and Mobile Bays—ever put in his mouth," wrote Apple.

The late R. W. Apple Jr. casts a large shadow on the enterprise of oyster journalism. I felt like I had a long way to go and a lot of oyster bars to visit before I could begin to hold forth on the subject. Visiting Moran's on the Weir was a first step, and one of several reasons I had traveled to the west coast of Ireland in September of 2004. The other big draw was the 50th Annual Galway Oyster Festival.

The oyster has inspired more than its share of festivals, feasts, and celebratory gatherings around the world. Oyster feasts generally occur at the opening of the oyster season, a date that falls close to the first day of autumn.

In the British Isles, oyster celebrations were part of the feast of St. Michael, or Michaelmas, celebrated around September 29. The United States inherited the oyster-festival tradition, along with a lot of our oyster culture, from England and Ireland. There are fall oyster festivals in Oyster Bay, Long Island; South Norwalk, Connecticut; Wellfleet, Massachusetts; and lots of other U.S. cities.

The Galway Oyster Festival is the biggest in the world, it was celebrating its golden anniversary in 2004, and it's the home of the Guinness World Oyster Opening Championship, so it seemed like a worthy representative of the genre.

I tried to ignore rumors that the three-day festival was little more than a Guinness-fueled bacchanalia. An estimated ten thousand pints of Guinness are consumed at the affair every year, I was told. I wondered how many oysters got washed down with all those suds.

While I had eaten quite a few Belon *(O. edulis)* oysters in France, I had never tasted the Irish *(O. edulis)* natives. Americans tend to call all the oysters of this species "Belons." But the English and the Irish hate it when you call their oysters by French names. They refer to them as "native" oysters, seemingly unaware that the moniker becomes utterly useless as soon as you leave the cradle of the bivalve's nativity.

In Ireland, I wanted to spend some time considering the nuances and trying to describe the differences in flavor between the appellations of the ancient European oyster.

And then there were the libations to consider.

The French insist on a tart white wine with oysters. Texans tend toward cold Lone Star beer. But the Irish have long held that Irish

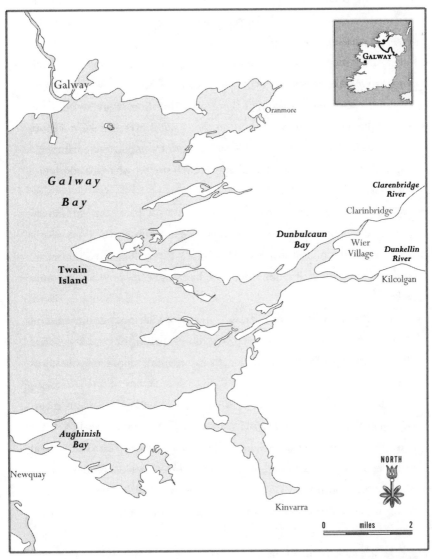

Galway

Oranmore

Galway
Bay

Clarenbridge
River

Clarinbridge

Dunbulcaun
Bay

Wier
Village

Dunkellin
River

Twain
Island

Kilcolgan

Aughinish
Bay

NORTH

Newquay

0   miles   2

Kinvarra

Galway Bay, Ireland

native oysters and Guinness stout is the ultimate pairing. And as everyone knows, the Guinness we get in the United States doesn't taste the same as it does in Ireland. I would have to have my Irish oysters with authentic Irish Guinness to do the subject justice.

Kelly volunteered to come along. Though we had begun our experiments to test the effectiveness of oysters as an aphrodisiac over Valentine's Day in New Orleans, I thought there was a lot more work to be done. Would the higher mineral content in the *O. edulis* oyster make it a more potent aphrodisiac? We would be eating them by the dozens, drinking a lot, and staying in romantic bed-and-breakfasts. So why not conduct a few more field trials?

I even looked up the names of a few marine biologists in Galway. Maybe I could find one who would meet me in a pub. By the time we got on the plane bound for Shannon, I had a long list of things to accomplish. And I brought my golf clubs along too, just in case there was some time to kill.

We had a lovely time. Galway is the most charming destination on the western coast of Ireland. Its cozy pubs and inviting old buildings offer all the comforts of civilization, yet it's close to the moors and seashores of wild Connemara.

The afternoon we first set eyes on Galway's town center was magically bright and sunny. Kelly and I grabbed a table on the sidewalk in front of a pub on a lively section of Quay Street. There, before the oyster festival had even begun, we sampled our inaugural dozen native Irish oysters.

The American Gulf Coast and the west coast of Ireland have much in common when it comes to oysters. Just as the Gulf is the last place in the United States where wild oysters of the native *Crassostrea virginica* species are still abundant, Ireland is one of the last places where Europe's native species, *Ostrea edulis*, are still plentiful enough to be harvested in any quantity.

The native *(O. edulis)* oysters harvested in Ireland are sold mostly on the European continent. According to Irish oystermen, the French buy Irish oysters in bulk and rechristen them with French names. Then they are retailed in Paris for outrageous prices. The French version of the story is obviously a little different.

Whatever water it comes from, *O. edulis* is the fullest-flavored oyster in the world. It is the oyster lover's oyster, the one that Brillat-Savarin ate, the one that the Roman emperors and the Sun King loved.

In her famous 1959 book, *The Oysters of Locmariaquer*, Eleanor Clark wrote of its flavor, "You can't define it. Music or the color of the sea are easier to describe."

One thing she was sure of: "It has no relation at all to the taste of the U.S. restaurant oyster . . . Or rather yes, it has the relation of love to tedium, delight to the death of the soul . . . "

Then, in one long paragraph, Clark provided perhaps the most lyrical description of the flavor of European oysters (or any other variety) ever written. It reads, in part, "It is briny first of all . . . there is the shock of freshness to it . . . Intimations of the ages of man, some piercing intuition of the sea and all its weeds and breezes . . . You are eating the sea, that's it . . . and you are on the verge of remembering you don't know what, mermaids or the sudden smell of kelp on the ebb tide or a poem you read once, something connected with the flavor of life itself."

With Clark's reverie in mind, I grabbed one of the oysters on the plate in front of me. I had eaten European oysters on several visits to Paris over the years, and I was eager to reacquaint myself with the fabled flavor. The *O. edulis* oysters on our plate had rounder, flatter, and more regular shells than Gulf *(C. virginica)* oysters. This was the first time Kelly had ever tasted one.

She wrinkled her nose in disapproval. "You don't like it?" I asked in amazement. She loved Gulf oysters. She often ate a dozen by herself. But she had her own opinion about the flavor of the European oyster—and it didn't have anything to do with mermaids or a poem she once read.

"It tastes like licking the bottom of a boat," she said.

That was actually a pretty fair description. I once asked San Francisco oyster maven Billy Marinelli how he described the flavor of a European oyster. He said it was like walking down to the beach, picking up a rock in the surf, and putting it in your mouth.

So, was it the flavor of life itself, or a rock in the surf, or licking the bottom of a boat? They were briny to start with, then I got a sweet nutty flavor around the abductor muscle. The chewy Irish oysters also had a seaweed sort of taste with a hint of iodine. They were strong, and I liked them a lot. And I can say with authority that the hard-to-describe flavor goes great with a pint of stout.

"Oh well, more for me," I smiled weakly at Kelly as I sucked down the remaining ten. So much for testing the aphrodisiac effect—on the female side of the equation, anyway. For the rest of the trip, Kelly would eat a token oyster when we visited an oyster bar or festival event and then wash the strong taste out of her mouth with lots of beer.

"There are those who like 'fishy' fish, and those who don't," I philosophized as she watched me eat. She rolled her eyes. I have embarrassed many of her friends who made the mistake of asking the waiter, while visiting a restaurant with me, if a particular variety of fish tasted "fishy." I inevitably follow that question up by asking the waiter if various beef dishes taste "beefy" and if the pork tenderloin is "porky." Making fun of people who don't like strong fish is one of my many failings.

But, like it or not, the truth is that in the twenty-first century, most people prefer mild-tasting seafood. Ask a seafood dealer or a chef at a seafood restaurant, if you don't believe me. And that change in tastes is part of the reason the magnificently full-flavored European flat (O. edulis) oyster is dying out.

On the day before the main event, I wrangled my way into a media briefing where the international oyster-shucking competitors were introduced. Six or eight photographers and a couple of local television crews were there. By far the largest media contingent was a Japanese television production company that was trying the patience of their festival hosts.

After chatting with a few of the oyster shuckers, I overheard a festival committee member named John Rabbit talking about taking somebody on a tour. I promptly butted into the conversation and asked if I could tag along.

"We'll see," he said without enthusiasm.

Rabbit was showing an important Canadian filmmaker around, and as it happened he had room in the backseat for Kelly and me. The fact that my wife is a good-looking blond wasn't lost on Señor Rabbit.

The filmmaker was a great big bear of a guy, and he turned out to be quite pleasant. He asked what my oyster book was going to be about, exactly. If I knew, I would have told him. I obliquely described a book about good places to eat oysters and whatever beverages they served with oysters once you got there. And I said that if I came across any low-hanging fruit of the philosophical or cultural variety, I might throw some of that in too.

When I asked him about his oyster film, he was equally vague. There was a book coming out with the film, he said. We turned west off the N18 highway just south of the village of Clarenbridge, and the filmmaker made us stop at the oyster flats. He got out of the car and jotted notes on what I took to be a shot list.

It was rainy and gray, and the scene in front of us was empty and gloomy. But in the 1800s, it would have been hopping.

Dunbulcaun Bay forks into two long fingers. The northern part ends at the mouth of the Clarenbridge River at the village of Clarenbridge, and the southern finger ends at the mouth of the Dunkellin River at the old port of Kilcolgan. This port on Inner Galway Bay was once crowded with the beautiful little freight-hauling sailboats called hookers, which were designed to haul blocks of peat cut from the bogs of Connemara and seaweed fertilizer from the Aran Islands across the rough seas.

Ireland's best oysters are dredged from the Clarenbridge oyster beds in the northern part of Dunbulcaun Bay. The locals claim the oysters from this seven-hundred-acre tidewater area are the sweetest in the world. Twice a day, the tide brings an influx of salty water from the bay up into the beds, where it mixes with the freshwater, providing a perfect environment for oysters.

For centuries, locals came to the port in horse-drawn wagons to meet the boats and load turf to burn in their fireplaces and seaweed to fertilize their fields. The thirsty work of toting and hauling sent the farmers, sailors, and oystermen to the local village in search of refreshments.

On the north shore of the river, there was a small village called "the Weir." It took its name from a weir (a low overflow dam) constructed across the Dunkellin River to trap salmon. Of the nine houses in the tiny village, three were licensed to sell liquor.

Daniel Moran came to the Weir in the 1760s and became one of those license holders. His license has passed down through six generations of Morans. The Moran family pub thrived during the heyday of the port of Kilcolgan. But in the 1940s, trucks took over the business of hauling turf and fertilizer, and Moran's pub at the Weir began to decline.

Clarenbridge oysters were always part of the local fare, and the Moran family had long harvested oysters from their own oyster beds.

But Moran's didn't become known as an oyster bar until it was included as a venue in the oyster festival of 1966.

In that year, the Guinness company threw a party at Moran's that the owners catered with oysters from the Moran's beds and brown bread baked by Kitty Moran. Only twenty people attended, but the publicity that followed about this beautiful oyster pub in the "middle of nowhere" put Moran's on the map for oyster lovers the world over.

The pub reinvented itself as an "oyster cottage" shortly thereafter and began to compete with the legendary Paddy Burke's pub a few miles up the road as the best place in Ireland to eat the native *O. edulis* oysters. What gives Moran's the edge (in clear weather, anyway) is an al fresco dining area—a grove of picnic tables that overlooks the river.

But Daniel Moran was a newcomer when he opened his pub in the 1760s—at least compared to Paddy Burke's, which has been serving the people of Clarenbridge since 1650. Moran's became famous thanks to the local oyster festivals; Paddy Burke's is the place where the festival business started.

There were actually two oyster festivals. The Clarenbridge Oyster Festival was held early in September to celebrate the September 1 opening of the oyster season, and the Galway Oyster Festival was held the last weekend of the same month.

After a draft of stout, I persuaded Mr. Rabbit to explain the strange history of the two oyster festivals. In the beginning, there was just one, he said. The first was held in Clarenbridge in 1954. In that year, thirty-four oyster lovers, most of them Dubliners, gathered at the invitation of Paddy Burke, who proposed that the party travel by boat to Galway to eat oysters, return by bus, then eat more oysters at Paddy Burke's pub. Dubbed "The Clarenbridge Oyster Festival," the party was mostly a bust. The boat malfunctioned and the musicians didn't show up. But the gathering and the oysters at Paddy's were immortalized in an *Irish Times* food article by Monica Sheridan. Benedict Kiely also covered the event for the *Irish Press*.

For the first few years, the festival was a sort of roving semi-private party, a moveable picnic of oysters, beer, and music. Eventually, the lawn of Paddy Burke's pub became the headquarters, but groups of revelers would frequently head off on pub crawls into Galway.

As the event grew and began to attract "oyster tourists," the festival's Galway sponsors wanted to change the date. The logic was that early September was prime tourism season. But by late September, the tourists were starting to disappear. By holding the festival a few weeks later, Galway could fill empty hotels instead of struggling to accommodate an influx of tourists in the peak season. But the Clarenbridge tribe liked things the way they were.

So the original oyster festival split into two festivals. Both count 1954 as their first year, and both celebrated their fiftieth anniversaries in 2004. If there were hard feelings when the split occurred, they are largely forgotten now.

The two events don't really compete. The Galway Oyster Festival is a huge celebration with a worldwide following. The Clarenbridge Oyster Festival is a charming little party at Paddy Burke's pub.

I asked Mr. Rabbit, who was sitting in the snug at Moran's with Kelly and me, if we could stop by Paddy Burke's on our way back. He said we would have to see what time it was when we finished our itinerary. First, we had to visit Michael Kelly Shellfish Ltd., better known as Kelly's Oysters, the company that supplies the oysters for the festival. The little oyster company is headquartered at Michael Kelly's farm on the other side of the river.

Mr. Kelly, who was wearing a dapper houndstooth jacket and a patterned purple tie, appeared to be in his mid-sixties. He had a thin face with expansive but well-kempt eyebrows and a forehead that protruded from under his comb-over. He held his hand to his forehead a lot, and he looked very nervous.

Mr. Kelly walked us through what looked like a four-car garage, where workers were packing miniature bushel baskets with thirty oysters apiece. A clump of wet seaweed was placed on top of the mollusks to keep the basket from drying out, then a round wooden lid was fastened in place. These were the oysters that would be used in the Guinness World Oyster Opening Championship. It wouldn't reflect well on Mr. Kelly if any of the oysters were D.O.A.

"We only sell around two hundred and fifty thousand oysters a year," Michael Kelly told me. "We are in it in a small way. Paddy Burke got me started in 1951," he said. "He was my first customer." Paddy died in 1971. I asked Mr. Kelly if he still sold oysters to the pub.

"I always did, and I always will," he said firmly.

But the Irish don't eat many oysters. And unfortunately, for many years Irish oysters were unfamiliar to the European customers who were willing to pay top dollar. (Never mind that the French were reselling Irish oysters after a little "finishing" in French waters.)

"It took me twenty-six years to get an outside market," Mr. Kelly laments. Today Kelly's Oysters sells most of its bivalves to Germany and Switzerland.

I asked Mr. Kelly what the water temperature was and if Irish oysters were fat now. He said the water temperature was around sixteen degrees Celsius (just under sixty-one degrees Fahrenheit) at the moment. The oysters would get bigger and sweeter when the water temperature reached ten degrees Celsius (fifty degrees Fahrenheit), he said.

While we were standing in the parking lot saying goodbye to Mr. Kelly, a big white passenger van pulled into the parking area and a gaggle of earnest young Japanese folks in black jackets and black-and-white Nike sneakers started unloading video equipment.

"Good God, it's the Japanese TV crew again," Mr. Kelly said in horror.

It seems that a Japanese reality television program had entered a contestant in the Guinness World Oyster Opening Championship. The comedic catch was their guy had never shucked an oyster before they grabbed him off the street in Tokyo. It was an amusing concept, but it was the interaction of the Japanese producers and their Irish hosts that was really funny.

On a previous visit to Kelly's Oyster Company, the Japanese crew had dragged their video cameras and lighting equipment into the Kellys' private residence to show the folks back home what a typical Irish household looked like. Unfortunately, the language barrier made it impossible for Mr. Kelly to explain that this might not be the best time for such a visit, as Mrs. Kelly was taking a bath. Unwilling to appear on Japanese television in her dressing gown, Mrs. Kelly was trapped in her own bathroom for over an hour.

As the video crew began to set up equipment and take over the place again, we wished Mr. Kelly the best of luck. I suggested to Mr. Rabbit as we got in the car that maybe this would be a good time to visit Paddy Burke's.

Paddy Burke's Oyster Inn is quite different from Moran's. When you walk into Moran's Oyster Cottage, the first thing you see is a lovely snug by the fireplace and a small bar. Beyond that, there's a large dining room that my wife describes as "cafeteria-like" because of the generic-looking Danish modern furniture. Paddy Burke's Oyster Inn, on the other hand, is an old Irish pub with some disturbing modernizations of both the menu and the interior decoration.

I winced to find Buffalo chicken wings, barbecued spare ribs with Texas barbecue sauce, and Chinese spring rolls on the bar menu. A dozen native oysters on the half shell went for Đ21.90. A dozen oysters baked in garlic butter and bread crumbs were Đ22.50. (The euro was worth about $1.20 at the time.)

I ordered raw oysters for the four of us to split and Guinness all around. The oysters weren't quite as fresh and plump as the ones down the road at Moran's, which come from Moran's own beds. Granted, Mr. Kelly's oyster company was stretched thin at the moment. And back in Texas, the waters of Galveston Bay were still above seventy degrees Fahrenheit, so the oysters hadn't even started to fatten. I wasn't complaining.

I can't say I had ever studied the decorating schemes of dimly lit Irish pubs before. But there was nothing about the standard decor of mismatched dark-stained woods, dingy stone walls, and lace curtains that bothered me. And I'm right at home with the aroma of wet wool, spilt beer, and oyster juice. My wife Kelly, who makes her living in art and interior design, finds this kind of ambiance depressing.

I thought the fringed burgundy-colored damask window treatments and the mauve linen napkins sticking jauntily out of the water glasses at the tables in the dining room were cute little touches. She described them as pathetic attempts at elegance.

If you take interior design into the equation, you should take my enthusiasm for both Moran's Oyster Cottage and Paddy Burke's Oyster Inn with a grain of salt. But if you're interested enough in oysters and Guinness to overlook minor flaws in the decor, put these two Irish pubs on your life list of oyster bars.

In the end, Paddy Burke's is a nice enough place, but Moran's has an edge because they own their own oyster beds. If strong-flavored European oysters accompanied by Guinness stout are to your taste, you will probably agree with the late R. W. Apple Jr. in ranking Moran's on the Weir among the best in the world.

❖

It was standing-room only inside the gigantic red-and-white-striped festival tent on the morning of the oyster-opening championship, the main event of the Galway Oyster Festival. I got six oysters on a paper plate for me and some smoked salmon for Kelly and took them outside to a picnic table between the tent and the concrete pier called the quay. Kelly met me there with a pint of Guinness for me and a pint of Harp for her.

We sat down and took in the wild scene. One spectacle after another competed for our attention. Old-fashioned sailboats showed off in the bay. A huge flock of ducks squawked for handouts. And there were lots of people wandering around in outlandish costumes.

One of the partiers was outfitted in a powdered wig, a three-cornered hat, and an old-fashioned redcoat. Four Elvis impersonators had their pictures taken together. And then there were the Irish college boys dressed up as the scarecrow, the tin man, the lion, and Dorothy. The guy playing Dorothy was a brawny six-foot-two, and he wore a blue gingham dress, pigtails, and freckles painted on his face just above the stubble.

The festivities started early in the morning of September 25, 2004, when Her Honor Catherine Connolly, the mayor of Galway, ate the first oyster, pronouncing the opening of the season and kicking off the 50th Annual Galway Oyster Festival.

She led the oyster festival parade, along with several local beauty pageant winners known as "the pearls." They marched from the town square to the marquee on the quay, where the major events of the festival were held. We watched the parade from the front of the marquee. There were the usual marching bands and convertibles carrying notables.

My favorite parade group was a class from a Galway elementary school. The students had constructed huge papier-mâché oysters with anthropomorphic eyes on their top shells and pearls inside their slightly opened jaws. The cartoonish oysters were mounted on long sticks and carried above the kids' heads. The students wore all-white clothing and had painted their faces blue; I think they were supposed to represent the sea. They were both touching and hilarious.

The marquee itself was a thing of wonder. It was a tent on a mammoth scale. I have heard that the largest marquees can hold ten thousand people. I'm not sure if this was the largest size, but it was certainly big enough to accommodate thousands of partiers. There were stand-up tables scattered around and an area roped off in front of a stage.

The picnic tables outside were prime territory if you wanted to eat sitting down. There, I considered my first half-dozen oysters for a moment before I dug in. There were two tiny ones, two medium-sized ones, and two enormous ones. I guessed that the shuckers were trying to spread the wealth around.

Oyster Grades

Oysters are often served "by the number" in Europe. The bigger the oyster, the higher the price.

European *(O. edulis)* Oyster Grades:

No. 000	> 105 grams
No. 00	95–105 grams
No. 0	85–95 grams
No. 1	75–85 grams
No. 2	65–75 grams
No. 3	55–65 grams
No. 4	45–55 grams

The larger oysters draw the most money, but few oyster lovers I have met like them the best. Most of the oyster-bar proprietors I've talked to recommend No. 2s or No. 3s for their concentrated flavor. And as I had already learned, for many female oyster aficionados, "the smaller, the better" seems to be the rule.

The European oysters I ate at the festival were a little more dried-out than the ones at Moran's and Paddy Burke's. They were tougher and not quite as plump. I chalked up the difference in texture and the slightly deflated quality to the logistics of feeding a crowd of thousands. What do you expect when you are eating oysters that were shucked hours in advance?

The flavor was also brinier, but with a nice touch of sweetness. The mineral taste, which in American *C. virginica* oysters is often compared to the flavor of "sucking on a penny," was in this case more like sucking on a mouthful of change. They were strong-tasting, and I was very grateful to the Guinness gang for handing out those endless pints.

The Đ95 entrance fee to the "Oyster Tasting," as the main event of the Galway Oyster Festival is known, got us into the Guinness World Championship Oyster Opening Competition, all-day admittance to the gigantic festival tent, all the draft Guinness or Harp we cared to imbibe, and a ticket with six food coupons along the bottom.

One of the stubs was good for the main course of hot seafood chowder, salad, Irish brown bread, and dessert. The others could be used for a plate of half a dozen oysters or a plate of smoked salmon on brown bread. Kelly wanted only the chowder and a plate of salmon, which left me quite a few oyster coupons to work with.

It was cloudy and cool but it wasn't raining, which is excellent oyster-eating weather in Ireland. Since there wasn't any seating inside the marquee, we passed a few hours at the picnic table while we waited for the oyster-shucking contest to start.

I was intent on my oysters, but gregarious Kelly struck up conversations with various festival-goers who came along and shared our picnic table. An Austrian couple sat with us awhile; they had been to the oyster festival before.

"This is our fourth time," the woman told us in heavily accented English. "The oysters cost twice as much in Austria, and they aren't nearly this good."

Later we were joined by Brendan Dolan and his wife Kate Ray Dolan, two American newlyweds who had chosen the Galway Oyster Festival for their honeymoon. Brendan was a student at the Atlantic Culinary Academy in Dover, New Hampshire. He told us his father, who was a master oyster shucker, went oystering near the University of New Hampshire Marine conservatory.

I asked the young chef how he would compare the flavor of these Irish *O. edulis* oysters to the *C. virginica* oysters of New England.

"These are wild oysters," Brendan declared. "They are saltier and cleaner than our cultivated oysters. They taste green. And they're meaty. You gotta chew these, you can't just slide them down."

Brendan and Kate predicted they'd celebrate their anniversary by returning for another festival. I thought about asking if they thought oysters were really an aphrodisiac. But what answer would you expect from a couple on their honeymoon?

"Go, George!" I screamed. If I had brought an American flag, I would have been waving it. After a half dozen or so pints of beer, I found myself packed shoulder to shoulder with a crowd of screaming supporters in front of the stage at the Guinness World Oyster Opening Championship. Irish and Norwegian flags were waving wildly, and cheers were screamed in several languages at once.

After doing my best to encourage American oyster-shucking champion George Hastings, of Maryland, I was bitter when he lost to the

French competitor. Suddenly I understood the behavior of English soccer fans. I might even have engaged in hooliganism myself had my better half not intervened.

The contestants in the Guinness World Oyster Opening Championship were already the national champions of their respective countries. To win the world title, they lined up side by side on the stage with a basket of thirty oysters and a plate in front of them. It took several flights of five or six shuckers at a time to arrive at a world champion.

The winner was determined by a score based on the fastest time, with deductions for penalty points. Judges examined each plate of thirty oysters for presentation after the times were recorded with a stopwatch. "Scrambling" the oyster's flesh, failure to detach the foot from the shell, grit in the oyster, and traces of human blood were all grounds for penalty points.

The 2004 world champion, Norwegian Ola Nilsson, opened his thirty oysters in two minutes and thirty-nine seconds, incurring twenty-two seconds in penalty points. "Keep your cool," Nilsson said, explaining his technique to the press. "Don't stress. You have to find a rhythm, and if you just go for speed you lose."

A former Irish champion who is now a judge offered his theory of why Scandinavians have dominated the competition in recent years. "The northern Europeans have developed a better technique," he told reporters. "We use an ordinary single-blade knife, and they use a double blade, which means they can open the shell and release the oyster in the same move." Oddly, the Japanese reality-TV competitor didn't come in last. He came in second to last. Singapore took the booby prize.

There was a black-tie ball at the Radisson Hotel that evening. It is the grand finale of the Oyster Festival and the social event of the year in Galway. But the gala was all sold out when I bought our tickets, so we couldn't go. I was disappointed about it back then. But by the time we walked the couple of miles to our bed-and-breakfast, I was extremely thankful I didn't have to be anywhere that evening. I passed out around eight thirty.

Rules for the Galway International Oyster Opening Championship

1. A sub-committee of the judges will select only the finest Galway Bay oysters *(Ostrea edulis)*, which shall be not less than seventy-six millimetres in diameter.

2. The opening tables will be approximately ninety centimetres from the ground.

3. Each competitor will receive a sealed box of oysters on stage. He/she will ensure it contains thirty oysters prior to the start.

4. Each competitor will be required to open thirty oysters.

5. The boxes will be allocated to the competitors by lottery and each competitor's tray will bear a code name.

6. The oysters must be opened on the board provided and presented on the tray provided. Nothing else can be used for presentation purposes.

7. The competitors must present their oysters face upwards and may present them all either on the deep or flat shell.

8. In opening the oysters, the competitor will only use a knife, a cloth, and any board supplied by the Committee. The competitor cannot use any support, holder, or any other implement whatsoever—the knives must also be approved by the Judges.

9. Competitors must be aged eighteen or over.

10. Competitors must wear the aprons provided.

11. Competitors may wear gloves or any protective covering on their hands.

12. The Festival M.C. will start each heat of the competition. Each competitor will start opening oysters on his order.

13. Each competitor must indicate that they are finished, by ringing the hand bell provided. The competitor must not touch the tray after ringing this bell or disqualification may result.

14. Each competitor may be requested to carry their own tray of oysters to a designated point, and they will be responsible for the safety of their tray up to that point.

15. Judges will examine the trays of oysters with the following points in mind:

   - Good appearance
   - Well opened, without flaws
   - Totally severed from shell
   - Muscle intact—not torn, cut, sliced, wounded, and without blood
   - Orderly and neat appearance

16. Points are awarded primarily for the speed of opening thirty oysters. Judges award bonus points for presentation of the tray of opened oysters. A bonus of from one to thirty points is awarded by the Judges at their discretion for a tray of oysters that are presented in a neat and orderly manner. The test for the Judges is how attractive the tray would look for a customer in a hotel or restaurant.

17. The following penalty points may be imposed:

   a. An oyster not severed from it's shell—four points
   b. An oyster with blood—thirty points
   c. An oyster with shell or grit on its flesh—four points

d. An oyster, the flesh of which is cut or sliced—four points

e. An oyster not presented upright—four points

f. For each oyster not opened or presented—thirty points

(If an oyster shell is presented empty, or the flesh only is presented, the oyster will be deemed not to have been presented.)

18. The winner will be determined by the lowest combined time and penalties. In the event of a draw, the competitor with the lower penalty shall be deemed the winner. If they are still equal the competitor with the highest bonus award will be declared the winner.

19. These rules have been prepared by the Galway International Oyster Opening Competition Committee of Judges and the decision of the Judges in relation to the interpretation of these rules is binding on all competitors and is final.

"They aren't Pacific oysters," the waiter told us. "They're local oysters." We had set off to the north in search of more Irish oysters and found ourselves eating dinner at a restaurant called The Waterfront Bar on Rosses Point, a stylish little resort area at the tip of the peninsula that juts into the Sligo Bay just north of the town of Sligo. We had ordered a dozen "Rosses Point" oysters, but we weren't sure what we would get.

When they arrived, I took one look at the deeply cupped shell and the elongated shape and knew they were *C. gigas*. They were about four inches long and an inch deep. Kelly loved the mild flavor, but I found them a disappointment after all the funky *O. edulis* oysters I'd been eating.

"These are Pacific oysters, just for your information," I told the waiter. When the waiter expressed doubts, a guy at a nearby table turned around in his chair and joined the conversation.

"He's right—those are Pacific oysters," he said, backing me up. When the waiter was gone, the guy and I kept talking.

I told him we had just come from the Galway oyster festival and that we were headed to Donegal because I heard it was an oyster region. He told me that there were indeed oysters in Donegal, but they were all of the Pacific *(C. gigas)* variety. In fact, he was from Donegal, but he said we could find the same kind of oysters in Westport on the road south, and it was a prettier drive.

"If you want to eat oysters, go to Moran's on the Weir," he said. Excellent advice, I mused as I made a mental note to return.

He also advised that the lobster at the Waterfront Bar came fresh every day from a local fisherman. So I had an Irish lobster for dinner, which turned out to be like a miniature Maine lobster. Kelly got the hake with "cucumber noodles," skinny strips of cucumber that were marinated to resemble pasta and served with a baby leaf salad and chive dressing. Both of our dinners were outstanding.

When we got up the next day, we decided to skip the Donegal oyster research and head back to Galway by the scenic route. We reached Westport around noon and stopped into a place called Asgard Bar and Restaurant on the Quay, where Kelly and I split another dozen *C. gigas* oysters. They were about half the size of a Gulf oyster. I speculated aloud that I could probably eat twenty dozen. Kelly thought that wouldn't be a good idea.

Kelly isn't much of a golfer, but we played golf together on a weird little par-three course fashioned out of a cow pasture near Westport. I also got a tee time at the Connemara Links, an old course situated on an elephant's trunk–shaped peninsula that sticks into the Irish Sea. Our most exciting romantic interlude occurred one morning while I waited for the rain to abate so I could play golf.

We had spent the night in a bed-and-breakfast in Ballyconneely. But I am not sure whether it was the oysters of the previous evening, the plush bed on a rainy morning, the prospect of playing the ancient links, or the sight of my gorgeous girlfriend that was the aphrodisiac in that case— maybe all of the above.

Before we left Galway, I decided to visit the National University of Ireland's Galway campus, where I heard they had an outstanding marine biology department. It was an hour's walk from our bed-and-breakfast. I set off one morning while Kelly slept in. I didn't have an appointment with anyone. I just barged into the Martin Ryan Marine Science Institute and asked if anybody had time to talk to me about oysters.

I ended up in the office of Declan Clarke, the marine institute's development director and manager of its experimental station at Carne. He gave me way more information than I was prepared for.

I asked Clarke about the health risk of eating oysters in Europe compared to back home, where *Vibrio* was a concern. European waters are classified Grade A, B, C, or D, the marine scientist told me. Oysters harvested in Grade A waters are fit to eat without treatment. Grade B waters are areas where naturally occurring contaminants like algae blooms or runoff raised the bacteria count above acceptable levels. Oysters from Grade B waters had to be purified before they can be sold.

Grade C waters are more contaminated, and the treatment of oysters from these areas follows a complicated process. Consumption of shellfish from Grade D waters was always prohibited.

Clarke reassured me that nobody died from eating oysters in Europe. Gastrointestinal distress is the most common problem. But quality standards in Ireland are far more strict than in the United States. "There are no oysters on the market in Ireland that haven't been tested," Clarke said.

Clarke also told me that the oysters I had been eating at the Galway Oyster Festival weren't from Galway Bay, which came as something of a shock. Oyster deseases were killing off the *O. edulis* oysters, he said. "While Ireland is one of the few countries with any native *(O. edulis)* oysters left, the Galway Bay population is quite small."

But I thought Michael Kelly got his oysters from Dunbulcaun Bay, I argued. Clarke, who works with oystermen all the time, explained to me that Kelly buys his oysters from fishermen who harvest wild oysters in distant waters. Then he stores them in mesh bags in Dulbaucaun Bay until he's ready to sell them.

But isn't that the same sort of "finishing" that the French do with Belon oysters? I asked naively. I thought that Kelly had said something about fattening his oysters in the nutrient-rich waters.

The marine scientist chuckled at the notion. He allowed that oysters did pick up the flavor of local waters when they were transferred, but it would take a lot more than a couple of days to fatten them up. Listening to him describe the nuts and bolts of the local oyster market, I realized that much of what I had been told about European oysters was romantic fiction.

A lot of the *O. edulis* oysters sold in Paris under French names like Belon came from Spain and Ireland, Clarke acknowledged, but he didn't have the same sense of outrage about it that others did. *O. edulis* oysters have become a rare and expensive luxury item for a few gourmets—less than one percent of the oyster market.

The French currently produce about a quarter of the world's supply, but they consume far more than they produce. *O. edulis* oysters are disappearing, and you have to buy them where you can find them these days.

As the price escalates, the market for *O. edulis* oysters is becoming more and more insignificant.

"There are modest commercial prospects [for the native *O. edulis* oysters]," Clarke said, "but we will never go back to the halcyon days." The major market for the strong-tasting *O. edulis* oysters has always been France, he explained. But a demographic shift has taken place.

"The older generation [in France] paid a premium for native *[O. edulis]* oysters," he said. But the younger generation in France doesn't have the taste for them anymore. They prefer the milder flavor of the *C. gigas* oysters. "Now when you say 'oysters,' everyone in Europe just assumes you are talking about *gigas*," he said.

In 1961, thirty thousand tons of *O. edulis* oysters were harvested. In 1996 the figure had dropped to 7,996 tons. The harvest has stabilized at around sixty-five hundred tons since 2000. Spain is responsible for more than sixty-five percent of that, with most of the rest coming from France, Ireland, and the UK.

Researchers are working with survivors of the oyster-related disease outbreaks to try to find a resistant strain of *O. edulis* oysters that could be propagated successfully.

It takes *O. edulis* five or six years to reach maturity; the mortalities from disease usually occur after the third year. *C. gigas*, on the other hand, matures in three years with little susceptibility to disease.

The waters of Ireland are too cold for the *C. gigas* oysters to reproduce naturally. Using oyster-farming techniques perfected by the French, Irish cultivators buy oyster spat (tiny baby oysters) and raise them in mesh bags anchored to frames in intertidal areas. As the oysters grow larger, they are divided into an increasing quantity of new bags.

In his capacity as an advisor to the aquaculture industry, Clarke works with oyster cultivation projects on the Irish coast. Efforts to cultivate *O. edulis* are flagging, he says. There's no incentive to work with them anymore because the demand is disappearing.

Before Kelly and I headed out for Shannon Airport, we stopped by Moran's on the Weir one last time. And I ate each one of the *O. edulis* Irish natives as if it were my last.

IRISH BROWN BREAD

Thickly spread with Irish butter, this is the ultimate accompaniment to a dozen Irish oysters and a pint of Guinness.

2 cups whole-wheat flour
2 cups bread flour
½ cup toasted wheat germ
2 teaspoons sea salt
2 teaspoons brown sugar
1 teaspoon baking soda
1 teaspoon baking powder
1 stick (½ cup) Irish butter, cut into ½-inch cubes
2 cups well-shaken buttermilk

Put oven rack in middle position and preheat oven to 400° F.

Whisk together flours, wheat germ, salt, sugar, baking soda, and baking powder in a large bowl until combined well. Blend in butter with a pastry blender or your fingertips until mixture resembles coarse meal. Make a well in center and add buttermilk, stirring until a dough forms. Gently knead on a floured surface, adding just enough more flour to keep dough from sticking, until smooth, about three minutes.

Transfer dough to a greased baking sheet and form into a loaf shape. With a sharp knife, cut an X (½ inch deep) across top of dough (five inches long). Bake until loaf is lightly browned and sounds hollow when bottom is tapped, about forty-five minutes. Cool on a rack for about one hour.

Slice thick and spread with butter. The bread will keep for only a day or two.

FIVE
Grand Central Degustation

Sandy Ingber was down on one knee rapping a big Pacific *C. gigas* oyster on the concrete floor of the New Fulton Fish Market. "It sounds a little hollow," he complained. "Hollow means dried out. They should sound like rocks." He passed on the hollow *C. gigas* oysters, but he liked the sound of the Olympic Miyagis. "Give me four of those," he told the fishmonger, who made a mark on his order sheet. He meant four cases, each containing a hundred oysters.

As the head chef and seafood buyer for the Grand Central Oyster Bar, Ingber goes through around four thousand half-shell oysters a day. "During the holidays we were selling six to eight thousand a day," he said. "I don't think anyone else in the country is selling more than we are. Except for maybe Acme Oyster House in New Orleans. But they have only one variety."

He was wearing wire-rimmed glasses and a long white coat that looked like a lab jacket. The tall, bald chef looked like a scientist as he moved from stall to stall examining specimens. It was three thirty in the morning and the New Fulton Fish Market was running at full steam.

While I was waiting for Ingber to arrive, I had a near-death experience with a speeding forklift loaded with wooden crates of fish. It nearly hit me as I zombie-walked out to the catering truck to get a cup of coffee. "Stay to the right," the driver yelled at me as he sped by. He graciously saved the "you idiot" until he was out of earshot.

I took a few photos of the fish with my digital camera until one fish seller asked me what the hell I thought I was doing. New York fishmongers are a notoriously cantankerous bunch. But they have every reason to be suspicious. Enforcement agents from all sorts of agencies prowl the place looking for infractions. One stall was busted recently for selling fish from restricted waters.

But attitudes changed drastically when Ingber showed up and I started walking around with him. Suddenly I was free to take all the pictures I wanted. And there were even free samples.

Ingber is one of the few New York chefs who shows up at the market anymore. When the Fulton Fish Market was located down by the South Street Seaport in lower Manhattan, lots of chefs used to prowl the aisles looking for bargains and trying to strike up the sort of personal relationships that might cause a fishmonger to set aside a prize tuna or a basket of rare shellfish. But since November of 2005, when the market moved to the Hunt's Point Food Distribution Center, a maze of enormous metal warehouses in the Bronx, the chefs stopped coming.

The old Fulton Fish Market was the product of one hundred and eighty years of tradition. It was a visually captivating tangle of fishmongers' booths and signs lettered in ancient graphic styles, and it was a favorite subject of artists. The New Fulton Fish Market is a 400,000-square-foot metal-and-concrete behemoth that looks like an airplane hangar and cost $86 million to build. The stalls are simply spaces on the concrete floor.

Each of the thirty-seven wholesalers at the New Fulton Fish Market has its own specialty, Ingber tells me. There are stalls with local fish like porgies and jumbo fluke, and there are stalls with giant tuna flown in from South America. There are sea urchins and baby conch and just about every peculiarity of the seafood world. It is the largest seafood market in America.

Much has been written about how soulless and austere the new location looks compared to the old one. But Sandy Ingber had another opinion. "The old market was horrible. The floor was covered with filthy black water, and it stunk. I used to have a box in the car that I put my clothes in after I went to the market. I couldn't stand to wear them." At the new fish market, the concrete floor is hosed down and scrubbed with bleach every day.

Ingber likes to keep on top of the market. Ninety percent of the oysters sold at the Grand Central Oyster Bar are purchased directly from producers. The ten percent he buys at the New Fulton Fish Market are mostly Pacific oysters. He buys them to insure that the Grand Central Oyster Bar has the best selection in the city. "I think we have thirty-two varieties of half-shell oysters today," he said.

The Grand Central Oyster Bar has long-standing arrangements with their East Coast suppliers. "We used to get our Long Island oysters from Tallmadge Brothers in Connecticut; in fact, in the early 1970s, the Grand Central Oyster Bar bought its own oyster lease from them," Ingber told me. The lease and the Grand Central Oyster Bar account is now under the care of Norm Bloom & Sons, which is a company that was spun off when Tallmadge Brothers split up.

When we were done shopping for Pacific oysters, Ingber showed me around the rest of the market. We were walking by the stall of M. Slavin & Sons when I noticed a box of oysters. On closer inspection, they turned out to be Texas oysters from Espiritu Santo Bay.

Due to the risks associated with *Vibrio*, it is a long-standing policy of the Grand Central Oyster Bar not to serve Gulf oysters, Sandy had told me. Even so, I thought he might be interested in the peculiar case of oysters from Espiritu Santo Bay.

I explained to him that when the Texas oyster season opened in November, the southern waters around Matagorda Island were closed to fishing due to the influx of a "red tide," as harmful algal blooms are known. And so all the harvesting was concentrated farther north on Galveston Bay, which has by far the largest oyster reefs in Texas. Some four hundred oyster boats exhausted the Galveston public reefs by Christmas.

As the water cooled, the red tide cleared, and after the biologists from the state were satisfied that the oysters were safe, the waters of Espiritu Santo and San Antonio Bays were opened to oystering. The closings gave the oysters a chance to put on some glycogen, so by the middle of January they were exceptionally sweet. It was odd that oysters from so far south should taste so good, but this year they were the best oysters you could eat in Houston.

One of the guys who worked for M. Slavin & Sons walked toward us. I opened my mouth to ask him who in New York was buying Texas oysters. But he cut me off with a loud gravelly voice.

"You know what that is?" he bellowed, pointing at the box of Espiritu Santos. "That's shit oysters for Middle America. Right, Sandy?"

"C'mon," said Sandy, pulling me away from the stall. When we were out of earshot, he said, "That's Herbie Slavin. He's one of the biggest characters in the fish market. Don't take him seriously." But I was a little miffed.

"Is that what people here think?" I asked. "Gulf oysters are shit?"

"It's not that they're shit," Ingber responded. "It's that warm water oysters carry *Vibrio*."

"But not in January!" I said. We walked a little more, and I noticed a box of Apalachicola oysters in the Blue Ribbon Fish Company stall.

I walked over to check them out, and the shellfish guy asked me if I wanted to try one. I said I did, and encouraged Sandy Ingber to try one too, but he wasn't interested.

The big three-inch oyster was briny and sweet with that creamy beige flesh unique to Apalachicola Bay. "Wow, that's good," I said.

The big shellfish man with a bushy beard introduced himself as John Guttilla. I told him about my encounter with Herbie Slavin, and he laughed. "Warm-water oysters have a stigma in the Northeast," Guttilla said. "It's a shame, because the people in Florida are doing such a good job with water quality and conservation." I asked him where Apalachicola oysters were served in New York. He said most of them would probably go to private chefs.

At the end of the aisle, we came to The New Sea Food Co. Inc., which had the biggest display of East Coast oysters at the fish market. The current proprietor, Anthony DeVito, was a third-generation New York shellfish dealer, Ingber told me.

A sign propped up above the boxes and bags listed the fourteen kinds of oysters available that day. It read: Delaware Bay, Glidden, Malpeque, Caraquet, Belon, Tatamagouche, Copps Islands, Cedar Point, Blue Point, Watch Hill, BeauSoleil, Pipes Cove, Wellfleet, and Glidden Point.

"He just ate an Apalachicola oyster over at Blue Ribbon," Ingber told Anthony DeVito, a wiry young guy who reminded me of Tony Danza. DeVito made a disgusted face.

"You wanna taste a real oyster?" DeVito asked me. "Try one of these Blue Points," he said, slicing open a mesh bag. He shucked the oyster and handed it to me. It was a little shriveled and not as sweet as the Apalachicola I had just eaten. But I hesitated to respond. If I told them the truth, that the Florida oyster was clearly superior, they would think I was basing my opinion on parochial loyalties.

"So, which one tasted better?" DeVito wanted to know.

"Let me go get a couple Apalachicolas from John Guttilla," I offered. "You taste them side by side with the Blue Points and you tell me which ones taste better."

"No way!" DeVito shouted, "Gulf oysters are Russian roulette." Sandy wasn't interested in doing a taste test either. The Apalachicolas were selling for around half the price of the Blue Points.

In his truck on the way back to Manhattan, Ingber told me a story. "In 1990, when I first started working for the Grand Central Oyster Bar, I got a great deal on some Apalachicola oysters," he said. When the manager of the restaurant saw the Gulf oysters, he threw them in the trash and gave Ingber a tongue-lashing. It doesn't have anything to do with what they taste like. It's a company policy, Ingber said.

I knew exactly what he meant. On the Gulf Coast, it's the insurance companies that are behind the drive to ban summer oysters. And I suspect that the reason New York chefs and seafood dealers avoid Gulf oysters has nothing to do with flavor and everything to do with liability insurance.

A few days after our fish market tour, Ingber and I sat at the oyster bar and ate every one of the thirty-two oysters on the menu that day. I proposed the tasting to test my theory that many of these varieties were identical oysters from within a few miles of each other.

Experience suggested that, regardless of the fanciful place names, oysters from the same general area tasted the same. We ordered the oysters in flights. First, two each of all the Canadian oysters, then two each of all the varieties from New England, followed by pairs of Long Island and Chesapeake oysters. Then we turned our attention to the Pacific oysters of Washington, Oregon, and California.

The results were mixed. There were similarities, but there were also some significant differences between oysters from a given locale. The Canadian oysters tasted the same except for the wild-harvested

Malpeques, which were stronger. The small varieties of farm-raised oysters from the Great Peconic Bay area all tasted identical, but the oysters from the Atlantic side of Long Island were saltier and firmer.

The large Chesapeake oysters tasted similar to Louisiana oysters. The flavor of the *C. gigas* oysters from Oregon and Washington seemed to change with the size. The little ones were delicate, while the bigger ones had strong seaweed flavors.

The large Miyagi oysters from Vancouver that we had bought at the New Fulton Fish Market turned out to be full of milky reproductive material. Ingber spit that one out. He was so disgusted by the taste, he ordered all of the Miyagis to be returned. And he encouraged me to tell people that anytime they got a bad-tasting oyster at the Grand Central Oyster Bar, they should send it back immediately.

I was standing on the dock in South Norwalk waiting for Captain Hilliard Bloom Jr. who was coming in from the oyster beds on the *Eben A. Thacher*, an eighty-foot steel-hulled oyster boat that once belonged to the Tallmadge Brothers oyster company.

I had come to Connecticut to learn more about Blue Points and the history of the Long Island oyster business. You'd think Long Island would be the place to go. In fact, I had read an article in the *New Yorker* by Bill Buford that described a boat trip with some small oyster farmers way out on Long Island. Buford raved about the unique flavor of the tiny oysters. So I asked a major New York oyster dealer if he could introduce me.

The veteran oysterman was more than a little derisive about the *New Yorker* article and the new breed of oyster farmers on Long Island. These retired stock brokers and lawyers were a bunch of hobbyists, I was told. They took a break from their golf games to run a couple hundred oysters in to a few Manhattan restaurants every now and then. "It's all a little too precious," the oyster dealer said.

If I was serious about understanding the Long Island oyster business, I needed to go to Norwalk, Connecticut, and see the old Tallmadge Brothers operation, I was advised. Connecticut was where the Long Island oyster business had long been headquartered. Currently, the state was home to thirty oyster concerns selling somewhere in the neighborhood of $50 million worth of oysters each year. So I made an appointment to meet a few Connecticut oystermen while I was in New York on other errands.

Kelly usually came with me when I went to New York; she loves the city—but not in January. I called her on my cell phone as I took a weirdly nostalgic drive from Saugatuck to South Norwalk. When I was in high school, my family kept a very old wooden boat at a marina on the Saugatuck River. I slowed down my rental car as I drove right by the slip on my way to the oyster docks.

It was odd, I thought, that I didn't know anything about those oyster houses, even though I spent part of my youth right down the road from the operation. My mother and father loved oysters, and we ate them in restaurants all the time. But in those days, nobody I knew went to South Norwalk unless they were looking for drugs. It was considered one of the most dangerous slums in the state.

When I arrived in South Norwalk, or "SoNo," as they are calling it these days, I was shocked. The place has undergone a massive restoration. In the 1970s, the historic oyster port was about to meet the wrecking ball when a coalition of citizens and civic officials banded together to save it. The Maritime Center, a museum that celebrates the shipping and oystering trade with exhibits, field trips for school kids, and a boatbuilding shop, anchored the SoNo renaissance. Today, the area is home to trendy restaurants and retail establishments. Hilliard Bloom Shellfish,

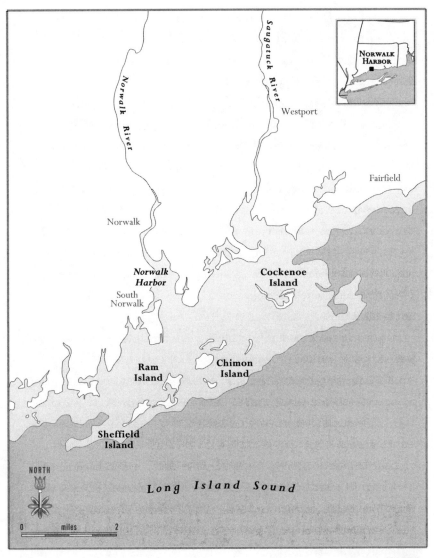

Saugatuck River

Norwalk River

Westport

Fairfield

Norwalk

**Norwalk
Harbor**

**Cockenoe
Island**

South
Norwalk

**Ram
Island**

**Chimon
Island**

**Sheffield
Island**

NORTH

Long   Island   Sound

0   miles   2

NORWALK
HARBOR

Norwalk Harbor, Connecticut

Inc. played a big role in the renovations, rebuilding some of the historic oyster buildings along the old dock.

When the *Eben A. Thacher* finally pulled in, I walked the length of it, admiring the gigantic hold and the mechanical hoists on the foredeck. "I've been oystering since I was a kid. I've been captain of an oyster boat for the last six years," Hilliard Bloom Jr. told me as he showed me around. It was really more like a ship, by far the largest oyster boat I have ever seen.

Hilliard Bloom Jr. was a tall, muscular kid with blond hair and a cleft chin who looked like he could play tight end for a college football team. He wore a navy blue hoodie and baseball cap and didn't talk much.

We rode in his pickup truck to go eat lunch. The young oyster-man was named after his uncle, Hilliard Bloom, who helped revive the Connecticut oyster industry in the 1960s. We sat down at the SoNo Seaport Seafood restaurant and talked about the oyster business over a pint of Guinness and a couple dozen Blue Points. The oysters were exceptionally juicy with a nice briny taste, and probably no more than a day out of the water.

"So you must be a third- or fourth-generation oyster man?" I asked him, slurping down some oyster juice.

"No, more like eighth or ninth," he said quietly. "My uncle Hilliard Bloom was in the business, but his wife was a Cavanaugh. They had the Bell Oyster Company way back when." And Joan Cavanaugh's mother was a Tallmadge.

As Bloom explained it, the modern Connecticut oyster business is a hybrid, part oyster farm and part fishery. If the oysters reproduce naturally creating lots of tiny oysters, or what's called a good "spat set," the company takes advantage of it. They can stretch the bounty by moving the small oysters around.

Some oysters are moved to deep-water spots where the colder water slows down growth. Others are moved to shallow spots near the shore where warm water speeds their development. And the rest are kept at medium depths where they grow at a natural pace. With careful management, a natural set can be turned into three years worth of oysters, I was told.

On a nautical chart mounted on the wall of the restaurant, Bloom pointed out some of the company leases and the spots where oysters are held in Long Island Sound. After the oysters are harvested, the company stores them in several caches close to the South Norwalk docks, where they can quickly be fetched and processed for shipment. One of those spots was in between a couple of sandbars called Grassy Hammock and Cockenoe Island, just off the Saugatuck River.

The name Cockenoe brought a smile to my face. Our family outings in the summer often consisted of a short trip on the boat over to Cockenoe Island, where we would anchor and spend a day swimming and lying around on the secluded beach. Little did I know back then that I was swimming alongside a couple zillion oysters.

Today, the Bloom company relies mainly on seed oysters. They run a small hatchery facility at their headquarters in South Norwalk, and buy the rest of their seed oysters from other operations.

Since they have no shucking house anymore, they don't have a steady supply of new oyster shells to use for cultch. Attempts to import oyster shells from elsewhere haven't worked out. A load of oyster shells from Maryland is the suspected cause of a disastrous outbreak of Dermo and MSX diseases that killed ninety-five percent of the oysters in Long Island Sound in 1998.

To cope with the cultch challenge, Hilliard Bloom Shellfish outfitted their boats with vacuums that suck up empty oyster shells from underwater beds. The shells are cleaned and dried in the sun, then returned to the oyster grounds. Hauling oyster shells around accounts for much of the time that Captain Bloom spends on the water these days.

But there is cautious optimism in the Long Island oyster business. "The future is looking good," said Leslie Miklovich, Hilliard Bloom's daughter, Hilliard Jr.'s aunt, and the co-owner of Hilliard Bloom Shellfish, Inc. The oyster population has now recovered from the die-off in 1998. There was a small set in 2006, and those oysters are beginning to mature. The healthy supply coincides with a stronger demand for oysters than ever before.

"Oyster bars are making a comeback," Leslie Miklovich told me in the company's office. "Younger people are getting interested in oysters. There are so many people who have never tasted an oyster before."

Miklovich confessed that she doesn't eat raw oysters herself, and neither did the company's founder, Hilliard Bloom. "He liked them fried," she said. Cooked oysters were long the main focus of the East Coast's oyster culture.

A tour of the company's archives taught me a lot about the history of oystering on Long Island. I looked at photos of the sailboats once used for oystering. The nimble, shallow draft boats looked a lot like the English oyster boats. Most of the underlying legal system by which oyster beds were deeded came from the English as well.

As I leafed through the boat records and deeds of oyster leases I came across some grants of "franchise" acquired by the Tallmadge Brothers company. I had never heard of a franchise before. Oyster leases are granted by the state and require a yearly payment, but franchises were once sold outright. "Franchises were granted by the King of England before the American Revolution," Miklovich explained. The rights to the underwater acreage purchased in the 1700s are still valid, even though the practice is extinct. "We have to pay property tax on them, but we own some of our beds."

Tallmadge Brothers was founded in the late 1800s, during the glory days of the Connecticut oyster business. In 1874, Norwalk oystermen were the first to begin harvesting oysters from steam-powered boats. By converting from sail-powered dredging to steamship dredging, an oysterman could triple his oyster haul. By 1880, Norwalk had the largest fleet of steam-powered oyster boats in the world.

In the early 1900s, the Long Island oyster business began a long period of decline. In 1957, the owner of Tallmadge Brothers, Inc. invited two fraternal twins named Hilliard and Norman Bloom to come to work for him.

Things didn't go so well. Storms and poor sets decimated the oyster population. For a while the Tallmadge Brothers company got by fishing for clams. By the 1960s, oyster companies were going belly up all over Long Island. Rather than give up, the Blooms bought up the failing oyster companies and their leases. And in 1967, they bought Tallmadge Brothers as well. The Bloom twins had cornered the Long Island oyster industry, but unfortunately the oysters had all but disappeared.

"My dad always said that an oysterman is lucky if he has one big set in his lifetime," Leslie Miklovich told me. Hilliard and Norm Bloom were extra lucky. In 1972, the oysters of Long Island Sound came back in a big way. It was one of the greatest spat sets in history. And it came just in time to turn around the Long Island Sound oyster industry.

In the year of the big set, the Bloom boys adopted the Tallmadge Brothers name for all of their operations, creating an oyster industry giant out of the empty shells of all the little failed oyster companies they had acquired. Eventually, Tallmadge Brothers became synonymous with Blue Point oysters.

"Blue Point" was a trade name for oysters first used by Joseph Avery, who got into the oyster business after he returned home from the War of 1812. He was the first to plant oysters off of Blue Point, Long Island, his boyhood home. He brought a load of Chesapeake Bay oysters by ship and planted them on beds he had acquired in the Great South Bay. The name "Blue Points" became so popular that from 1817 on it was used to describe all the large oysters produced in the Great South Bay.

Legend has it that when sewage pollution ended oystering in the Great South Bay, the Blue Points were dredged up and replanted all over Long Island Sound so their strain could continue.

Miklovich showed me some of the cans that shucked oysters were sold in. The brand names were all taken from idyllic-sounding places on Long Island Sound. Cedar Point was another famous name. My favorite was the can with a red-and-white checkerboard pattern and the name "White Rock and Grassy Hammock Oysters."

In albums of old black-and-white photos, I saw mountains of empty oyster shells sitting beside the shucking plants of South Norwalk. There were also photos of the shuckers, who were mainly African Americans.

It was a bit of a shock to look at those photos and then consider what South Norwalk looked like today. No doubt it was the shucked oyster business that helped make South Norwalk a slum. Oyster shucking is a poor-paying job, and a major shucking house requires lots of shuckers.

Minority workers who were recruited from New York to come to South Norwalk for low-paying jobs like shucking oysters formed a pocket of poverty that stood in stark contrast to the rest of the "Gold Coast" of Southern Connecticut, one of the most affluent areas in the country.

The piles of smelly oyster shells and the tenement houses where the shuckers lived must have been considered eyesores by the neighbors, many of whom were high-paid executives who commuted to New York every morning. No wonder we never came to South Norwalk when I was a kid.

After the huge set of 1972, Hilliard Bloom and his brother Norman bought the Bivalve Packing Company, whose assets included the entire town of Bivalve, New Jersey. The shucking house there had once been the largest on the East Coast. Tallmadge Brothers revived it and began to move its shucking operations there.

Another huge set in 1985 brought on the modern heyday of Tallmadge Brothers and Connecticut oysters. But the bad times returned with the die-off of 1998. In 2001, after the death of Hilliard Bloom, Tallmadge Brothers, Inc. was split up and divided between the heirs of Norman Bloom and Hilliard Bloom. Tallmadge Brothers held a reported 22,000 acres of oyster beds in Long Island Sound at the time of the breakup.

Today the two Connecticut companies that were formed by the breakup of Tallmadge Brothers—Hilliard Bloom Shellfish, Inc., in South Norwalk, and Norm Bloom & Sons, in Norwalk—are major sources of Long Island oysters.

I asked Hilliard Bloom Jr. about the small producers on Long Island that Bill Buford wrote about. He had never heard of them.

"The only major oyster business left on Long Island is an oyster hatchery called Frank M Flower & Sons," the young Captain Bloom told me. "They grow a few of their own oysters in Oyster Bay, but mainly they sell seed oysters. Connecticut is the dominant force in the Long Island oyster business."

Hilliard Bloom Shellfish, Inc. is located in a big, red, barn-like structure. It's actually a replica of a building that used to sit in the same spot on the historic South Norwalk docks. It was called the Radel Oyster Company building.

Though South Norwalk was once considered the oyster capital of the East Coast and is still one of the most important oyster docks in America, for a long time there wasn't any place to buy oysters there. And so, in 1983, Leslie Miklovich opened a retail outlet called SoNo Seaport Seafood. The business was such a hit that the oyster bar and seafood restaurant was added in 1984.

As I sat at the SoNo Seaport Seafood oyster bar eating another dozen Blue Points, I thought about how the area had changed. Once upon a time, the East Coast oyster industry was just like the Gulf Coast oyster industry. Both produced shucked oysters for the mass market. But now Connecticut oystermen are no longer involved in the messy business of shucking.

The recent surge in demand from oyster bars and upscale restaurants has provided enough of a market for Connecticut oystermen to concentrate on the half-shell market.

And once the smelly oyster-shell piles were removed and the poor black and Latino shuckers left, civic groups suddenly took an interest in the history of the oyster-fishing industry and the waterfront area. The gentrification of South Norwalk was made possible by the gentrification of the American oyster industry.

GRAND CENTRAL OYSTER PAN ROAST

The traditional oyster pan roast is made in a steam jacket, the unique cooking vessel mounted on the work table behind the oyster bar. In it, oyster stews and pan roasts are gently heated so they never boil over. Thanks to Sandy Ingber of the Grand Central Oyster Bar for the recipe.

¼ cup clam broth or juice
1 tablespoon sweet butter
¼ teaspoon celery salt
½ teaspoon Lea & Perrins Worcestershire sauce
6 select shucked oysters with juice
2 tablespoons Heinz Chili Sauce
2 cups half-and-half
1 slice buttered white toast
Dash of Hungarian paprika
Oyster crackers

In a double boiler with the water boiling on high, combine the clam juice, butter, celery salt, and Worcestershire sauce. Once the butter melts, add the oysters and cook for thirty seconds, stirring constantly. Add the chili sauce and stir well. Add half-and-half and cook for a few minutes until the soup is hot, but not boiling.

Place the slice of buttered toast in a warmed flat soup bowl. Using a slotted spoon, put the oysters over the toast. Remove the top pan and pour the hot soup over the oysters, filling to about ¼ inch beneath the rim. Garnish with a dash of paprika and serve with oyster crackers.

Serves one.

A MODERN OYSTER PAN ROAST

New York chef Tom Valenti serves an updated version of an oyster pan roast at Ouest restaurant on Upper Broadway. Valenti published the recipe in his cookbook *Welcome to My Kitchen*. His addition of potatoes and bacon adds a chowder-like heartiness to the soup. I understand why a great chef would want to replace the flavored ketchup with oven-roasted tomatoes, but I liked the Heinz Chili Sauce. So here's my adaptation; it's a "two steps forward, one step back" compromise.

> 3 cups potatoes, peeled and cut into ½-inch dice
> 6 ounces bacon, finely diced, about 1 ½ cup
> 1 clove garlic, minced
> ½ cup dry white wine
> 1 cup oyster liquor or clam juice
> 4 tablespoons Heinz Chili Sauce
> 1 ½ cup half-and-half
> 1 tablespoon butter
> Dash of Lea & Perrins Worcestershire sauce
> Dash of celery salt
> 12–24 oysters, shucked, juices reserved
> Buttered toast slices
> Tabasco sauce (optional)

Cook the potatoes until tender and set aside. Fry the bacon in a large frying pan; remove with a slotted spoon and drain on absorbent paper. Remove most of the bacon renderings, leaving a teaspoon of grease in the pan. Sauté the garlic in remaining grease for a minute or two, or until limp. Deglaze the pan with the white wine, leaving the garlic in the pan juices. Add oyster liquor or clam juice and transfer to a small soup pot or large saucepan over medium-high heat and bring to a boil. Add potatoes, bacon, and Chili Sauce, mixing well, and heat until the liquid returns to a boil. Turn down the heat to low and add the half-and-half, butter, Worcestershire sauce, and celery salt. Heat, but do not allow to boil. Add the oysters to the stew, stirring over low heat until the oysters' gills curl and they are just cooked through, about three minutes.

Prepare the desired number of bowls by placing a piece of buttered toast in the bottom of each. Divide the oysters among the toast slices and then spoon the rest of the soup into the bowls.

Serves two to four.

SIX

English Oyster Cult

My NEW FRIEND DON QUINN motioned to the waiter, and a huge platter with two dozen oysters on ice with lemon wedges and a crown of parsley were grandly brought to our table. The oysters had been specially ordered for my arrival. But they weren't exactly what I was expecting.

In October of 2004, I traveled to England to witness the world's oldest oyster celebration, the Colchester Oyster Feast. Half an hour northeast of London by train in rural Essex, the town of Colchester is connected by the River Colne to the North Sea. Thanks to the frigid water temperatures, the oysters here put on extremely high levels of sweet-tasting glycogen.

The Roman emperors prized Colchester oysters above all others. The Romans dragged them back in nets thrown over the sides of their ships. In the winter, they packed them in snow and shipped them across the continent. I had been looking forward to eating Colchester oysters fresh out of the water ever since I first heard about them.

Before I left Texas I had arranged a meeting with Quinn because he was the organizer of something called the "Alternative Oyster Feast" in Colchester. We emailed back and forth and I suggested we meet at a restaurant, pub, or oyster bar where we could conduct our conversation over some Colchester oysters and a beer.

That was when I first learned that there wasn't anywhere in Colchester that served oysters. Quinn said not to worry, he would find some for our dinner. But I was a little shocked. It was like finding out they didn't serve lobsters in Maine.

Britain is, after all, the source of American oyster traditions. Byron, Shelley, Wordsworth, Thackeray, Dickens, and Swift made comments about the oyster. Shakespeare made its vulnerability part of our culture's symbolic language with the line, "the world's mine oyster." And Lewis Carroll spoofed the macabre nature of our relationship with the living foodstuff in "The Walrus and the Carpenter."

I expected every Englishman to be an expert on the subject of oysters, but the folks I met knew diddly-squat about them. When I arrived in Colchester that afternoon, I had tea with a local newspaper reporter named Robert Mead. I was shocked to discover that Mead, like most residents of Colchester, had never eaten an oyster.

Looking over the huge platter of oysters that Quinn had so kindly arranged to be delivered to our table at the Lemon Tree restaurant on St. John Street, I could barely believe my eyes. I sent my compliments to the chef and toasted Quinn with some wine. Then, after eating a few, I pointed out the embarrassing fact that the oysters we were eating weren't Colchester *(O. edulis)* natives.

The chef at the Lemon Tree had ordered two dozen crinkly lipped, Pacific *(C. gigas)* oysters, which are known as rock oysters in Britain and Ireland. Nobody knew the difference anymore, Quinn shrugged.

Nobody ate raw oysters around here anyway. An oyster on the half shell may be a common sight in New York or London, but not in rural Essex, Quinn told me.

When I asked him what it was about a raw oyster that Essex folk didn't like, he told me bluntly, "It looks like a boogey—and it's alive."

I was a bit surprised by that, and I was even more dumbfounded by Quinn's description of the Colchester Oyster Feast, the event I had crossed the Atlantic to witness.

"It's a bunch of rich bastards leeching off the ratepayers," he seethed.

"And don't fall for the phony history," he told me. The Colchester Market was chartered in the 1300s, he said, and there was a market festival going back to that date that included oysters, among other things. But the earliest oyster festival wasn't actually held until 1618, and the feast didn't take its current form until the mid-1800s. While these dates were intended as a refutation of the Colchester Oyster Feast's claim to ancient origins, they only served to impress me more.

I first read about "the world's oldest oyster festival" in Waverly Root's encyclopedic book *Food*. When I found out the festival was still going on, I resolved to attend it. But it wasn't easy.

There was very little information on the Internet, so I looked up the local newspaper in Colchester, the *Essex County Standard*, and contacted the reporter Robert Mead. In an email, I explained that I was a fellow newspaper man from Texas writing a book about oysters and that I wanted to come to the Colchester Oyster Feast. The reporter kindly put me in touch with the mayor's office, which was in charge of issuing tickets. And the Mayor of Colchester's office politely informed me that all the tickets were taken.

I had no idea what exactly the Colchester Oyster Feast was, but having experienced the madcap Galway Oyster Festival, I had every reason to believe it was another oyster-eating and beer-drinking bacchanal. And I couldn't imagine that tickets were really all that hard to come by. So I called the British Tourism Office and told them I was a food and travel writer who wanted to cover the Colchester Oyster Feast and wondered if they could get me a ticket somehow.

Prodded by the tourism folks, the Mayor of Colchester's office contacted me again and told me that I would be admitted to the feast along with other members of the press, but that members of the press were not seated or fed. Kelly was hoping I was going to get two tickets to the affair. When I informed her that I couldn't even get one ticket and that I would be herded behind the velvet ropes with the rest of the journalists, she decided not to join me on the trip.

I didn't really mind the treatment. I had no desire to make chitchat with the upper-crust society types who evidently attended the event. And the mayor's office actually took great care of me. Since I was traveling from so far away, the mayor offered to take me on a tour of the oyster grounds off Mersea Island the day before the festival and then host an oyster lunch at "the Company Shed."

Early the next morning, Dick Barton, a member of the Guild of Registered Blue Badge Tourist Guides, picked me up at my hotel to take me to meet the mayor. Barton was an earnest man who apologized profusely for not having memorized a sufficient inventory of oyster facts. With his badge and his jacket and tie, he reminded me of a very old Boy Scout.

Our route from Colchester to Mersea took us along the salt marshes and intertidal mudflats where our system of oyster cultivation began. The oyster-loving Romans harvested oysters from distant reefs and stored a big supply in brackish pools closer to their settlements. The oysters got fatter and sweeter in the plankton-rich backwaters, where freshwater from the River Colne mixes with saltwater from the North Sea.

Following the Roman example, early English oystermen created "oyster layings," where large oysters were stored for later sale and small oysters were fattened. In the northern latitudes of the North Sea shore,

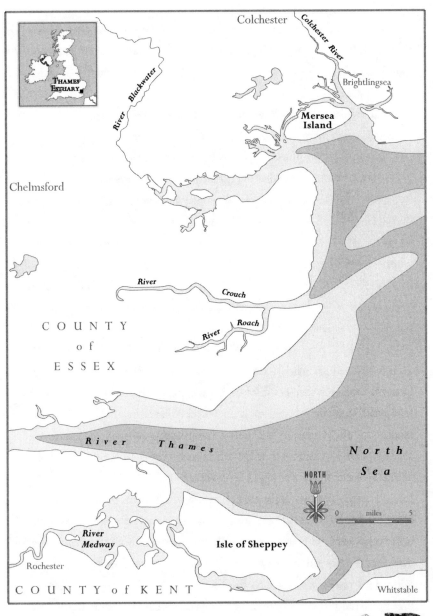

Thames Estuary, England

the tides fluctuate so drastically that the muddy flats are exposed during the low tide. Oystermen dug pits in these intertidal areas for their layings. When the water receded at low tide, the pits remained full of water, so the oysters stayed wet.

The British noblemen who owned the foreshore leased lots in their intertidal lands to oystermen. These little tenanted oyster farms were privately owned, but the oyster reefs themselves were common grounds. The English system gave birth to the American oyster lease.

There were no fishing regulations until the late 1600s, when Britain's first fishing guild was formed. The guild drafted rules protecting the property rights of the owner of oyster layings and limiting when and where oysters could be taken. This led to a cooperative system of husbandry. The guild would require all oyster boats to show up on a given day to assist in grooming the public areas to prepare them for the spat set. All the oystermen would then share in the harvest.

I asked Barton what he thought of the Colchester natives. "We didn't eat shellfish when I was a kid," he said. "I ate my first oysters at the Colchester Oyster Feast when I was forty years old. I got sick and I never ate them again."

John Bouckley, the mayor of Colchester, was sitting on the opposite side of the small aluminum boat, smiling hugely in a red windbreaker and black wool cap. He was giving me the promised tour of the Colchester oyster beds. The tide was low and the mayor pointed out some swimming-pool-sized pits dug into the mud flats. He didn't know whether they were old unused oyster pits or ones that were still being used.

Colchester oysterman Peter Vince piloted the johnboat out past the yacht docks of West Mersea. Vince was a tall, lanky man who looked like a caricature of an English fisherman, with long white hair, a big salt-and-pepper beard, and yellow, gnarled teeth. He had been oystering in Colchester since 1944.

He pulled up alongside a twenty-eight-foot oyster boat and helped us climb aboard. Captain Allan Bird, a friend of Vince's, had agreed to take us along for a ride as he dredged an oyster bed in the Blackwater River basin.

"The big freeze in the winter of 1962–63 changed the way we do things," Vince said. When the bay froze, every oyster in the water was killed. Today, Bird, Vince, and many other Colchester oystermen buy half-grown rock *(C. gigas)* oysters from hatcheries that they can raise to a marketable size in a year or two. The *C. gigas* oysters grow more rapidly and are much heartier than the natives.

I said it was a shame the Colchester natives *(O. edulis)* were being lost. "To most people, an oyster is an oyster," Peter Vince said with a shrug. The natives were delicate and died from diseases, they took five years or more to grow to maturity, and they tasted very strong. The *C. gigas* are very hard to kill, and the softer texture and milder flavor are more palatable to a wider number of people.

Vince is a member of the Slow Food movement, and he is spearheading an effort to acquire a Protected Geographical Identity (PGI) from the European Union for Colchester oysters. The PGI designation is akin to the French *appellation d'origine contrôlée* (AOC) and is intended to protect consumers and producers from fraudulent marketing.

There was a bushel basket of Colchester native *(O. edulis)* oysters sitting on the stern, but the point of the dredging wasn't really harvesting. Captain Bird was grooming the bed to remove debris and pests.

I picked one up with the intention of shucking it, but I was reminded that Colchester waters are "Grade B" and the oysters require "depuration," as the purifying process is known. After our cruise, we took a tour of the seafood plant on the other end of Mersea Island. "Colchester Oyster Fishery Ltd.," read the sign out front. It was an industrial shed where oysters were sorted by grade, purified, and packed for shipping all over the world.

"These are going to Gordon Ramsey," one of the packers told me, pointing to a bag of oysters. I have no idea if he was telling the truth or pulling my leg.

The purification setup is called an ultraviolet recirculator. The oysters are placed in square plastic tubs, and brackish water is pumped in so that it flows from tub to tub. In between tubs, the water passes through an intense dose of ultraviolet radiation, which kills the offending bacteria. For forty-eight hours the water recirculates through the oysters and the ultraviolet lights, at which point the oysters are certified free of contaminants. Ultraviolet recirculators kill most offending bacteria. Unfortunately, they don't work on *Vibrio*.

My tour of the Mersea oyster fishery ended at the Company Shed in the village of West Mersea. The establishment is actually a fish store with picnic tables. It's also the only place anywhere near the town of Colchester, England, that serves the city's famous oysters. At a lunch in my honor hosted by the mayor, each of us seated at the table got a half dozen Colchester natives on the half shell. They were large, extremely salty, very sweet, and not quite as aromatic with iodine and ebb tide flavors as the Irish natives. The texture was extremely firm and it took quite a bit of chewing to get one down.

My host, the mayor, brought a bottle of Mersea white wine that he poured all around. We were joined by the mayor's wife and several other local dignitaries. It was quite a party. But I was a little surprised when a photographer from the *Essex County Standard* stopped by and took a picture of the mayor and me holding up a plate of oysters.

On Friday morning, the day of the Colchester Oyster Feast, I went down to the hotel lobby to get some tea and pick up a newspaper. I was shocked to see a photo of the mayor and me with our oysters on page two of the *Essex County Standard*, with the headline "Texan Robb Goes Native." The story by Robert Mead read in part, "A Texas food writer has called it a 'civic crime' that people cannot sit down and enjoy oysters in Colchester."

Later that morning I was in my hotel room getting ready for the Oyster Feast when the phone rang. It was a reporter from BBC Radio. Having read the story in the *Essex County Standard*, she wanted to do a phone interview on the subject of Colchester and oysters.

I was a little baffled by all the attention. I suppose I did call it a "civic crime" that a town famous for its oysters didn't have a single oyster bar. But I'm not used to being taken quite so seriously. It must have been an awfully slow news day.

But I was on a roll, so I told the BBC Radio reporter something I'd found out from the mayor's office. Of the 280 guests invited to the Colchester Oyster Feast this year, only 120 ordered oysters.

"Why go to an oyster feast if you don't like oysters?" I asked rhetorically. That seemed to satisfy her desire for a sound bite. I assume the interview aired, along with the rest of the coverage of the Colchester Oyster Feast, on the BBC's regional news program, although I didn't get a chance to listen.

At the appointed hour, I headed over to Colchester Town Hall, a building with a tall steeple-like clock tower that looks something like a church. When I arrived, a line of town cars and limos were pulling up to the building's main entrance.

I got in line to get into the building behind a guy who was wearing a navy blue suit. Draped across his shoulders was the official regalia of his position. I leaned forward and studied it closely. It looked like a charm necklace with two kinds of charms repeated over and over. There were silver oyster shells alternating with two crossed herrings, bound together with links of silver chain. If you like oysters and herring (and I do), it was some pretty impressive jewelry.

I tapped the guy on the back and asked what office the regalia represented. He told me he was the mayor of Brightlingsea, an oyster provenance I had heard a lot about. His wife was wearing official regalia too, and so were a lot of other guests.

The guests weren't being let in to the hall yet; they were mingling in a downstairs salon. But photographers were going in to the feasting hall early to shoot the elaborate place settings, so I waltzed in with the rest of the media lowlifes, bejeweled in the regalia of our office—plastic press badges.

I got a briefing from a press liaison on the event's history. The original Oyster Feast was part of the St. Dennis Fair and dates back to at least 1318. St. Dennis Fair was Colchester's version of Michaelmas, a traditional October harvest celebration. Contracts, including oyster leases, were renewed at this time of year. In the 1790s, a "gift" of October oysters from the Colne dredgermen became a part of their annual oyster charter.

The oysters were consumed at a civic feast thrown by politicians to win favor with the Freemen, the hereditary gentlemen who were the town's only voters. In 1835, new laws were passed nationwide to clean up corrupt local government. They specifically forbade civic feasts held at taxpayer's expense.

In 1845, a mayor named Henry Wolton invited two hundred people to be his guests at an oyster lunch held in town hall. He paid for the whole thing out of his own pocket, except for the oysters, which were still being donated to the city as part of the dredgerman's charter. Wolton was reelected several times, and the tradition of the Colchester Oyster Feast was continued.

Over the years, each mayor of Colchester has vied to get bigger names to attend his Oyster Feast. Royalty, cabinet ministers, and London dignitaries were the big catches in past years. The Oyster Feast of 1931 was attended by HRH Edward Prince of Wales—the man who five years later ascended the throne as Edward VIII and, two months after that, abdicated in order to marry the woman he loved.

In modern times, media celebrities, military brass, and members of Parliament have attended. And to this day, the oystermen's contract still requires them to provide the mayor with two thousand oysters for the Oyster Feast every year. In 1902, when the current Colchester Town Hall was built, the design included a Moot Hall built specifically for the Oyster Feast.

The press liaison showed me into the Moot Hall and left me with the other press types. I stood there dumbfounded for a minute. The room looked like a cross between a ballroom at the Waldorf-Astoria and the inside of a cathedral. Shafts of colored light poured in through the two-story stained-glass windows. There were stately white columns between the windows and a giant oil painting of the queen hanging on the wall. The room was three stories high, with a barrel-vaulted ceiling.

The tables were already set. At each seat was a menu with a color portrait of the mayor in his robes and regalia on the front. The head table for the dignitaries was set up in front of the stained glass windows on a raised platform several feet above the rest of the crowd. Perpendicular to the head table, on the floor below, were long tables with twelve place settings on each side. Place cards designated where each guest would sit.

"Guests are seated in order of social prominence," one of the photographers told me. The big shots sat up on the high table with the mayor. Speakers that year included Margaret Thatcher's former press secretary, Bernard Ingham, and Labour MP Bob Marshall-Andrews, QC. The tables on the main floor had a lot of military guys sitting on the ends closest to the mayor's table.

The rank of the guests on the main floor could be determined by their proximity to the mayor's table, he explained. "So the guys sitting on the ends of the tables farthest from the head table are the least important?" I asked.

"That's the idea," he said.

I walked along the far end of the tables looking at the place cards of the lowly and asking him if he knew who they were. He identified a few as seafood distributors and oystermen.

Looking over the ornate feasting hall in the stillness before the ceremony began, I decided that Colchester's Moot Hall was the Cathedral of the Oyster Faithful, and the mayor of Colchester was their archbishop.

When the doors opened, an orchestra seated in a loft above the hall struck up some light classical music and the crowd of guests entered and took their places. When everybody had been seated, the big time pomp got going.

The dignitaries were led into the room by the Town Serjeant, who wore a white tie, white gloves, and a blue coat with brass buttons and tails, with a large blue medal around his neck and three more medals hanging from his breast pocket. Over his shoulder he carried the mayor's mace, a five-foot-long golden shaft with a big crown on top.

The mace was set on the table in a pair of wooden holders in front of the mayor's throne, a huge, ornately carved wooden chair that was taller than the mayor. There were birds over each of the arms, a crown over the headrest, and the red-and-white crest of Colchester set into the backrest.

The mayor was wearing a full-length black robe with gold braid over a white shirt and white ascot with the enormous medallion of office around his neck on a maroon ribbon. The white fuzzy hair on top of his balding head was magnificently backlit by the stained-glass window as he sat down in his great big chair.

When the mayor was seated, the Town Serjeant reappeared in the doorway of the banquet hall holding a silver platter with a dozen Colchester natives on the half shell. He paused there for a minute and then, to the cadence of "Fanfare to the Colchester Native," a classical composition by Nigel Hildreth, M.Mus PGGE, he marched with the plate of oysters up to the front of the room and handed them up to the mayor.

The mayor stood up and took the oysters. Holding the silver platter in his left hand, he held up one Colchester native in his right for all to see. And then, with all the drama he could muster, he slurped it down to thunderous applause. The mayor had eaten the first oyster, and the Feast had begun. Wine was poured and toasts were made.

It was a stunning thing to witness. The Colchester Oyster Feast is nothing short of an oyster sacrament. It is one of the most unique food events in the world. That a community should still honor the food that made it famous centuries ago is both touching and ironic. Colchester has carefully preserved the world's oldest oyster ceremony, but has lost the joy of eating oysters. Plates of opened oysters stood ready, but hardly anyone asked for seconds. You call that an oyster feast?

If I were king, the money changers would be driven out of the temple, and Moot Hall would be returned to the true believers. No one would be invited to the Colchester Oyster Feast unless they loved oysters. As the waiters began to serve the entrées, I looked over a serving table on the back wall loaded with dozens upon dozens of opened oysters that would soon be thrown away. With a waiter's permission, I grabbed a couple of plates and some bread and butter and ducked down the back stairs.

Looking for somewhere to sit down, I came upon the first-aid station, where two elderly women in nurses' uniforms sat drinking tea. I asked if I could join them and they invited me to sit down at a table. When they noticed the oysters, they were horrified. One said she had never seen an oyster before, never mind eaten one. She looked at mine and declared them disgusting.

"Martinis and oysters are a natural combination, especially in London where people love gin," the bartender at J. Sheekey in Covent Garden told me as he set my martini down in front of me. It was a Beefeater martini, dry with a twist of lemon. I asked him to shake it hard and make it slushy, but he refused. Shaking bruises the liquor and dilutes the cocktail too much—a martini should be stirred, not shaken, he said. And he wasn't kidding.

I couldn't get a reservation at J. Sheekey—it's considered the top fish restaurant in London—but I found an open seat at their oyster bar at around three on a Saturday afternoon. The bartender at Sheekey's recommended a half dozen No. 2 Mersea *(O. edulis)* oysters.

Sheekey's Mersea oysters were pretty impressive. The combination of the oysters and the icy martini, with its herbal aroma and the hint of lemon, was sublime. The bartender was waiting for a reaction, but my mouth was full. I made a grateful groaning sound to show my approval.

"Gin and oysters—it's just like vodka and caviar," the bartender said with satisfaction.

My plan had been to spend a weekend in London touring the city's famous oyster bars. The martini part of my oyster-and-martini weekend came about by accident.

On Friday night, after I arrived from Colchester, the first oysters I came across were at an oyster stall out in front of Bibendum Oyster Bar in the Chelsea neighborhood near my hotel. It looked just like the oyster stands you see in front of restaurants in Paris. So I went inside and sat down at a table.

Eavesdropping on the other tables, I surmised my fellow patrons weren't British. There was an Italian couple, a French couple, and a Japanese guy with several Asian women. All of them had wine bottles in ice buckets.

I really didn't want to drink a whole bottle of wine by myself, and the waiter indignantly told me they didn't serve beer. I ordered the national cocktail, a gin martini. And so my first oyster-and-martini pairing came about by accident. But I liked it—a whole lot. While martinis might overpower more delicate oysters, they went perfectly with the *(O. edulis)* natives. The cold fire of a gin martini, with its juniper berry and botanical aroma, stands up to the briny "licking the bottom of a boat" flavor of the natives like nothing else I've tried. And it cleanses the palate brilliantly. I had that first one with an olive.

As for Bibendum's oysters, they were shucked in the French style, with the bottom foot still attached. The half dozen Belons I sampled were shriveled up; I suspected they had been shucked hours ago. If a half dozen sounds conservative, consider that six oysters along with one martini set me back more than $50. Sad, when you consider that in 1864, laborers in London were buying four oysters for a penny.

J. Sheekey's was the one London restaurant I would most like to visit again. A warren of booths and snugs furnished in dark wood paneling and decorated with black-and-white photos of old London, the restaurant is charming but utterly unpretentious.

Sheekey's got started in 1896, when Lord Salisbury made a deal with a Covent Garden fish stall operator. Josef Sheekey would open an oyster bar in Lord Salisbury's building at a favorable rent, provided he supplied the Lord's private theater parties with the very choicest oysters in London.

After I left J. Sheekey's in Covent Garden, I walked to an even older restaurant located nearby. Rules on Maiden Lane is said to be the oldest restaurant in London. It was opened as an oyster bar in 1798 by a playboy named Thomas Rule, who had promised his parents he would abandon his dissolute life and run a proper oyster bar.

Over the years, the restaurant has hosted such literary luminaries as Charles Dickens, H. G. Wells, and William Makepeace Thackeray. It is decorated with hundreds of cartoons and artworks hung on the walls by patrons.

Rules is still quite proud of its oysters. The menu features Lindisfarne rock *(C. gigas)* oysters from Northumberland and Strangford Lough *(O. edulis)* from Ireland. When I visited, six oysters on the half shell were £10.95 for rock oysters, and a comparatively reasonable £13.50 for the Irish natives. I got six of each.

They were brought to the table on a large, round tray of ice with a stand placed underneath, much the way pizzas are served at some Italian restaurants in the States. The ice was garnished with seaweed. Mignonette was served in a little steel cup in the middle of the platter, flanked by two half lemons with sprigs of parsley on top.

Tucked under the platter were salt, pepper, Tabasco sauce, and a shaker bottle of red wine vinegar with mixed peppercorns soaking in it. The table was set with lots of silver, linen, and bread and butter.

The rock oysters had a very salty flavor. I sprinkled a little of the peppercorn vinegar on some and doused others with the mignonette, which made for an interesting variation. The natives were chewy and sweet. I was pleasantly surprised by how diluted the Rules martini tasted. Is it possible the bartender at the oldest restaurant in London is shaking the martinis instead of stirring them?

The next day, I made my way to Harrods Department Store. At Harrods seafood counter, the oysters were displayed neatly in a bed of crushed ice, in perfect rows and columns with their pointy ends sticking up. Colchester natives went for £2 apiece, while rock oysters were seventy-five pence (the exchange rate was roughly $2 to the pound then.) I got six Colchester natives, which were served at the bar with toast points, vinegar, and shallots. There weren't any martinis available, so I had a London Pride beer.

The oysters were exceptionally sweet, but utterly brineless. There was no hint of salt in the flavor whatsoever. Looking back at the seafood counter, I realized that while the display looked impressive, sticking the oysters in ice sharp end up was probably responsible for the loss of brine. The little card stuck in the ice beside them said "Natives, Catchment Area: Colchester." "Where exactly are these oysters from?" I asked the seafood manager.

"All I know is that they are from somewhere in the Essex estuary," she said. "They are actually oysters that are harvested in Ireland and deposited in the Colchester area," she told me.

Irish oysters? In Colchester?

At Bentley's, one of the toniest oyster bars of the West End, they serve only Irish oysters. Which is ironic since Bentley's was opened in 1916 by the Bentley family, who made their fortune selling Colchester oysters.

"We don't serve Colchester oysters anymore. It's Grade B water. It's a compromise," the bartender at Bentley's told me. "We serve only Strangford Loughs."

Doubts about the cleanliness of Colchester waters began to arise in the 1890s. Thanks to the Industrial Revolution, the population of London was increasing rapidly at that time, and so was the amount of sewage being dumped into the Thames Estuary. A report titled "On Oyster Cultivation in Relation to Disease," issued in 1896, identified four different places where oyster beds were exposed to sewage outflows.

Oystermen ridiculed the alarmist report. Then, six years later, in 1902, the Dean of Winchester and several other people died of typhoid from contaminated Brightlingsea oysters served at a public banquet. A systematic study of water quality ensued, but oysters had gained a dangerous reputation. In 1930, a sanitizing facility was built to purify oysters taken from Colchester's "Grade B" waters. Colchester oysters still must be treated before they can be served.

The bartender at Bentley's explained that Irish oysters were the only ones in Great Britain that came from Grade A waters. I found his honesty refreshing. But then again, Bentley's was owned by Richard Corrigan, a famous Irish chef.

Sitting at Bentley's lustrous marble bar, I ordered three No. 1 and three No. 2 Strangford Loughs and a martini. I was promptly set up with a dark green and gold placemat, a napkin, silverware, a bread plate, an oyster plate, some fresh bread, a plate of deep yellow butter rounds, vinegar, red pepper, Tabasco sauce, and a saucer full of lemons wrapped in cheesecloth. Bentley's is a very serious oyster bar.

When the bartender asked me if I wanted olives or a twist, I asked him which garnish he liked better with oysters. He recommended both. I had never seen both garnishes served together, but he told me he combined them all the time. When he served me the cocktail, there was a toothpick loaded with olives and a piece of lemon peel in it.

Like all the martinis I drank in London, Bentley's was much more potent than the more diluted style of martini we drink in America and not quite as cold. The V-on-a-stem martini glass was small, and it was chilled by being filled with ice water for a few minutes, not stored in the freezer like my martini glasses at home. The lemon and olives did go well together, and they tasted great with the oysters too.

Bentley's was the only place I remember seeing oysters Rockefeller on the menu; six went for £18.50, five or six times what they sell for in New Orleans. A half dozen Irish *(O. edulis)* native No. 1 oysters on the half shell were £18.50 at Bentley's, while a half dozen No. 2s went for £16.50. I decided to compare the No. 1s and No. 2s, so they kindly made up a plate with three of each.

The texture of the No. 1 oysters was very different from the smaller oysters. As I bit into them, they came apart in pieces in my mouth, like a big bite of scrambled eggs. Some of the firmer pieces required more chewing than others. The big oysters were salty, with lots of marine and mineral flavors. I sat back and savored the last oyster, the dregs of my martini, and the olives.

"I make the best martini you will ever drink," the bartender at Green's Restaurant and Oyster Bar, a short walk from Bentley's, told me. He pooh-poohed my usual choice of Beefeater and recommended I go with the bar gin, which was Tanqueray. His preparations—chilling the glass, carving and trimming a large hunk of fresh lemon peel—were quite elaborate. But then again, I was the only customer at three in the afternoon.

Green's is located in such an exclusive neighborhood, it is sometimes given the title "Green's of Duke Street, St. James." The restaurant feels more like an exclusive men's club than the sort of oyster saloons we have in Texas. It was founded in 1982 by Simon Parker Bowles, the brother-in-law of Camilla Parker Bowles (now better known as HRH

The Duchess of Cornwall, second wife of Prince Charles). Along with the best martini-maker in London, Green's also employs the city's best oyster shucker. Or so he says, anyway.

Shucker Jack Pasinski moved to London from Poland, where he was trained as a chef. He had been shucking oysters for six years in London, four of them at Green's. When I spoke with Pasinski, he said that, in his opinion, No. 1s were too big and too chewy. They were also thirty-five percent more expensive. Colchester No. 2s were his recommendation. A half dozen Colchester *(O. edulis)* natives went for £15.50.

The oysters were perfectly shucked and daintily presented with a profusion of silverware, linen, and china. They tasted sweet and a tad salty. The martini tasted quite different from the others I had been drinking, owing mainly to the difference in gin. Tanqueray is heavier on the juniper than most other gins, while Beefeater has a bit of coriander in the nose. The bartender gave me the oft-repeated bit about stirring rather than shaking so as not to bruise the liquor.

The contention that shaking "bruises the gin" is so rampant among London bartenders that you have to wonder what's behind it. A martini-loving scientist once wrote a treatise that theorizes that shaking causes the aldehyde molecules in the alcohol to bond with more oxygen, resulting in a nasty oxidized taste. I think he was spoofing us. I prefer W. Somerset Maugham's explanation: "Martinis should always be stirred, not shaken, so that the molecules lie sensuously one on top of the other."

For whatever reason, the martini I drank at Green's was distinctive. "What is the secret of your martini?" I asked the bartender.

"It's love," he said with a smile.

❖

The Walrus and the Carpenter

(Excerpt from *Through the Looking-Glass and What Alice Found There*, by Lewis Carroll, 1872)

"O Oysters, come and walk with us!"
The Walrus did beseech.
"A pleasant walk, a pleasant talk,
Along the briny beach:
We cannot do with more than four,
To give a hand to each."

The eldest Oyster looked at him,
But never a word he said:
The eldest Oyster winked his eye,
And shook his heavy head—
Meaning to say he did not choose
To leave the oyster-bed.

But four young Oysters hurried up,
All eager for the treat:
Their coats were brushed, their faces washed,
Their shoes were clean and neat—
And this was odd, because, you know,
They hadn't any feet.

Four other Oysters followed them,
And yet another four;
And thick and fast they came at last,
And more, and more, and more—
All hopping through the frothy waves,
And scrambling to the shore.

The Walrus and the Carpenter
Walked on a mile or so,
And then they rested on a rock
Conveniently low:

And all the little Oysters stood
And waited in a row.

"The time has come," the Walrus said,
"To talk of many things:
Of shoes—and ships—and sealing-wax—
Of cabbages—and kings—
And why the sea is boiling hot—
And whether pigs have wings."

"But wait a bit," the Oysters cried,
"Before we have our chat;
For some of us are out of breath,
And all of us are fat!"
"No hurry!" said the Carpenter.
They thanked him much for that.

"A loaf of bread," the Walrus said,
"Is what we chiefly need:
Pepper and vinegar besides
Are very good indeed—
Now if you're ready, Oysters dear,
We can begin to feed."

"But not on us!" the Oysters cried,
Turning a little blue.
"After such kindness, that would be
A dismal thing to do!"
"The night is fine," the Walrus said.
"Do you admire the view?"

"It was so kind of you to come!
And you are very nice!"
The Carpenter said nothing but
"Cut us another slice:
I wish you were not quite so deaf—
I've had to ask you twice!"

"It seems a shame," the Walrus said,
"To play them such a trick,
After we've brought them out so far,
And made them trot so quick!"
The Carpenter said nothing but
"The butter's spread too thick!"

"I weep for you," the Walrus said:
"I deeply sympathize."
With sobs and tears he sorted out
Those of the largest size,
Holding his pocket-handkerchief
Before his streaming eyes.

"O Oysters," said the Carpenter,
"You've had a pleasant run!
Shall we be trotting home again?"
But answer came there none—
And this was scarcely odd, because
They'd eaten every one.

It was 1853 when the East Kent Railway first connected London with the beaches of Kent, making a day at the seashore convenient for Londoners. This was the heyday of English oyster eating, and the famous oyster beds of Seasalter and Whitstable were not far from the tourist areas.

In 1856, a Whitstable oysterman named Richard "Leggy" Wheeler set up his wife Mary Ann in a small shop selling local oysters, whelks, and shrimp to visitors. Wheelers Oyster Bar became a Whitstable landmark, and it has changed very little to this day.

In the 1950s, the restaurant came into the possession of a Wheeler relative named Bernard Walsh, who decided to become a restaurant entrepreneur by taking the famous Wheelers name to London. There he founded a chain of restaurants that became immensely popular.

The legendary London journalist, Max Hastings, remembers Wheelers seafood restaurant in Old Compton Street where his father was a member of the "Thursday Club" in the 1950s. The group included Prince Philip and Peter Ustinov among others.

Bernard Walsh eventually sold his empire to a big restaurant company and retired comfortably. And there are still a few Wheelers seafood restaurants left in London at last report. But in the twenty-first century, it is the original 150-year-old Wheelers Oyster Bar, housed in a hot pink edifice on High Street in Whitstable, that is once again capturing the attention of seafood lovers.

Some people think Wheelers in Whitstable is the best oyster bar in England. It may also be the quirkiest. It's a tiny space, with four bar-stools at a counter in front of an overstuffed seafood case. The woman behind the display handed me a plate of six Whitstable *(O. edulis)* natives. They were of medium saltiness and medium sweetness, but they were extremely mineral, like a mouthful of pennies.

After lunch, I wandered into the one-room Whitstable Museum farther up High Street. The curator, Manda Gifford, who also operated the gift shop, asked me if there was something in particular I was interested in. I told her I was looking for information about Whitstable's famous oysters. She told me I had come to the right place.

First, she asked me to sit down in a row of chairs in front of a television set while she cued up a videotape. I was mesmerized by a four-minute black-and-white silent movie made in the very beginning of the motion-picture era.

The movie begins with Whitstable oystermen rowing out to their sailing smacks in a dinghy. Cut to them under sail throwing dredges overboard and hauling them back up by hand. Now they are back on the beach sampling a few oysters before packing them up in barrels. Cut to a steaming locomotive. And finally, we see a bunch of London swells in dinner jackets slurping oysters in a fancy restaurant—the end.

I sat for a second wondering why the moviemaker had chosen oystering as a subject. Was it part of a series about food? Then I commented to Ms. Gifford that hauling dredges by hand looked like a miserable way to spend the day.

Then she handed me a pamphlet produced by the museum called "Farming Oysters: The Story of the Seasalter Oyster Fishery." From it, I learned that since the time of the Norman conquest, the oyster charter of Whitstable was owned by the monastery of Christ Church at Canterbury, and oystermen bought their leases from the church.

Until 1859, anyway, which is when a wealthy Whitstable ship owner named Thomas Gann bought the fishing charter for the Seasalter grounds for £2,000. With a partner, he also acquired the adjacent Ham grounds and founded the Seasalter and Ham Oyster Fishery Company.

In 1965, Seasalter and Ham Oyster Fishery Company was purchased by Associated Fisheries Ltd. The managing director, Gerald Gardner, was an early advocate of the oyster hatchery concept. Gardner hired a staff of scientists, including a biologist named John Bayes, to find a way to breed oysters artificially. But the considerable investment never paid off, and the Whitstable operation was scheduled for closure.

In 1987, biologist Bayes took over the operation and renamed it Seasalter Shellfish (Whitstable) Ltd. And, according to the pamphlet, everyone lived happily ever after.

"What happened to this guy?" I asked Ms. Gifford, pointing to a photo of a hippie with a long beard on a bicycle.

"You mean John Bayes?" she asked.

"Yes, if I wanted to interview him, where would I find him?" I asked the curator.

"I'll ring him up for you if you like," she volunteered, picking up the phone.

Within a few minutes, I had an appointment with the eccentric scientist. And my view of oysters and oystermen would never be the same.

The taxicab dropped me off in a maze of falling-down industrial buildings by the waterside. I couldn't find any sign or mailbox or front door. So I wandered around the compound of partially demolished nursery buildings, picking my way through heaps of refuse and empty plastic containers while yelling hello.

Someone finally opened a door in a warehouse-type building and motioned for me to come in. The inside of the place was cluttered with plastic buckets, plastic pipes and fittings, and various other debris. The walls were unpainted plywood framed with two-by-fours. Wires hung from exposed electrical switches, timers, and junction boxes. It was dark and dank, and there wasn't any heat in the building.

The headquarters of Seasalter Shellfish felt like the post-apocalyptic landscape of a *Mad Max* movie. And I was about to meet the leader of this dystopian seaside community.

John Bayes yelled for me to come up the stairs to his second-floor office. He stood up to shake my hand, then took a seat in a beat-up office chair behind a messy desk. He was wearing a filthy quilted blue nylon parka, blue jeans, and sandals with black socks. He was bald on top with long, stringy hair around the fringes, and he had a salt-and-pepper beard that reached his chest.

Within a few minutes of conversation, Bayes made it clear that he thought I was a twit. In retrospect, I can hardly blame him. I had a lot of silly ideas. He set me straight with some shockingly frank news.

Food writers have always romanticized the oyster business. In an age-old dance, oystermen blow smoke up journalists' asses about the unique flavor of their oysters, and the scriveners jot down the oystermen's clever quotes, eat the delightful shellfish, and then share the experience with readers.

But most oyster books and articles focus on the oysters and oystermen of one particular locale. I made the mistake of thinking that I could interview oystermen in lots of different places and get lots of lovely stories.

When I told Bayes that a very nice oysterman named Peter Vince was working on a Protected Geographical Indication (PGI) for Colchester oysters, Bayes blew a fuse.

Whitstable already had a PGI, he told me, or they had applied for one anyway, but the whole thing was nonsense.

"Why?" I asked him.

"Because it's impossible to identify where oysters come from, so it's impossible to police," he said. "The oysters you ate in Colchester were probably from Whitstable," he said. At Wheelers Oyster Bar, I had already learned that oyster bars in London were calling Whitstable oysters Colchester oysters because nobody wanted Whitstables anymore.

"It's all a lot of kidology," Bayes said bitterly.

"Kidology?"

"Bullshit," he said. "There is no traceability of oysters. Anybody can tell you anything about where their oysters come from and nobody can prove a thing."

Think about it, Bayes continued. When you harvest oysters in Ireland and dump them in Colchester, you are taking perfectly edible oysters from Grade A waters and putting them into Grade B waters. So then you have to use this expensive machinery to purify these oysters that were perfectly clean before you mucked them up.

It does sound pretty absurd. But the Thames Estuary ran out of oysters a long time ago. Oystermen around here have been bringing them in from elsewhere since the late 1800s because Colchester and Whitstable were the names that oyster eaters wanted to hear.

But how did a fishery that had been around for over a millennium suddenly disappear? I asked Bayes.

"Rapid transportation killed the oyster," he said. Suddenly the meaning of the little black-and-white film I watched at the Whitstable museum became clear to me. Audiences of the 1800s were meant to marvel that, thanks to the railroad, oysters harvested in the morning in Whitstable could be eaten in London that night.

Before the railroad, Bayes explained, there wasn't any incentive for oystermen to push their harvest to the limit because there was no way to get all they could catch to the market. But once the railroad arrived, you could sell all the oysters you could gather.

It was rapid transportation that caused overfishing.

The railroad to London arrived in Whitstable in 1860. The price of oysters hit its lowest point in London between 1862 and 1864, when a meal of oysters cost a few pennies. By 1889, the oyster fishery in the Thames Estuary went into serious decline, and prices rose with the decrease in supply. There were only two good spatfalls between the 1890s and the early 1900s. But there were still plenty of oysters to be had elsewhere.

"A hundred years ago, the owner of Seasalter and Ham Oyster Fishery went to France every spring, bought twenty million oysters, and relaid them on the Ham grounds," Bayes said. "They sold ten million of them a little at a time—the rest were lost. But it was still profitable."

Moving oysters around isn't so easy anymore. It's illegal to bring oysters in from France these days because of *Bonamia ostreae*, but the laws aren't well enforced, he observed. "The disease is everywhere, and fishermen just keep spreading it around," Bayes said.

"When I first came here in 1966, the idea was to resurrect the business. I was going to raise native *(O. edulis)* oysters. But I never did succeed," said Bayes.

"Why?" I asked.

"If I knew why, I would be doing it!" he barked at me as if I were a dolt.

One guy in Cork, Ireland, named David Hugh-Jones succeeded in cultivating native *(O. edulis)* oysters, Bayes told me. He built twenty-two ponds of a million liters each and lined them with mussel shells. Then he pumped seawater through them and put six hundred natives in each. He got a spat set on the mussel shells and then put them in beds in the open water. He had only a four percent survival rate, but he was producing millions.

Hugh-Jones was undone by local sewage works that discharged pollution into his oyster beds. They said it was an accident, but it just kept happening, Bayes told me. His waters were rated Class D, and he was wiped out. "He is still fighting it," Bayes said. "But he shouldn't have to. The pollution is illegal. And there is no such thing as a regular series of accidents."

But the whole idea of cultivating *(O. edulis)* natives has been undone by the oyster disease called *Bonamia*, which arrived from California and New Zealand in the 1970s, Bayes told me.

Seasalter Shellfish ended up as a hatchery selling *Crassostrea gigas* oyster seed and clam seed to shellfish farmers around the world. (Seed is the word used for the tiny oysters and clams that shellfish farmers raise to maturity.) But while he relies on *C. gigas* oysters for his livelihood, Bayes doesn't have a high opinion of the species.

"*C. gigas* is as far from an oyster as a man is from a monkey," he told me. "It's a faster-growing, coarser animal. It dedicates sixty percent of its body weight to gonad!" While an *O. edulis* oyster produces around two million eggs, the average *C. gigas* produces fifty million.

"This is their northernmost limit; they don't reproduce naturally in England and Ireland," he said. "But they do in France. Most years, they have more of them than they know what to do with."

Bayes once visited the oyster operations of the United States. He had a pretty dim view of the situation. As long as you can harvest oysters for free, as they do on the Gulf Coast, there is no incentive for investment, he said. The oyster concerns on the East Coast were a lot of "tin pot affairs," in his view. He was very impressed, however, by a hatchery he visited in Seattle. It was built on a massive scale, he said. The oyster tanks were bigger than swimming pools. The Pacific Northwest might actually challenge France some day, he thought.

But oysters were finished in England. "People in England eat one million oysters a year. That's nothing. In the 1920s, this company [Seasalter and Ham Oyster Fishery] alone sold twenty million oysters a year and the Whitstable Oyster Company sold the same amount."

I asked Bayes what happened. "When oysters rose in price, they became a luxury product like caviar," he observed. "It has been said that the real competitor to oysters is smoked salmon." In the same time period that the price of oysters skyrocketed, salmon farming brought the cost of smoked salmon down. "Smoked salmon has gotten cheap and easy," Bayes said. "It's practically fast food now."

I asked him if there was any hope for oysters. "For all intents and purposes, the English oyster business is dead," said John Bayes.

❖

The mystery of why oysters disappeared from England was addressed a few years ago by a retired Cambridge economics professor named Robert Neild. Intrigued by the abundance of oysters in France and their scarcity in the United Kingdom, Neild submerged himself in the sort of statistical research that economists love and food writers loathe.

The result was a wonderful book called *The English, the French and the Oyster* that was published in 1995. In the book, Neild follows the government responses in both countries to the crisis in the oyster industry that occurred around 1850. Oysters were dying off in both places, but the two governments took a radically different approach to the problem.

An English commission created to study the failure of the oyster harvest concluded that there was a bad spat set and no evidence of over-fishing. Their recommendation was to suspend all local and national government regulations that might limit oystering, so that individuals would have economic incentives to restock the oyster beds. The fishery recovered for a while and then failed.

Across the English Channel, facing the same dilemma in the mid-1800s, Napoleon III slapped a ban on fishing until the oyster population could recover, strictly regulated the season afterward, directed government development of oyster parks in the intertidal areas for use by oystermen big and small, and had scientists begin research that would lead to a national system of oyster farming.

In 1902, when people started falling sick and dying because English oysters were contaminated with sewage, the British government responded to the public outcry with investigations and reports, but little in the way of real action. The result was a steady decline in oyster sales. The oyster, which was considered the most common food of the poor in the time of Dickens, completely disappeared from English food culture. As I discovered in Colchester, most English people don't even consider oysters edible anymore.

In 1915, the French created sanitary commissions that inspected oysters and oyster beds to prevent unhealthy oysters from getting onto the market. In 1930, the first steps were taken to stop pollution that might affect oyster beds. A comprehensive national system to ensure the purity of French oysters was established in 1939 and became the model for the E.U. regulations that were enacted in 1993. Today French people of all economic classes enjoy oysters—most often in their homes.

The English laissez-faire economic system, which relied on market forces and individual initiative, functioned beautifully during the Industrial Revolution. The French mercantile economic system, in which government intervened on behalf of key industries, was arguably less successful in the nineteenth century. But in the particular case of oysters, a resource which requires some management, government regulation proved good for business.

In the mid-1800s, England and France both produced around 500 million oysters a year. Today England produces around 10 million oysters a year and France produces 2 billion oysters a year. History has proven that the French approach was the right one.

"But the main point that stands out in a comparison of Britain and France," writes Robert Neild, "is the absence in Britain of a coherent government policy toward the production of oysters . . . The oyster growers are left to respond to market forces within an incoherent framework of higgledy-piggledy institutions."

England may never regain its former stature as an oyster-producing country, but the oyster is about to make a comeback at the British table thanks to the country's growing enthusiasm for gastronomy. There are more than four dozen celebrity chefs featured on the BBC, and their televised antics are followed by a wide cross section of English society.

But there is no better example of the change in English culinary culture than the career of Don Quinn. The night I arrived in Colchester, I told Quinn I wanted to join up with him after the Oyster Feast to go to the Alternative Oyster Feast and eat some oysters there too. I had read that Quinn started the Alternative Oyster Feast twenty-five years ago.

"There are no oysters at the Alternative Oyster Feast, and there never were any," he railed at me as if I were a dolt. "The Oyster Feast was a lot of conspicuous overconsumption subsidized by the ratepayers [taxpayers]. The Alternative Oyster Feast was a protest—it was a free meal we distributed to pensioners."

The Alternative Feast isn't held anymore. Things have changed in the last twenty-five years. In the late 1970s, Quinn was a leftist radical who saw Colchester oysters as a symbol of upper-class snobbery. In 2004, he founded the Colchester Food and Drink Festival.

Quinn's Colchester food festival was held under a marquee in a local park. Merchants offered samples of sausages, cheeses, and Colchester oysters, among other edibles. Quinn expected the first-year attendance to be around two thousand; instead, six thousand people showed up. The festival has gotten larger every year since.

"Instead of battering the doors down," Quinn told me, "I started an oyster festival that's inclusive instead of exclusive."

A LONDON MARTINI

Try one of these with your next dozen on the half shell. And remember, gin, not vodka; always stirred, never shaken.

6 ounces Tanqueray, Bombay, or Beefeater gin
1 ounce Noilly Pratt dry vermouth (or to taste)
2 pieces lemon peel and/or 2 olives (or more to taste)
2 toothpicks

Fill two martini glasses with ice, then add water to the brim. Fill a glass martini shaker most of the way to the top with cracked ice. Pour the gin into the shaker and allow it to sit for one minute. Add the vermouth and stir gently with a glass rod or long cocktail spoon, three times clockwise, then three times counterclockwise. Dump the ice water out of the martini glasses. Strain the gin mixture into the chilled glasses. Impale an olive and piece of lemon peel on each toothpick and add to the glasses. Serve immediately.

Makes two martinis.

SEVEN

Dreaming of a Huître Christmas

"THESE ARE THE BEST OYSTERS you will eat in Paris," the manager of Le Dôme announced while we stood on the street in front of the restaurant admiring the oyster fashion show in his stunning seafood display case.

Le Dôme, the art deco brasserie on Montparnasse where Hemingway got his morning coffee, not only served the best oysters I had in Paris, it also saved our honeymoon. Kelly was pregnant, and she spent most of the trip gastronomically incapacitated by morning sickness.

This morning she'd woken up feeling great, and said she wanted to go out for a nice lunch. I figured it was a great opportunity to visit Le Dôme, the most expensive restaurant on my Paris oyster hit list.

It was just after Christmas in 2005, and it had been snowing for days. The streets of Paris were white. The manager of Le Dôme greeted us at the door, and while someone took our coats, hats, and gloves, he asked us in excellent English where we were from. When we said we were from Texas, he beamed. He had traveled in the United States, and he even knew that Texas had a coastline. So I gave him my *Houston Press* business card and explained that I was writing about oysters. At home, I review restaurants anonymously, so I felt a little sheepish about announcing my-self. But it sure is nice to get special treatment sometimes.

After we were seated, the manager came to the table and escorted me outside to select some oysters. He also introduced me to the shucker. I was tempted to bribe the guy, but I don't think that's done in Paris.

I was soon totally absorbed by the view. There were a dozen varieties of oysters nestled in the shaved ice, representing all the latest specialties of France's top oyster producers. These weren't just oysters, they were designer oysters.

There were premium *pousse en claires* from the oyster farms of David Hervé, one of Marennes's most renowned producers. Then there were the *boudeuses de* Bretagne, tiny fluted oysters from Brittany. "Boudeuses" means "pouters," a name that aptly describes a fleshy oyster poking out of a tiny shell.

A three-year-old boudeuse is less than half the size of other "full grown" creuses, but the meat inside is as fat as many larger specimens. An oyster farmer named Yvon Madec from the north Breton port of Prat-au-Coum made the boudeuses famous, but now many other producers are using the name. Papillons are similar; they are small fat oysters from Marennes.

I smiled when I noticed that Le Dôme's oyster list included both plates de Cancale and Tsarskaya oysters. I had spent a day with the pro-ducer of these oysters, Stephan Alleaume at Les Parcs Saint-Kerber, on a trip to Cancale.

Back at the table, I discussed my oyster selection with the waiter. I probably should have tried the boudeuses and the papillons, but I had long ago come to the opinion that dainty oysters were for dainty eaters. I am a *fresser*; I like big oysters.

So I got four of the biggest oysters on the list. David Hervé pre-mium pousse en claires were the richest, creamiest Marennes oysters I have ever eaten. And, at the waiter's insistence, I got four of the trendy new Tsarskaya oysters from Parc Saint-Kerber, which I had sampled in Cancale. They seemed to taste better in the elegant environs of Le Dôme. And since I can never resist the good old *O. edulis*, I also got four of the meaty plates de Cancale.

When I picked a muscadet from the wine list to go with the oysters, the waiter made a face. He agreed that muscadet was the classic choice with oysters, but he recommended I try either a Quincy or a Menetou-Salon, which were appellations of the Loire Valley of which I knew nothing.

Since Kelly wasn't drinking, I ordered a half bottle of Pierre Clement 2004 Menetou-Salon, and it was the best oyster wine I had ever tasted. The Sauvignon blanc–based wine had plenty of acidity, but without the mustiness of Muscadet. The pinpoint tartness reminded me of raspberries rather than lemons.

Kelly wasn't eating oysters during her pregnancy, so she ordered the coquilles St. Jacques on the waiter's recommendation. The presentation was spectacular. Five scallops in red-pepper cream sauce surrounded two crescent-shaped slices of fluorescent orange pumpkin in the center of a white plate.

These small pumpkins were the rage that winter among Europe's top chefs; the flesh was not only intensely colored, it was very sweet. The big, nutty-flavored scallops were served with their red roe sacs attached, as is the custom in France. The combination of scallop, red-pepper cream sauce, and pumpkin was incredible.

Kelly had been cursed with morning sickness. This was the first time I saw her really dig into a meal since we had been in Paris. She loved the fish, but it was her dessert, an oversize napoleon made with layers of pastry and Bavarian cream, that brought a huge smile to her face. I took her picture as she ate it. The snapshot is slightly out of focus, but I will always treasure it anyway for the impish grin that Kelly gave me from behind the mountainous dessert covered with a snowcap of powdered sugar.

I took notes while I ate that lunch. Here's what I wrote in my note-book: "Biting into the first of the plates de Cancale after the Marennes oysters was like eating a bite of steak after a sushi appetizer. The second to last plate de Cancale was the sweetest one, it was pure sugar." I stuck my nose in the oyster shell and took a stab at describing the scent. I wrote, "It was the aroma of the beach at Cancale on a cold winter morning."

Nestled in a crescent cove east of Saint-Malo and across a wide bay from the famous Mont Saint Michel in neighboring Normandy, Cancale's his-toric buildings, fishing pier, and sailing ships look ancient to the American eye. The most common complaint about the place is that the weather is always bad.

"If you can see Mont Saint Michel, it's about to rain," the saying in Cancale goes. "And if you can't see Mont Saint Michel, it's already raining."

A lot of art buffs have a mental image of Cancale because of all the famous paintings done of the place in the late 1800s. Artists including Jacques Eugène Feyen, Henry Herbert La Thangue, and John Singer Sargent were drawn to Cancale's beaches because of the eerie gloom, the billowing clouds, and the play of light and dark when the rays of the sun cut through the haze.

But my first morning in Cancale was clear and bright. I took some photos while the women who ran the oyster stalls set up shop for the day. There were five stalls with bright striped awnings that lined the pavement on the ledge above the famous beach. Beyond the oyster stalls I could see the green curve of the shoreline and the dark blue sea. It wasn't an en-tirely peaceful scene, because the woman at the stall called Le Sirene was none too happy about having her picture taken. She emptied a bucket of

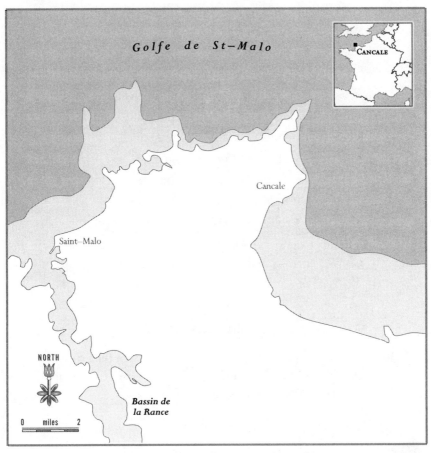

Golfe de St–Malo

CANCALE

Cancale

Saint–Malo

NORTH

Bassin de
la Rance

0   miles   2

Cancale, France

dirty water onto the sidewalk in my direction, to the amusement of her compatriots in the other stalls. To placate her, I bought a dozen oysters, despite the fact that it was only nine thirty in the morning.

I wasn't too clear on what I had bought. Since the No. 3 creuses sold for a mere Đ3 a dozen, I figured she would just hand me a sack with the oysters in it. But instead, she produced a shucking knife and a blue plastic plate with a dozen depressions in it, and proceeded to shuck my oysters.

She opened them so fast, I couldn't tell you anything about her technique. When she was done, she handed me the plate, complete with a wedge of lemon. The oysters were cold and crisp, with a lovely mineral flavor—just the thing with your second cup of coffee. And at $3.50 or so shucked, those Cancale creuses were among the cheapest oysters I have ever eaten. Wow! What a place!

I like the way the English and French order oysters by the numbers. It is a huge improvement over the game of grab bag we play in North America. Instead of getting oysters in a wild variety of sizes, you pay for exactly the size you like.

Oyster Grades

Here are the classifications for *C. gigas* oysters, from the French Comité National de la Conchyliculture. (For classifications of European flat *(O. edulis)* oysters, see page 73.)

Creuses *(C. gigas)*

No. 0	150 grams and above
No. 1	111–149 grams
No. 2	86–110 grams
No. 3	66–85 grams
No. 4	46–65 grams
No. 5	30–45 grams

Cruising the oyster stalls along Quai Gambetta, the street that runs along the beachfront, I noted big differences in price. Creuses *(C. gigas)* were cheap; plates de Cancale *(O. edulis)* were expensive. They call the *O. edulis* oysters "plates" in France because they are flat and, when opened, resemble a dinner plate.

No. 3 plates de Cancale were selling for Đ7 a dozen, while No. 4 plates were going for Đ5.50 a dozen, and the enormous No. 000 plates de Cancale were selling for Đ3 apiece. The most interesting oysters on the street in Cancale were wild oysters. I didn't even know they existed in France. But there they were—*sauvage de* Cancale—selling for Đ6 a dozen.

The showstopper was a stall at 10 Quai Gambetta called Au Pied de Cheval, where they sold wild oysters of enormous proportions. *Pied de cheval* means "horses hoof" in French, which is what they call these giant oysters. I couldn't resist the temptation. For Đ3, I bought a wild plate de Cancale that measured five inches across and did indeed resemble a horse's hoof. You can tell the age of an oyster by counting the rings in the shell. This one looked to be more than ten years old, maybe twelve. The proprietor of the stall wedged it against the wooden leg of the table with his shoe and opened it with a hatchet. I cut it into several pieces with a knife and fork. It was the chewiest oyster I have ever eaten.

I had hoped to spend some time with a Cancale oysterman on this research trip, but my planning left a lot to be desired. Repeated emails to the French tourism and fishery offices had yielded absolutely nothing in the way of help—probably because none of them were written in French. I finally decided to just show up in Cancale and see what happened.

So after my tour of Colchester and Whitstable, I crossed the English Channel on the ferry from Dover to Calais. Then I rented a car at the ferry port and started driving toward Cancale. I thought I'd have time for lots of sightseeing along the way, but the drive took a lot longer than I had imagined.

It was almost five o'clock when I pulled into town, and the tourism office was about to close. I handed the lady behind the counter a business card from the *Houston Press* and told her I was writing a story about oysters.

That got me into the office of the director, Gregoire Choleau, who, as luck would have it, spoke perfect English. Choleau listened briefly to my pitch, then picked up the phone and called Stephan Alleaume, one of Cancale's most prominent oystermen.

Within a couple of minutes, Choleau had arranged for a tour of the Saint-Kerber oyster facility, a visit to an oyster museum, and an interview and oyster tasting with Alleaume. I got a hotel room and toured the waterfront. Then at noon, I drove up the hill to the headquarters of Saint-Kerber to keep my appointment.

A young man wearing blue jeans and a gray V-neck sweater shook my hand and introduced himself as Stephan Alleaume, *président et directeur général* of Les Parcs Saint-Kerber. With his stylishly shaved head and French-accented English, he reminded me more of a film director than an oysterman.

I asked him a few questions about the history of French oysters, but Alleaume was much more interested in talking about modern marketing techniques. He showed me a new oyster that his firm was promoting. It was called a Tsarskaya oyster, in honor of the oysters that used to be shipped to the Russian czar, he said. He disappeared for a few minutes and returned with a dozen Tsarskaya oysters on a plate, freshly shucked.

They were large creuses *(C. gigas)* oysters with an iridescent purple shell. They had black lips like the *fine de claire* oysters from Marennes. The flavor was pleasantly nutty. I asked Alleaume if the color came from some kind of salt pond.

"No," he said. "Actually, they came from a new park that was just established farther east." The oysters are being grown at half the usual density, which has given each oyster more access to the food supply. Workers noticed that oysters from the new park had darker shells and black lips, so the company decided to market them differently.

"They're pretty, but they don't really taste much different from the other creuses," I told the oysterman.

"Yes, but there's a story behind them. If you have a story, customers like it better," Alleaume said. "That's marketing."

On the road into town, I had noticed several oyster stores with little ponds in front of them and the words "fine de claire" painted on the side of the building. I always thought "fine de claire" referred to oysters finished in the seaside ponds (claires) once used to create sea salt. I asked Alleaume if dunking the oysters in a pond in your backyard was legitimate.

"Sure," he shrugged. Marennes in the south is where most *fine de claires* come from. That's where the old salt pans are. Some of the oysters really are kept in the algae-rich water for a long time, until they turn green. But Marennes is the smallest oyster region in France—and it sells more oysters than any other area. So how do they do it?

"Follow the oyster trucks from Brittany," says Alleaume. There are all kinds of schemes to quickly turn the oysters green. *"Fine de claire* is another story that customers like," Alleaume said. "But it's usually just a story."

But Cancale has a better story than anywhere else because the oysters have an identifiable flavor, Alleaume asserted. In a blind tasting, Cancale oysters are almost always singled out for their strong iodine flavor and the high level of salt. Cancale oysters are the strongest-flavored oysters on the market.

The name Cancale is associated with the oldest oyster traditions. Cancale was made a city in the sixteenth century because of the oysters. The city status made it possible to collect taxes and develop the oyster beds. "The waters here are almost all Grade A," said Alleaume. "We can sell oysters directly from the sea."

And Cancale is one of the last places with plates, the young oyster-man said. There are only two thousand tons of plates *(O. edulis)* produced a year in France. Half of them come from Quiberon, and half of them come from Cancale.

I asked him if he thought the species was disappearing.

"A few Cancale producers get together sometimes to discuss the philosophy of consumption," Alleaume told me. "We see sales of plates are going down and the cost of producing them going up and up. We wonder what we could do to shake the coconut tree?

"In Paris, we visited some restaurants with oyster displays—I won't mention any names—but what they were selling weren't French oys-ters," he said. "You could tell from the darker color of the shells that they were Irish oysters. They are good quality, but they are cheaper."

You don't lower the price of a luxury product; it's counterproduc-tive, Alleaume said. It just makes it less desirable. So how do you com-pete? "I am not sure the guy in the restaurant even knows what he is buying," he said. "But somebody knows, maybe everybody knows."

I asked him about the stories I heard in Ireland about Belon oysters actually being Irish.

"You can buy some Irish plates, put them in the water here, and after two weeks they can be sold as Cancale oysters," he said. "There are no regulations. I don't think it's fair, so I don't do it. But have we ever done it? Yes. When we run out of the big size. We don't label them plates de Cancale, but we have sold them."

And if a customer in Canada or somewhere wants them labeled Belons because that's what they call plates there, then why not label them Belons, he said with a shrug. "In Belon they are buying Irish oysters and . . ." Alleaume started to say. And then he stopped himself. He realized he had already said too much.

"In the old days we caught oysters in a dredge pulled behind a sailboat," Alleaume said. "We put the little ones in beds by the shore until they grew up. Then we started to catch the spats on collectors, and we put those in the beds too. But the silt on the bottom was a problem. So in the 1960s, we started using the metal tables to keep them off the bottom and the mesh bags to keep them from washing away."

The spat are collected in Quiberon. They use mussel shells packed into large plastic pipes as collectors during the larvae season in the summer. The following spring, the mussel shells are cleaned out of the pipes and deposited in Cancale waters. The larvae are about as big as your fingernail. As they grow, the mussel shell fragments and dissolves. You can see a tiny curve of the mussel shell attached to the tiny oyster. Cancale oyster growers put the little oysters into bags. As the oysters grow too large for the bag, they are dumped out three or four times a year, cleaned, and divided among more bags so they have room to grow.

"But if all of Cancale's oysters are grown in bags on racks, then where do the wild plates and the *pied de cheval* come from?" I asked Alleaume.

"There is a protected wild oyster bed in the Bay Saint Michel," he said. "Every three or four years, they allow limited dredging to keep it healthy." The wild oysters are prized by high-class restaurants in Paris, he explained. The wild oyster harvest is conducted in the old-fashioned "caravan" style.

"In the old days, when they dredged oysters from sailboats, they went out in a caravan," Alleaume told me. The oyster boats all sailed out together and they all started oystering on the same signal.

It sounds like some charming old ceremony, but it's nothing of the kind. The caravan was invented in Cancale as a way for French oystermen to keep an eye on each other.

Alleaume's account of French oyster-farming history makes it sound like the French oystermen were a good-natured bunch who gladly accepted government regulations back in the 1850s when the fishery was failing, and subsequently built a successful oyster-farming culture through amiable cooperation.

But that's not how it happened. In fact, French oystermen were persuaded to cooperate with government regulations only when a gun was held to their heads—literally.

In the 1700s, Cancale was an important oyster center because it was close enough to supply Paris, even before the railroads were built. It was Cancale oysters that Louis XIV had delivered to his palace at Versailles. So when the Cancale oyster fishery began to fail in 1766, the French admiralty enacted regulations to conserve the oyster beds from overfishing.

Oystering was prohibited from April until October 15. Each oyster bed was tested at the beginning of the season and opened only if there were enough healthy, mature oysters. Outside boats were strictly limited. And anyone caught cheating was severely punished.

But enforcement was a problem. French oystermen were extremely adept at cheating. The genius of the new regulations was that the masters of the oyster boats were directed to elect four of their own members to serve as *gardes jurés*. The *gardes jurés* made the rules. They tested the oyster beds and decided when and where oystering would take place.

To ensure that every oysterman complied with the regulations, the boats all sailed out together on the appointed tide in what came to be known as the caravan. A signal was given and everybody started fishing at the same time. And on another signal, all oystering ceased. Anyone caught oystering on his own was punished.

Under this system of regulated fishing, Cancale enjoyed its heyday. From 1836 to about 1847, Cancale's production peaked at an average of fifty-six million oysters a year. But the oystermen were never very happy about the government regulations.

In 1845, there was a rebellion in Cancale. The oystermen asked for an additional day of fishing because of a national famine. The officials at Cancale waffled, and eventually the oystermen took matters into their own hands. Two hundred oyster boats sailed out and gathered oysters out of season. They were met by two naval cutters in the bay and two brigades of gendarmerie on the land. The military forced the fishermen at gunpoint to return the oysters to the oyster beds.

Armed intervention may sound like an overreaction to a tussle over fishing rules. But the way the rebellion was crushed ensured that when Napolean III enacted new regulations in the face of failing oyster harvests in the 1850s, they were taken seriously.

The regulations and the caravan system developed in Cancale were applied to all oyster fisheries in France, and they effectively curbed over-fishing. At the same time, the government began the modern system of oyster farming as a way of restocking the depleted oyster beds.

A scientist named Jean Jacques Marie Cyprien Victor Coste was the brains behind the French system of oyster farming. He was working on the aquaculture of fish when he encountered the oyster farms in Italy that dated back to Roman times. In the enclosed salt ponds at Lake Lucrino and Lake Averno, oyster spats were captured on branches or ropes, and oysters were grown in a way that made them easy to harvest.

The Roman aquaculture concept was developed by a famous huckster named Sergius Orata, who grew the oysters in ponds for convenience and then launched a marketing campaign to convince Romans that his cultivated oysters were tastier than the ones that came from the natural oyster beds at Brindisi.

In 1855, Coste published a book about the aquaculture methods he had encountered in his travels. In 1858, he wrote a letter to Napolean III asking for money to try to restock the bay of Saint-Brieuc, just west of Saint-Malo, using a system of submerged sticks, much like he had seen in Italy. He got all the money he wanted. A year later, he wrote back to the emperor to say the experiment was a huge success and to recommend that the entire coast of France be similarly restocked. And Napolean III took on the challenge.

From then on, the French worked with two systems of oystering— deep-water dredging from ships, and farming of cultivated spats on the intertidal flats. But the success of the farming method eventually won out. Aracachon, south of Bordeaux, and the Gulf of Morbihan, in Brittany, became the principal oyster-culturing regions.

In the 1860s, France began importing Portuguese oysters *(C. angulata)* to help make up for the shortages of French oysters. The Portuguese oyster species originated in Asia and was introduced into the Bay of Lisbon in the early 1800s. In 1865, a ship named *Le Morlaisien*, bearing a cargo of Portuguese oysters, was delayed by a storm and sought refuge in the Gironde Estuary, north of Bordeaux. When the cargo began to smell, the captain dumped the oysters overboard. (Or so the story goes, anyway.)

The disease-resistant Portuguese oysters thrived on the French coast and began to be cultivated. By 1914, Portuguese oysters accounted for half of France's total production. In 1920, the plates *(O. edulis)* died off in massive numbers.

The production of Portuguese oysters hit a historic high after World War II, but gradually a malady called "gill disease" began to infect the Portuguese oysters, prompting a return to the native *O. edulis* among oystermen. The harvest fluctuated dramatically from year to year.

Beginning in 1966, more and more successful experiments with the Pacific oyster *(C. gigas)*, a close relative of the Portugese *(C. angulata)* oyster, encouraged French oystermen to put their faith in this non-native species. The oystermen lobbied the fisheries ministry, and soon a massive switchover to *C. gigas* production got underway.

By the early 1970s, more than five hundred tons of *C. gigas* oysters from British Columbia were relaid in French oyster beds to serve as breeding stock, while over ten thousand tons of spat (more than 5 billion baby oysters) were imported from Japan.

Some scientists, notably the American marine biologist Carl James Sindermann, have suggested that while the *C. gigas* species is itself immune to most oyster diseases, it could be guilty of passing diseases on to other oyster species.

Sindermann pointed out that the introduction of Pacific *(C. gigas)* oysters to France coincided with the appearance of three major oyster diseases. The gill disease that killed the Portuguese *(C. angulata)* oysters may have been introduced with the first Pacific *(C. gigas)* oysters. And of the two diseases that are currently wiping out the native *(O. edulis)* oysters, *Marteilia refringens* first appeared in the early 1970s, and *Bonamia ostreae* appeared in 1979.

French oystermen are now almost totally dependent on the *C. gigas* species. When those oysters contract a disease as they did in the summer of 2008, there is no other species to turn to. And some marine biologists suggest that the French oyster industry is setting itself up future disasters by pushing production to hard.

The more oysters that are crammed into a small area, the less food there is for each oyster. As overcrowding increases, the oysters begin to grow weaker and become more susceptible to diseases. Marine biologists are encouraging oyster farmers to decrease their density to improve the health of the species, but decreased density means less profit.

Les Parcs Saint-Kerber's Tsarskaya oysters are an experiment in growing oysters at a lower density and then seeking a higher price for them. By combining sound management and good marketing, Stephan Alleaume is hoping to improve the health of his oysters without sacrificing profits.

Saint-Kerber ships oysters to seventy different countries around the world. In the packing room, Alleaume showed me how oysters are prepared for shipment. The oysters were being placed in the same sort of wicker baskets I had seen in Ireland. A wad of wet seaweed was placed on top before the basket was sealed.

"The oysters are kept refrigerated during shipping, but the air is dry, that's why the seaweed is required," Alleaume said. "Our oysters can survive a week to ten days," he said. "But only because they have been to 'oyster school.'"

"What's oyster school?" I had to ask.

In the middle of the packing house there was a huge concrete basin. It was about four feet deep and it looked like an enormous kiddy pool. A forklift lowered crates and crates of oysters stacked on pallets into the basin, and then seawater was piped up from the bay. After a set period, the water was drained and the oysters were exposed to the air—just as they were in their natural habitat. But after each dousing with seawater, the time the oysters were exposed to the air was lengthened. Gradually, the oysters were conditioned to "swallow" a lot of seawater to survive. Normally the oysters would gape open after two or three days. After conditioning, they could last up to two weeks.

Very few oysters were shipped during the summer, when the oysters are milky with reproductive material. "Some people like milky oysters," Alleaume told me with a shrug. The bivalves begin fattening in October and November, reaching their peak at Christmas. Ninety-nine percent of the company's oysters are eaten raw on the half shell.

"Oysters are a seasonal food. They are part of the holiday festivities in France," the oyster company president said.

I had heard that before. "Oysters are everywhere in Paris during the holidays," Bernard Brunon, a French friend of mine in Houston had told me. His family started opening oysters as soon as they woke up on Christmas morning. That's when I started thinking about spending the holidays in Paris some day.

Of the Saint-Kerber company's total production of 130,000 to 140,000 tons of oysters, an average of sixty to eighty percent are sold in Paris during the holiday season. Last year, sixty workers packed and shipped seventeen to twenty tons every day in the last two weeks of the year, Alleaume said.

After I left the young oysterman, I returned to the oyster stalls where I'd eaten my first dozen early in the morning. And I was astonished by how the scenery had changed. The blue water that had sparkled behind the oyster stalls when the tide was high that morning was gone. Where the water had once been, rows upon rows of metal tables with mesh sacks of oysters fastened on top of them had miraculously risen out of the sea. There was a whole field of them, row upon row upon row.

I went down to the beach to take some pictures. While I was snap-ping away, a woman pulled up in a pickup truck, grabbed a couple sacks of oysters off a rack, threw them in the bed of her truck, and drove away—now that's a convenient way to harvest oysters.

Cancale has over seven square kilometers of these "oyster parks." The intertidal area is enormous because of the long sloping beach, and because the difference in the water level from high tide to low tide at Cancale is almost fifty feet.

Thanks to the scenery, the history, a chance to see oyster farming up close, and lots of cheap oysters, Cancale gets my nomination for the world's best destination for oyster tourists.

On my drive back to Calais, I began to wonder: How could I write a book about oysters without visiting Paris during this holiday oyster-eating frenzy? And how was I going to sell the trip to Kelly? She didn't mind me traveling to distant oyster farms by myself once in a while. But there was no way I was going to fly to Paris without her.

A few flakes of snow fell on the basket of Belons as I stood there at the display in front of the fish market taking photos of them. It was around nine o'clock on December 27, 2005, our first morning in Paris. I was so excited to see some oysters, I had skipped breakfast and headed out to the market. Kelly was back in the hotel room sleeping. With the camera, I tried to capture an image that expressed the poignancy I felt. After all the planning and plotting I had done to get to Paris, watching the big soft snowflakes falling on these beautifully scrubbed French oysters choked me up.

When the fishmonger came out of the store and asked if he could help me, I bought the dozen Belons for Đ22. They were big No. 00 size oysters. While I was standing at the cash register, I noticed some oyster knives for sale, and I bought one of those as well. It had a lovely wooden handle and a sharp, angular steel blade that looked like it belonged on a pocketknife. It was a bargain at Đ12.

After Kelly and I were married in May, I proposed delaying our honeymoon until the holidays. She knew that oysters were the real reason I wanted to go to Paris during the holiday season, regardless of my rationalizations about how romantic it would be. She wanted a honeymoon at the beach. As a compromise, we took two honeymoons.

For the first one, we went to Rio de Janeiro and Salvador da Bahia in Brazil to lie around on the beaches. I actually got to sample some Brazilian oysters at Trapiche Adelaide, the fanciest restaurant in Salvador. I had hoped they might be one of the two native Brazilian oysters, the *Crassostrea gasar* or the *Crassostrea rhizophorae*. And maybe they were. Both of those species are "cupped oysters" just like *C. gigas*, so it's hard to tell them apart. But I'm pretty sure the ones I was served were ordinary, farm-raised *C. gigas* oysters. The modern waterfront restaurant was stunning, and so was my entrée of prawns in a mustard and pineapple sauce.

Our second honeymoon, a few months later, was the one I had been dreaming about—Paris during the holidays. Of course, I hadn't anticipated that Kelly would be pregnant by that time.

We got a ridiculously cheap fare because we were willing to arrive on Christmas Eve. We decided it would be too depressing to sit in a hotel room for Christmas, so we made plans to have Christmas with some old friends of Kelly's in rural Holland.

The next day we took a train into Amsterdam, and the TGV from Amsterdam to Paris. That night in Paris, we met my old friend Jim Haynes at Le Zeyer, a few blocks from our hotel. Jim had recommended the not fancy but pleasant Hotel du Midi on the Avenue Rene Coty, right across the street from the Denfert-Rochereau Métro station.

Kelly's pregnancy had entered a stage in which her morning sickness often stayed with her much of the day. At Le Zeyer, she was feeling okay until my platter of oysters arrived. Things took a sudden turn for the better when Jim Haynes turned up.

At the party in Houston where Kelly and I first met, I had mentioned Jim Haynes while telling a story about traveling. It turned out that Kelly knew Jim Haynes too. And that coincidence led to our first conversation, which led to our first date, etc., etc. The fact that he played a role in our love story made Jim pretty happy.

He suggested that Kelly try some ice cream for dessert. She hadn't eaten much dinner and she loves ice cream, so she dug into the three tiny scoops of chocolate, hazelnut, and vanilla ice cream from the legendary Berthillon with some enthusiasm. "Omigod," she mumbled with her mouth full.

Berthillon may be the best ice cream in the world. The Chauvin family, who are descendants of Monsieur Berthillon, use natural ingredients in intense concentrations. The vanilla is café au lait colored from all the natural vanilla bean. Thanks to Jim Haynes and Berthillon, the night ended on an upbeat note. Finding restaurants in Paris that had both oysters and outstanding desserts would prove critical.

The morning after our dinner at Le Zeyer, I tiptoed out of the hotel room and headed for the oyster market. One reason that Jim Haynes had recommended this particular hotel was because it was very close to the market street of Rue Daguerre. That's where I found the Belons. By the time I made it back to our hotel with the Belons and my new oyster knife in hand, the first flurry of big snowflakes was falling.

I was excited about my snowy Belons and generally in an ecstatic mood. I ran up the stairs of our hotel and burst into the room to tell Kelly all about it. She was still asleep. She woke up and tried to act enthusiastic, but she was feeling sick. I tried to cheer her up while I struggled to open a few Belons with my brand new oyster knife.

I didn't have a lot of shucking experience, but I knew that stabbing your left hand while wielding the knife with your right was a frequent problem, especially with a sharply pointed oyster knife like the one I had just bought. So I wrapped my left hand in a towel and struggled with the big No. 00 Belons. It took me five minutes to get the first one open.

My breakfast consisted of four Belons, crunchy bread, and French butter that I had bought in the market. The oysters were sensational—meaty and chewy with a big marine flavor. I wanted to go see another seafood market a few Métro stops away, but Kelly didn't feel like coming along. She wanted to stay in bed.

The other market was a bust. There were lots of scallops, but hardly any oysters at all. And the gentle flurry of snow had turned into a full-fledged snowstorm. There were almost no customers. The merchants started packing up and leaving the market early.

When I got back and opened the door to our hotel room, I was greeted by an aroma reminiscent of a fish market's trash can. I had discarded the empty Belon shells in the wastebasket next to the bed. With the snowstorm raging, the heating system in the old hotel was going full blast. It didn't take long for the strong-scented Belon shells to permeate the warm and stuffy little room with their ebb-tide perfume.

Kelly was so sick, she hadn't moved from the bed. Her face looked green. I opened the window and the door to the room and allowed the freezing fresh air to flush out the room. My wife is a good sport about my oyster obsession most of the time. But she was livid when she realized it was my oyster shells that had made her so sick that morning.

I believe that oysters can be an aphrodisiac. Unfortunately, on my honeymoon in Paris, oysters served as an anti-aphrodisiac.

The tiny restaurant called Huîtrerie Régis near the Boulevard St. Germain changed my mind about *fine de claires* and Marennes. After everything I had heard from their detractors, I had started to suspect that the *claires* of Marennes and the green oysters they produced were little more than a marketing gimmick.

Once I tasted the real thing, however, I understood what all the imposters were trying so hard to emulate.

Huîtrerie Régis is a little fourteen-seat "degustation" room run by a top Marennes producer who sells his oysters by the bag outside. It's also the best public relations promotion for Marennes oysters imaginable. There is no doubt that these are real Marennes *fine de claire* oysters, nor is there any doubt that they have been fattened according to the region's strict guidelines. Most importantly, they taste fabulous.

Before I came to Paris, I asked everybody with an opinion where I should eat oysters. Huîtrerie Régis was recommended by Patricia Wells, the author of the *Food Lover's Guide to Paris*. The restaurant may be tiny, but there's white linen, fine china, and crystal wine glasses on the tables. Oysters, bread and butter, wine, and coffee are about all you'll find on the menu. Since there was nothing Kelly could eat here, I went alone for an early lunch and promised to bring her something sweet when I came back.

I got a dozen oysters, a glass of wine, and an espresso for Ð25. My platter of six *fine de claires* and six *spécial de claires* were amazing looking. The color of the "mantle" (the edge of the meat) on these oysters was the most intense I have ever seen. They had an aroma of fresh-cut grass and a seaweed flavor that reminded me of the nori wrapper on a piece of sushi. Eating these explained a lot about the French infatuation with *fine de claires.*

If a lot of oysters that go by the name "fine de claires" spend hardly any time in the ponds, these looked like they had been there too long. They were so dense with greenish black color, I would have believed you if you told me that someone left them in the pond and forgot about them.

Sometimes called *les vertes* (the green ones), Marennes oysters were a special favorite of Louis XIV. The green oysters undergo a "refining" process after they are harvested. They are placed in *claires*, which are ponds dug into the clay of the former salt pans. An algae called blue navicula that is native to these ponds imparts a pigment to the Marennes oyster that gives it a green, blue, or black tint and also creates a distinctive taste. The micro-algae's scientific name is *Navicula ostrea* or *Haslea ostrearia*.

When marine laboratories succeeded in culturing and growing this micro-algae, the monopoly that Marennes once enjoyed on green oysters ended. Now the blue navicula algae is purchased by oyster producers all over France. An enterprising oyster grower could create green-tinged "fine de claires" anywhere. I am guessing this is what Stephan Alleaume was talking about when he mentioned the many scams for turning oysters green.

Alleaume insinuated that many oysters labeled "Marennes *fine de claires*" are actually green oysters from other parts of France. I'm glad I got to visit Huîtrerie Régis and taste the bonafide bivalves.

De Claire Definitions

These are the definitions used to identify authentic Marennes *claire*-finished oysters.

Fine de Claire
A true *fine de claire* is refined in a *claire* for one to two months at a maximum density of twenty oysters per square meter. The oysters weigh the same or slightly more than they did when

harvested and exhibit a small amount of bulge. The meat may
be green tinged or white.

Spéciale de Claire
Refined for at least two months with a maximum density of ten
oysters per square meter, the *spéciale de claire* is measurably fatter than the *fine de claire,* with a pronounced green color.

Pousse en Claire
Refined for at least four months at a maximum density of five
oysters per square meter, these oysters are extremely fat and
show intense coloring.

There were still eight Belons and some white wine in the little refrigerator in our hotel room. When I dared to get them out one afternoon,
Kelly had a fit. She told me to go eat them somewhere she couldn't smell
them. I thought about taking them to the park, but it was still snowing
and the sidewalks were slushy.

As a compromise, I was allowed to eat my oysters in the bathroom—
as long as I didn't leave the shells in the trash can. I sat on the only seat
available in that room, opening my Belons and drinking Sancerre from
the glass provided for tooth-brushing. A window in the bathroom over-
looked the roof of a lower part of the building. So I threw the shells out
the window and they landed on the roof. It wasn't exactly what I had in
mind when I planned an oyster holiday in Paris, but when life hands you
lemons . . . that's what I was missing, lemons.

Compared to my wife's travails, I had nothing to complain about.
She had been sick for two days straight, and I was very lucky she hadn't
yet murdered me with my sharp new oyster knife. She kept me company
at almost every restaurant I went to, even if she could only choke down
bread and water.

Of all the places to eat oysters in Paris, the ones most often recommended to me by fellow oyster lovers were brasseries, which seemed strange since *brasserie* means "brewery" in French, and the French always drink wine with oysters. But the ornate Belle Epoque brasseries of Paris don't look much like beer halls—at least, not anymore.

Brasserie Bofinger was a crude little one-room beer joint when it first introduced draft beer to Paris in 1864. Back then it served nothing but draft beer and charcuterie. But 1864 was also the year that the French vineyards were devastated by phylloxera. With no wine available, the demand for beer was enormous. Bofinger was in the right place at the right time.

France's beer brewers came from Alsace-Lorraine, a region on the eastern border that had been handed back and forth between Germany and France many times over the centuries. During the hostilities leading up to the Franco-Prussian War, Alsatians who wished to remain French fled to Paris. A number of brasseries were opened by Alsatian refugees around this time, including those with such German-sounding names as Zimmer, Zeyer, and Wepler.

In 1871, when France lost the war and the provinces of Alsace and Lorraine were again taken over by Germany, more Alsatians flocked to Paris. As the brasseries prospered, they became more ornate. But regardless of their successes, the brasseries remained famously egalitarian. It was not uncommon for tradesmen to sit down at the bar next to flamboyantly dressed aristocrats. Some brasseries, like Wepler, became known as meeting places for artists, writers, and politicians.

The brasseries introduced draft beer and the Alsatian sauerkraut dish called "choucroute" to Paris. And they also became famous for serving oysters, though why, exactly, I have never been able to ascertain. My best guess is that oysters were a common and inexpensive foodstuff in Paris at the turn of the century, so the brasseries responded to the demand.

I wonder if Parisians ate their oysters with beer during the phylloxera years. I imagine they must have.

During my oyster-eating binge the week between Christmas of 2005 and New Year's 2006, every brasserie I saw had an oyster stand on the sidewalk outside. It's both an economical way to keep the oysters cold in the winter and a come-on to passersby.

We were led to Brasserie Flo by an old friend of Jim Haynes named Cathy Sroufe Monnet, who lived not far from the restaurant. Her husband, Yves Monnet, was visiting his parents' house in Brittany. Marrying into a family from Brittany means that you have to know your oysters, Cathy said. She had returned early from the holidays because their son had a guitar lesson. And she was happy to join us.

I don't think we would have found the place without her. In order to find the "passageway" where Flo is located, you have to navigate a rabbit's warren of back streets and alleyways in the tenth arrondissement. But once you step inside the old restaurant, you have truly entered wonderland.

It was dark and snowy outside and then we stepped into this weird yet wonderful atmosphere. The electric chandeliers gave the place an uneven lighting that reminded me of a van Gough painting. The glasses above the bar glowed intensely bright, but the corners of the room were completely dark. The waiters, who were dressed in white shirts and black ties with calf-length aprons, moved quickly in and out of the shadows.

A romantic mural of the Alsatian countryside done in a series of large canvasses continued from one room to another. The blue sky and green forests covered the upper half of the walls, each section of the painting framed by elaborate dark woodwork. The lower parts of the walls were dark wood paneling accented with brass chair rails and brass coat hooks. Art nouveau mirrors and Christmas trees hung with red and gold ornaments made up the rest of the decorations.

We were shown to a banquette table covered with white linen. Every table in the restaurant was occupied, and the noise level was deafening. Kelly was trying hard to smile, but after a while she slumped back against the upholstery. She had a cheese plate and a half glass of wine that she didn't finish.

There were a variety of oysters available that evening. I ordered two each of six. They came on an elevated round pedestal made of aluminum. A huge mound of shaved ice sat in the middle with three half lemons in the center.

We got No. 00 Belons, which were fat and chewy and sweet; they were by far my favorites. The No. 2 Belons were more petite versions of the big boys. The Girardeau oysters were creuses from somewhere on the Atlantic, according to Cathy. Finestre Nord specials were huge creamy creuses with a black mantle; they were too big for me, and I like big oysters. Finally, we tried some lovely looking Marennes oysters that had more of that oceany iodine flavor than the others.

Cathy picked up the shell of an oyster I had just finished and pointed to the tiny piece of flesh that was still attached to the shell. In the United States, oyster shuckers cut both of the oyster's abductor muscles away from the shell so you can slurp the oyster out of the shell without any silverware.

In France, oyster shuckers cut the top muscle from the shell, but leave the oyster attached to the bottom shell by the other abductor muscle, which is commonly called "the foot." They say the oyster stays alive longer if it is left attached to one shell, and so it stays fresher. But in order to eat it, you have to cut it free.

In Brittany, where oysters are a way of life, the dense muscle of the foot is eaten by itself. It's savored for its nutty sweetness and chewy texture.

"In Brittany, if you don't eat the foot, they say, 'You eat oysters like a Parisian,'" Cathy said. "And that's not a compliment."

Our holiday oyster honeymoon in Paris went reasonably well, considering the circumstances. I did get to sample some wonderful oysters in Paris restaurants, but I was a little disappointed that there wasn't really a public frenzy of oyster eating to witness. Then I realized that I was thinking about oysters like an American when I planned the trip. Americans don't know how to shuck oysters, so when we go on an oyster-eating binge, we do it in an oyster bar. The French eat their holiday oysters at home.

We left Paris on the TGV for Milan in the early morning gloom a few days before New Year's Eve. We hadn't been listening to the news, since we don't speak much French, so we didn't realize that the snowstorm was actually a blizzard. The countryside outside Paris was covered in several feet of snow. It was a beautiful ride through the Alps.

Our original plan had been to take a ferry from Italy across the Adriatic to Croatia to visit the ancient oyster beds in the town of Ston. But the ferries weren't running, and the prospect of traveling on snowy mountain roads by bus once we got to Croatia didn't sound very appealing.

So we went to Rome, where I hoped to relive the exuberant oyster eating of the Roman Empire. I thought I would visit Nero's palace and see the mother-of-pearl-covered walls of the feasting hall where Nero ate oysters from every part of the Empire. It was said that Nero could tell where an oyster came from by the taste alone.

But Nero's palace was closed for repairs, and my search for oysters in the Eternal City turned up next to nothing. I found a box of French creuses at a fishmonger's stall at the Campo de Fiori market. It was Đ35 for a box of one hundred, which seemed like a reasonable price. But

Kelly gave me the evil eye when I picked it up, and I knew I would never get away with it.

The only oysters I ate in Rome were served to me in an upscale seafood restaurant called La Rosetta. I had one No. 000 Belon for Đ12, one No. 00 Belon for Đ9, and a couple of *fine de claires* at Đ6 each. It seemed silly, though; I might as well have eaten them in France.

The oyster tour of Rome was a bust, but Kelly's spirits revived. As our European honeymoon drew to a close, she felt so good that she decided to see if Rome had any after-Christmas sales going on.

EIGHT

Wild Bill on Hog Island

"This is the best oyster bar in the U.S.," said Billy Marinelli, the president and founder of Marinelli Shellfish, the day we met at Zuni Café on Market Street in San Francisco. Marinelli is an animated Italian American with an oversized belly, a loud voice, and a salesman's penchant for hyperbole. I sought him out because some people credit Billy Marinelli for introducing America to the Kumamoto oyster and for reawakening San Francisco's half-shell tradition.

Zuni Café had the best assortment of oysters in San Francisco. I was astonished to see five species on the oyster-bar menu, each identified by its Latin name. The market names and locations were also spelled out. It was certainly the most detailed oyster-bar menu I had ever seen. But unfortunately, all five species of oysters weren't available that day. The native Olympias were out of season.

I told Marinelli that I thought there were a couple places that might give Zuni a run for its money in the competition for best oyster bar in the United States. But Marinelli wasn't interested in debating. He was already on to the next subject—oysters from my neck of the woods.

"Gulf Coast oysters are criminal," he told me. Gulf oystermen were a contemptible bunch, as far as he was concerned. "They shouldn't be allowed to sell any oysters outside their home states until they stop killing people," he railed. At that point, I was glad Kelly had decided to stay home. She would have ended the interview by slapping Marinelli in the face.

Interviewing Billy Marinelli was hard enough as it was. It was like questioning a passing train. I finally got him to stop at my station by appealing to his considerable ego. I asked him to tell me about how he'd single-handedly built the San Francisco oyster business. He soon had me laughing so hard I could barely take notes.

"In the late 1970s, the Pigeon Point Shellfish Hatchery was set up near the Pigeon Point Lighthouse, between San Francisco and Half Moon Bay," he began. It was the first successful hatchery in the country. A self-taught biologist named Ron Zebal made the oyster-seed business cost-effective. "The guy was an oyster genius," Marinelli said.

Zebal employed a system in which the oyster spat attaches to a tiny fragment of oyster shell, so it can be grown as a single oyster instead of in a cluster. The bag of precisely sized oyster-shell fragments is called "oyster shell flour" because it looks like a bag of flour. It's very difficult to manufacture because all the larger and smaller bits of shell have to be removed. Once the oyster larvae attach themselves to a bit of shell, they transform into tiny "oyster seeds" and can then be shipped anywhere and grown to maturity.

"I was just looking for a job when I started working there in 1978," said Marinelli. It was a wild time to be in the oyster hatchery business. "There were no regulations. Fish and Game had no idea what we were doing. You can fit ten million oyster seeds in a Fed Ex box—that's $20,000 worth of oyster seed. New Zealand, Ireland, we were sending them all over the world."

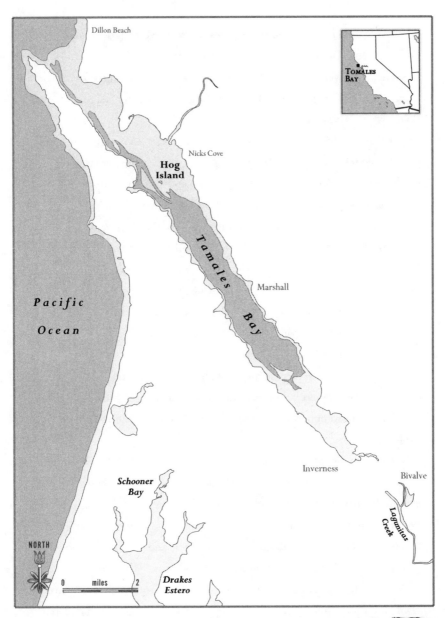

Dillon Beach

Nicks Cove

Hog
Island

T a m a l e s

B a y

Marshall

Pacific

Ocean

Inverness

Bivalve

Schooner
Bay

*Lagunitas
Creek*

NORTH

0   miles   2

Drakes
Estero

TOMALES
BAY

Tomales Bay, California

"We started growing our own oysters too. We called them Pigeon Point oysters." But there wasn't really any market for them.

Then an investor named Tony Weaver came along and took over the place, Marinelli remembered. Weaver wanted to start selling Pigeon Point oysters to San Francisco oyster bars.

"I'll never forget this meeting we had where Tony announced his plan," Marinelli said with a laugh. "We were all wearing shorts and rubber boots—listening to the Rolling Stones and smoking dope while we worked. Tony asks us, 'Who wants to be a salesman?'"

"Two of us became the marketing guys. We didn't have a clue what we were doing," Marinelli said. "The competition was the Eastern Blue Point. It was a big meaty oyster. Our oysters were two and a half to three inches, and they were smaller than most people were used to. At the end of the day, we were selling off all the leftover oysters out of the trunks of our cars in Chinatown for a dollar a dozen."

Then Marinelli read an article in *California* magazine about chef Alice Waters at Chez Panisse and her insistence on using local ingredients. "I was twenty-six years old and eating mac and cheese out of a box for dinner," he remembers. "But all of a sudden, I became the poster boy for local oysters."

Slowly he developed a market for his Pigeon Points. But the restaurants wanted a variety of oysters. "I had some friends growing oysters in Tomales Bay, so I started selling those too. Then we got some beach oysters from Canada. They broadcast them right on the rocky intertidal beaches, so they looked different from the rack-and-bag oysters we were growing. We called them Portuguese oysters."

Marinelli worked in an Oakland oyster bar from five to ten every night, then got up at eight in the morning and drove out to the airport twice a week to pick up oysters and deliver them to upscale San Francisco restaurants including Hayes Street Grill, Chez Panisse, and René Verdon's.

"When places like Zuni started to open, I needed more different kinds of oysters," he remembered. "In 1982, when I was first starting Marinelli Shellfish, I called the chief oysterman up in Humboldt Bay, Twig LaBranche. Believe it or not, that's his real name. The Pigeon Point hatchery had been sending him Kumamoto oyster seeds for years, and I wondered what happened to all those oysters. Turns out he had millions of Kumamotos on his oyster beds, but they never grew large enough to sell.

"'I would love to get rid of these things. Make me a deal,' Twig told me. I started out paying him $2 a dozen." At first, Marinelli tried to sell the little oysters to San Francisco's traditional oyster bars. But he found San Franciso's old oyster culture slow to warm to the Kumamotos.

San Francisco has always been a great place to sell oysters. During the gold rush era, when oysters were selling for $1 to $1.50 a basket in New York, they went for $7 a basket on the dock in San Francisco.

Beginning in 1851, oyster schooners loaded up with the small native oysters that we now call Olympias collected in Washington's Shoalwater Bay (now Willapa Bay) made the treacherous run to San Francisco. The Native American tribes who collected the oysters were paid $1 a basket. A schooner could hold as many as two thousand bushels. A good run took as little as a week, but a delay due to bad weather meant the shipment was lost.

When the railroad arrived in the 1880s, oysters were shipped by the trainload to San Francisco, and the oysters in Willapa Bay were rapidly fished out. In 1895, Eastern *(C. virginica)* oysters were introduced to the Pacific Coast, including Willapa Bay, where they coexisted with what was left of the native oyster fishery.

Once known as the California oyster, the Olympia oyster got its current name from Olympia, Washington, where it remained abundant after the San Francisco Bay population was wiped out during the gold rush. Gold miners displaced some twelve billion tons of earth in the Sierras with picks, shovels, and high-pressure water hoses. The hoses were outlawed in 1884, but by then the mercury-laden silt had already reduced the depth of San Francisco Bay by six feet. The huge population of oysters that had inhabited the Bay were wiped out and never recovered.

In 1905, Pacific *(C. gigas)* oysters from Japan were introduced to the West Coast. At first the beds had to be restocked with seed oysters from Japan. Eventually, populations of *C. gigas* oysters in the United States and British Columbia began to spawn, and seed could be collected on this side of the Pacific. But while the Pacific oysters flourished, they grew in clusters that made a half-shell presentation impractical. They were sold mainly as shucked oysters until the hatchery system made it practical to grow individual oysters.

The tradition of eating half-shell oysters never died out in San Francisco. At vintage seafood restaurants like Swan Oyster Depot on Polk Street, you could always find East Coast *(C. virginica)* Blue Points. But San Francisco's old-fashioned oyster bars resisted the new wave of Pacific Coast oysters.

Billy Marinelli still bristles at the mention of Swan Oyster Depot. Its legendary owner, Sal Sancimino, refused to do business with Marinelli and told him that Kumamoto oysters would never sell in San Francisco.

"My dad was from the World War II era," Sal's son Jimmy Sancimino explained when I stopped by Swan's to eat some oysters and chat one day. Billy Marinelli was trying to sell oysters with Japanese names, Jimmy pointed out. But Sal was old-school. San Francisco was a Navy town, and people were still sore about Pearl Harbor. Sal Sancimino wasn't going to buy Japanese.

But the new wave of California restaurant owners and chefs were crazy about Kumamotos. "Alice Waters tried a few," said Marinelli, "and she loved them." The fact that they were grown in California and nobody in the United States had ever tasted them before was a big selling point, Marinelli said.

"I charged thirty cents apiece at first. Then they really caught on. We sold 250,000 in eight months." That's what got his company started, he said, a lot of nickels and dimes. "Now I have offices in Bali, San Francisco, and Seattle, and employees who have been with me for twenty years. We sell a million oysters a week."

Marinelli lives in Bali and concentrates on the lucrative Asian market. He told me that Marinelli Shellfish is the largest oyster distributor in the world. Then he thought for a minute. "Well, maybe some of those shucking plants down on the Gulf Coast are bigger. Who knows?"

When I told Marinelli I'd be traveling around the Bay Area writing about the best places to eat oysters, he invited me to join him on Saturday at noon at the Hog Island Oyster Company picnic grove on Tomales Bay. "That's the best place to eat oysters around here," he said.

"Hog Island! Hog Island!" screamed Billy Marinelli like a small crazy child. He pointed to a rock outcropping with a small copse of trees, visible off the port side of the boat. John Finger, the founder of Hog Island Oyster Company, was piloting the oyster lug, and he was inured to Marinelli's antics. The two were once roommates at Southampton College in New York.

Finger was a gaunt, serious man dressed in a gray sweatshirt and rubber boots. He spoke with the gravity of a scientist describing his latest experiment. He was quite a contrast to his wild man of a former roommate.

When I arrived at Hog Island Oyster Farm at noon, Billy Marinelli asked me if I'd like a tour of the oyster beds. It was a bright, sunny Northern California afternoon, and I couldn't think of a better way to work up an appetite for an oyster picnic.

"When we started the company we were looking for a name," Finger explained as we chugged along over the glassy water of Tomales Bay. "Tomales Bay Oyster Company was already taken." Finger thought the most promising spots for oyster beds were in the quiet flats not far from the saltwater outlet to the Pacific. The flats were right across the bay from the knot of trees and rocky beaches of Hog Island, named for the feral pigs that were its only inhabitants.

"So we called ourselves Hog Island Oyster Company. When restaurants sell our oysters, we insist that they use our name. We have to get a return on this investment in quality."

It was Billy Marinelli who got Finger into the oyster business. Marinelli had already created a market for local half-shell oysters in San Francisco, but he needed more varieties. Finger and his partner, Michael Watchorn, were marine biologists working in the aquaculture business in Monterey, California. Marinelli promised them he could sell all the oysters they could produce.

He was right. Ever since Finger and Watchorn started selling oysters in 1982, their small operation has never produced enough to meet the demand. Their ten-acre lease has expanded to 160 acres. They now sell about three million oysters a year.

Finger maneuvered the boat up to the rows of racks that held the seaweed-strewn oyster bags, and he and Marinelli jumped off, holding on to the boat by a rope, while I took pictures of them. Billy clowned with a giant oyster he found lying in the mud.

"These are called Stanley racks," Finger said, demonstrating the motion of the cylindrical bags, which revolved around an overhead pipe.

"It's an Australian system." The bags flip from one side to the other with the incoming and outgoing tide. The water flow gives the Pacific *(C. gigas)* oysters a thicker shell and a more uniform shape. I asked Finger which variety of oysters Hog Island cultivates.

"We grow Pacific oysters and Atlantic oysters—they are very hardy. The Kumamoto oysters do okay; we are even reviving the Olympias. We used to grow [European] *O. edulis* oysters. We have the last of them in a deep-water channel. We can harvest them at a year and a half or so. They look great until they're about one year old, then they suddenly die [of *bonamia*]. We are giving up on them. It's a species that's at the end of its evolutionary days," Finger prophesized. "They are weak, sensitive animals. I think the *edulis* is doomed."

When the boat returned, Finger showed me Hog Island's UV depuration system. It's the same sort of sanitizing plant used by European oyster growers whose beds are in Grade B waters, the California equivalent of "restricted" waters.

Finger argued that going the extra step of depurating shellfish increased their quality. But, on further questioning, he admitted that, in fact, the system was installed after what Finger called "The 1998 Mother's Day Disaster," during which more than one hundred people got a sickness traced to Hog Island oysters."

The Mother's Day storm cloud had a silver lining, Finger insisted. "Tomales Bay was thought to be so pristine that nobody bothered with water quality issues. It forced us to clean things up." Every possible source of *E. coli* was tracked down. Dairy farms were forced to fence off the creeks, campsites were equipped with toilets, and septic systems of houses near the water were tested.

"Tomales Bay still goes from 'approved' to 'restricted' every time it rains," Finger said. Hog Island opted to install a purification system to sanitize the shellfish because they couldn't afford to shut down due to weather.

I asked Finger where he stood on selling and eating oysters in the summer. "When we started, we didn't sell any oysters in the summer," he admitted. "And I am afraid that, in the interest of developing a year-round market, we are getting too far away from the sustainable food wisdom of every food in its season. Oyster season is in the winter. I wouldn't want to lose my summer sales. But you can't treat oysters the same way in the summer that you do in the winter. I have seen trucks full of Gulf oysters arriving in San Francisco in the heat of summer with no refrigeration. The problem with Gulf oystermen is that they are taking oysters from the warmest waters in the country and not taking any responsibility for how they are treated once they leave the boat. I think part of it is the difference between a wild fishery and oyster farming. They are a bunch of cowboys down there, and they have a different attitude from people who are nurturing a crop."

John Finger returned to Hog Island's headquarters building while Billy Marinelli and I grabbed a few bags of oysters from the retail area. We sat down at the table he had reserved in Hog Island's picnic grove and started shucking oysters. He had invited six more guests to the picnic, so we had some work to do. But it was quite a place to sit and shuck. When Billy said this was the best place to eat oysters in the Bay Area, for once he wasn't exaggerating.

At the entrance to the picnic grove where we were sitting, there was the front half of a wooden sailboat buried standing up with the bowsprit serving as a flagpole. A dozen or so tables surrounded the boat, each with a barbecue grill. The picnickers at the next table had laid out a red-and-white-checkered tablecloth, which they decorated with a centerpiece of Gerber daisies and chrysthanthemums in a Mason jar. They had brought a gorgeous salad and stemware, and they were drinking Champagne they kept in an ice bucket.

Our table wasn't nearly so fancy. Billy's guests arrived and we all ate scads of Hog Island Pacific *(C. gigas)* oysters on the half shell with some tart Sauvignon blanc that we drank from plastic cups. Then we lit some charcoal and put some Portuguese linguiça sausage and some opened oysters topped with a little salsa on the grill. We ate the grilled oysters and linguiça with cold Anchor Steam beers.

If you want to eat in Hog Island's picnic grove, you have to reserve a table months in advance and pay $35 just to use it. But on a sparklingly sunny day, with the boats bobbing on the blue water of Tomales Bay and the shore at your feet, it's an experience of a lifetime.

While I was in the San Francisco Bay Area, I stayed at a friend's apartment in the Berkeley Hills in a building owned by an elderly Frenchman named Ray. He had grown up near Arcachon, and when he found out I was writing a book about oysters, he invited me over for a glass of vermouth. We spent a long time talking about French oyster traditions.

He knew I was going to Tomales Bay for the day, and he was waiting for me on the front porch when I got back. "Well," he said, "where are they?"

"What?" I answered in genuine surprise.

"The oysters, where are the oysters?" he said.

"Oh, I ate them there. I didn't bring any back," I said.

"You drove all the way to Tomales Bay, went to the oyster farm, and came back without any oysters?" he asked with raised eyebrows.

"I will never understand Americans," Ray fumed. Then he went back in the house and slammed the door.

HANGTOWN FRY

Two different legends are told about this oyster omelet, invented in the California hamlet of Hangtown. Both agree that eggs and oysters were among the most expensive foodstuffs of the gold rush era. One has it that this was the last meal of a condemned man; the other claims that it was the most expensive dish a gold miner who just struck it rich could think of.

    2 slices best quality bacon
    1 tablespoon unsalted butter
    6 oysters, shucked
    3 eggs, lightly beaten
    3 or 4 dashes Tabasco sauce
    Salt and pepper

Fry the bacon until crisp. Transfer to paper towels to drain. In a clean skillet, melt the butter over medium heat. Add the oysters and sauté for about one and a half minutes, or until they just plump up. Crumble the bacon and toss it with the oysters. Pour the eggs into the pan. Season with Tabasco sauce, salt, and pepper to taste and cook for five minutes or until the eggs are set, turning the cooked eggs to let the uncooked eggs run underneath. Transfer to a plate and serve immediately with sourdough toast.

Makes one large serving.

NINE

Will Shuck for Food

Music from *The Big Chill* blared while Jon Rowley and I shucked
oysters on the front porch of the Fairview Grange Hall on Washington
State's Olympic Peninsula. I had volunteered to serve as an oyster shucker at a Christmas party in order to spend some time with Rowley and ask
him about what he has called the "Great American Oyster Renaissance."

"It's mostly marketing," Jon Rowley chuckled when I asked him
again about the grandiloquent name. But Rowley is dead serious when
he predicts that the rise in popularity of oysters on the East and West
coasts of the United States is the start of something big.

A steady increase in consumer interest, a spate of new oyster-bar
openings, and soaring oyster sales over the last three decades is more
than a passing fad, he argues. It has reached a tipping point all across
America—Rowley sees us returning to our roots as an oyster-loving
culture.

I'd been trying to get Rowley to agree to a meeting for weeks, but he
couldn't find a time for us to get together until I sent him an email titled
"Oyster Moments." It contained a batch of digital photos taken during

my research for this book—snapshots of oyster eccentrics, oyster bars, and oyster boats in Connecticut, California, Texas, England, Ireland, and France (you can see it at www.robbwalsh.com). After looking at the photos, he agreed to let me put on an apron and shuck oysters at somebody's Christmas party.

The sixty-two-year-old turned out to be an impressive figure. He stood just over six feet tall, with thick white hair that hung down in bangs over a round baby face. It was a cold and drizzly December night, and he wore a quilted blue coat and a knitted wool cap with a Cowichan tribal design. Both of us had white aprons tied around our bellies.

"Try one of these Totten Inlet *virginicas*," Rowley would say when somebody came to get an oyster. "They are Eastern oysters that are born and raised in Washington. They are my nominee for some of the best oysters on the planet," he would say, with an emphasis on "the best oysters on the planet." After the sales pitch, most people tried the big *virginicas*, and nearly everybody loved them.

I was willing to risk stabbing myself with an oyster knife to meet Rowley because he is the John the Baptist of this "Great American Oyster Renaissance." He has also been called the P. T. Barnum of the oyster world.

He has been working with oysters for some thirty years and is generally acknowledged as the leading seafood expert of the Pacific Northwest. *Gourmet* keeps him on as a contributing editor and *Saveur* put him on their Top 100 list for 2008. But he is, first and foremost, a marketing genius.

Before he became an oyster evangelist, Rowley changed the way Americans ate salmon. A former Alaskan salmon fisherman, he is the guy who thought there was something special about Copper River king salmon and started bringing it to market unfrozen in 1983. Today he is also trying to establish a market for Yukon River king salmon, a fat-bellied fish harvested by Yupik Eskimos in Alaska.

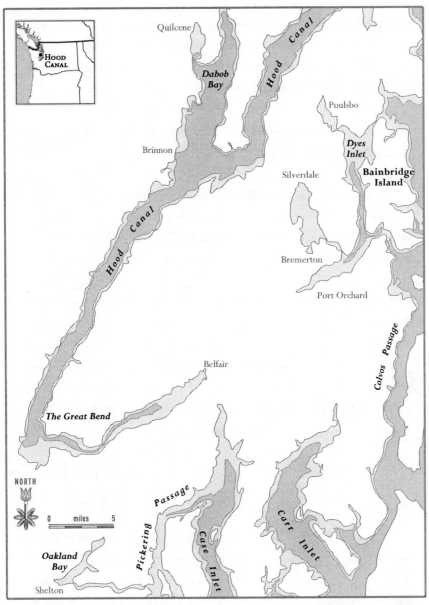

Quilcene

*Dabob
Bay*

Hood Canal

Poulsbo

*Dyes
Inlet*

**Bainbridge
Island**

Brinnon

Silverdale

Hood Canal

Bremerton

Port Orchard

Colvos Passage

Belfair

The Great Bend

NORTH

0   miles   5

Passage

Pickering

Case Inlet

Carr Inlet

*Oakland
Bay*

Shelton

Hood Canal, Washington

In his marketing of Copper River king salmon, Rowley showed a knack for tapping into the culinary zeitgeist. Wild salmon had always been differentiated in the Pacific Northwest, but the former Alaskan salmon fisherman turned it into a product, gave it a trade name, and brought it to the rest of the country. At the beginning of the season, never-been-frozen Copper River king salmon has been sold for up to $30 a pound, three times the price of most salmon. And consumers couldn't get enough of it.

Since the 1980s, Rowley has been doing the same thing for oysters. Drawing on French oyster culture for inspiration, he began to set up half-shell programs for restaurants. "Place names add value," he told oyster-bar owners, encouraging them to charge more for oysters from particular places.

Identifying oysters by place names isn't new—it goes back to the Romans. But in the United States, the system had fallen into disrepute. All over the country, *C. virginica* oysters served on the half shell were called Blue Points, no matter where they came from. Rowley stressed what he calls "integrity of nomenclature," insisting that oyster bars avoid confusing or misleading oyster names and even encouraging them to include the Latin names on their oyster menus if they sold more than one species.

In the late 1980s, Rowley started oyster festivals in Seattle, Boston, Chicago, and elsewhere. Throwing a great party was only part of his motivation.

When Gulf oysters were identified as the cause of several deaths in the 1980s, the media sensationalized the threat. "Oysters will kill you," was the message the public was getting. Oyster-bar sales began to slow. Rowley organized his oyster events to involve local media celebrities. And he saw to it that the journalists were educated about oysters in the process.

Part of the education, of course, was that the potentially lethal oysters came from the warm waters of the Gulf of Mexico. And that the cold-water oysters didn't carry the deadly *Vibrio vulnificus* bacteria.

While Rowley and I talked, we struggled to keep up with the Christmas party's demand. Rowley had purchased a couple hundred oysters of three varieties, all from Washington State: Pacific *(C. gigas)* oysters from Totten Inlet, tiny Kumamotos, and a curious, cream-colored *C. virginica*. We tried to keep about two dozen oysters on the half shell in the ice-filled galvanized steel laundry tub in front of us, so the faster the crowd slurped, the faster we had to shuck.

Rowley, who once shucked at the oyster bar at Le Bernardin in New York, used an imported French oyster knife. He severed both abductor muscles in a flash, turning each oyster meat over in the shell so it looked perfect. I took up shucking only a couple of years ago, and though I can usually get the oysters open, they aren't always pretty. I got a few tips from Rowley. Over the course of the evening, my oyster shucking improved dramatically. It was the first time I shucked a lot of *C. gigas* oysters. The vast majority of oysters produced in Washington State are the Pacific *(C. gigas)* oysters that the French call *creuses*.

Washington State grows *C. gigas* oysters in the tidelands. At this northern latitude, the rise and fall of the tide is extreme enough to leave the mud flats along the bays and the Hood Canal exposed at high tide. Oyster farmers take advantage of the intertidal lands just as they do in France. But while the French "parks" are owned by the government and leased to oyster growers, here the oyster farms are privately owned.

Oyster farmers are far more engaged in marketing than oyster fisherman. Oyster fishermen bring their product to the market, and that's the end of it. Oyster farmers give their oysters brand names and write sales pitches describing their flavors with words like cucumber, melon, and sea breeze.

Eaten side by side with *C. virginicas*, *C. gigas* oysters taste more vegetal and less sweet to my palate. The tiny Kumamoto oyster, which was imported from Japan and is also popular in the Pacific Northwest, is a distant cousin to the *C. gigas*, with a similar flavor.

The Totten Inlet *C. virginicas* that Rowley was promoting were much larger than the Pacific and Kumamoto oysters on our little display. About half of the women who came out to the porch would balk at eating one.

"It's too big," they'd say.

"But it goes down really easy," Rowley countered. A few were convinced, but most opted for the daintier Pacific and Kumamoto oysters. One attractive woman picked up a Totten Inlet *C. virginica* and paused for a moment with the oyster in front of her mouth. A gaggle of guys who knew her heckled her from the doorway of the Grange Hall about "eating a really big one." She turned red and put the oyster down. Rowley sweet-talked her until she picked it up again and defiantly gulped it down while the gallery lustily cheered her on. It was a riveting little Christmas party flirtation at the oyster bar.

Jon Rowley does small events like this all over the country. He calls it "educating the public, one oyster-eater at a time." He says it keeps him in touch with people's tastes. It's part of his role as a marketing consultant for the Shelton, Washington–based Taylor Shellfish Farms, one of the largest oyster cultivators in the world.

Rowley helped develop the Totten Inlet *C. virginica* oyster marketing plan. The decision to harvest the Totten Inlet *C. virginica* at a three-and-a-quarter-inch shell size was a bold departure from the norm. Pacific *(C. gigas)* oysters are generally harvested at two and a half inches in Washington State, and Kumamotos are two inches and even less. But with oysters selling for $2 apiece, Rowley worried that people were starting to feel gypped.

"I hate tiny oysters," he complained. "You pay $24 for a dozen and you get like six tablespoons of membranous seawater."

To counter the image of Washington State oysters as undersized and overpriced, Rowley and the marketing department of Taylor Shellfish Farms settled on the relatively large size for the Totten Inlet *C. virginicas*. Eating a dozen of these oysters was intended to be a satisfying experience.

The Pacific Coast Oyster Wine Competition is another one of his projects that's sponsored by Taylor Shellfish. The competition is open to wines of British Columbia, Idaho, Washington, Oregon, and California. Leading West Coast food and wine writers eat oysters and drink wine, then select their top ten oyster wines. A total of 159 wines were entered in the 2006 competition. At the Christmas party, Rowley was pouring some of the winning wines.

Some of the winners are small operations that produce limited amounts of wine. But some perennial winners, like Geyser Peak Winery's Sauvignon blanc and Kenwood Vineyards' Sauvignon blanc, are made in large quantities and available all over the country at reasonable prices.

The *C. virginicas* were the first oysters we ran out of at our little oyster bar. But it was clear from our audience's reaction that there would always be a market for tiny oysters too. For a list of the winners of the most recent Pacific Coast Oyster Wine Competition, visit the website www.taylorshellfishfarms.com/oysterwine.

Xinh Dwelley came out of the kitchen carrying two shucking knifes, a couple of white towels, and a baking sheet mounded with oysters. The

Vietnamese American chef sat down at a table beside me and Bill Taylor, the president of Taylor Shellfish, and started shucking.

Before I got to the Christmas party on the Olympic Peninsula, Jon Rowley had set up an appointment for me to stop in Shelton, Washington, the headquarters of Taylor Shellfish, where I was supposed to pick up several Styrofoam boxes full of oysters and ice. Rowley had also arranged for me to interview Bill Taylor, who brought me to Xinh's Clam and Oyster House in Shelton, Washington, for lunch.

I told them I would be making my debut as an oyster shucker that evening and that I needed advice. I had never shucked a Kumamoto or a C. gigas oyster before. Xinh handed me a shucking knife and invited me to go at it. She had learned to shuck in a commercial oyster plant.

"Most commercial shuckers go in from the bill side," explained Taylor as we watched Xinh's technique.

"You have to break the top shell to get your knife into the bill," Xinh said.

After looking over the oysters on Xinh's baking sheet, I realized there were five different species on the table. It was the first time I had ever seen an Olympia *(O. lurida)* oyster. I picked one up and examined it closely; it looked like a small clam.

Only in the Pacific Northwest, where the native Olympia (*O. conchaphila* or *O. lurida*) oyster is making a comeback, will you see five species of oysters in one place. For this reason alone, the Pacific Northwest is the most exciting oyster region in the world.

I grabbed a knife and shucked my first "Olys," as they are known in Washington. The half shell was about the size of a fifty-cent piece. They tasted salty and coppery, amazingly similar to their cousins, the European *(O. edulis)* oysters. I fell in love immediately. Then I tried to learn Xinh's shucking technique.

Hanging on the wall near the front door of Xinh's Clam and Oyster House, there is a photo of owner Xinh Dwelley showing off a medal she just won in an oyster-shucking competition. She is the five-time winner of the West Coast Oyster Shucking Championship. I asked her to show me her scars, and she pointed to a divot in her left thumb.

"I did that on my second day as a professional shucker," she said. "The first day you get fast. The second day you get cocky," she said.

Bill Taylor is a fourth-generation Washington oysterman. "In 1890, my great grandfather, James Y. Waldrip, came to Seattle to help rebuild the city after the fire of 1889. He got into the Olympia oyster business in the Shelton area. He built a big oyster concern called the Olympia Oyster Company," Taylor told me over lunch.

Washington is one of the few states where tidelands, the lands exposed at low tide, can be privately owned. The laws were passed to protect the oysters, which could otherwise be picked up off the beach by anyone.

"We have a fifteen-to-twenty-foot tidal fluctuation, which gives you lots of land that is exposed at low tide," says Taylor. Taylor Shellfish owns more than eight thousand acres of tidelands, of which about thirty percent are used as oyster farms.

"My family bought some tidelands in the old days. They built dikes to create tidal pools that were three to four inches deep at low tide. That's where you kept your oysters," Taylor said. Olympia farmers used a system like the English one. They would harvest native Olympia oysters from common fishing grounds and then deposit them in the privately owned tidal pools until they reached market size. "My family helped develop the native Olympia oyster industry," said Taylor.

Oysters have a limited lifespan out of the water, and it took too long to sail up through the treacherous waters of Puget Sound and down the coast to San Francisco. It was a much shorter trip from Willapa Bay, and so the Willapa Bay oyster trade was established. But the railroad made overfishing possible, just as it had in Europe.

In the years between the 1890s, when the native *(O. lurida)* oysters were wiped out, and the early 1900s, when the Pacific *(C. gigas)* oysters were well established, West Coast oystermen cultivated *C. virginica* oysters imported from the East Coast.

"The Totten Inlet *virginicas* we sell actually have a long history," said Taylor. In the early 1900s, East Coast *(C. virginica)* oysters were shipped across the country by train. They came in during the cold weather in early spring. Then they were planted in the "Eastern bed" in Totten Inlet's South Sound, and in a few other places. After holding them for a few months, they sold them in the fall and winter.

Seed oysters were also purchased for cultivation in anticipation of establishing the *C. virginica* as the new West Coast oyster. There were a couple of natural sets of *C. virginicas* up near Canada and in Willapa Bay. But it takes three years for a *C. virginica* oyster to reach maturity.

Plans to grow *C. virginicas* on the West Coast were abandoned after the Pacific *(C. gigas)* oyster was imported from Japan. The Asian oysters were more profitable because they grew much faster. Pacific oysters planted from seed imported by ship from Japan grew to maturity in eighteen months. Eventually, the Pacific oysters began to reproduce, and it was no longer necessary to import seed.

But the West Coast oyster industry was shrinking. The bays and inlets that once held oyster beds were being polluted. The oysters of San Francisco Bay were the first to go. As industrial development made its way up the coast, Washington oyster beds began to disappear too.

In the 1920s, a pulp mill was built on Washington's Oakland Bay. Waste sulfates contaminated the water, and the runoff created a massive algae bloom that depleted the oxygen in the water. Within two years, the oysters were wiped out. Oystermen sued, but the mill just settled the matter by buying up the oyster beds. By the 1950s, the pulp mill was closed because it was no longer efficient.

When Bill Taylor's father, Justin Taylor, and his uncle, the late Edwin Taylor, took over the oyster company in the late 1960s, they bought the old oyster beds from the defunct pulp mill, among others. They bought up a lot of tidelands and started raising other kinds of shellfish. That set the stage for the Taylor Shellfish Farms of today.

When the Clean Water Act of 1972 cleaned up the water, Taylor Shellfish was in a unique position to restart the Washington oyster business. "We are now the largest Manila clam producer in the United States, and we cultivate a greater variety of shellfish than any other grower," Bill Taylor told me. Taylor Shellfish is also involved in efforts to revive the native Olympia oyster, the oyster that got the Taylor family started in the oyster business.

While I was picking up oysters at Taylor Shellfish, Austin Doctor, the plant manager, gave me a guided tour. Flipping through the inventory list attached to his clipboard, he told me that there were more than thirty thousand half-shell oysters from five different species on hand at Taylor Shellfish that day. The inventory listed them by size, by area of origin, and by trade name.

"The trade name and the place name are not always the same," said Doctor. For instance, Eld Inlet is the state of Washington's designation for oysters from that area, but Taylor Shellfish markets some oysters from Eld Inlet as "Maple Point oysters." Why? "Because it sounds better."

"Trade names come and go," says Doctor. In the case of Totten Inlet, the trade name and the place name are the same. But there used to be

some bag-cultivated oysters from Totten Inlet that came out very delicate, with beautiful fluted shells. "We called them 'Steamboat Island oysters' for a while," says Doctor. "Everyone called them 'Steamboats.'"

And then there were "quils," the extra-small oysters from Quilcene,
Washington, on the Hood Canal. "We don't even sell 'quils' anymore,
but we still have people asking for them," said Doctor. "We know that
when they ask for 'quils' they are looking for very small oysters, so
we suggest something small. There are hundreds of names for Pacific
(C. gigas) oysters at this point.

"'Blue Point' is an example of a trade name that's been abused," said
Doctor. The consumer is getting savvy; they know that Blue Point oysters
don't come from Blue Point, Long Island, anymore. But really, as long as
the characteristics remain the same, it doesn't matter, he told me.

I told him that I thought Washington State oyster trade names were a
scam. "Oyster bars want to claim they are selling twenty-seven varieties
of oysters, so you guys sell them the exact same Pacific (C. gigas) oyster
under twenty-seven different names," I argued.

I told Doctor about an experiment I had conducted at Elliott's
Oyster House on Pier 56 in Seattle. The day I stopped in, a waiter named
Trent Yarosevich bragged that the restaurant had twenty-three varieties
of oysters on hand.

But I said I thought there wasn't much difference between them.
The waiter said that there were big differences. For instance, he could
always tell a Hama Hama oyster from the others because of its distinctive
appearance.

So we made a bet. I had the shucker line up four kinds of Pacific (C.
gigas) oysters on a plate. The waiter studied them carefully and pointed to
what he thought was a Hama Hama oyster. He was wrong.

Austin Doctor wasn't impressed. He gave me an analogy: When you
go to Napa Valley and visit wineries, aren't you really drinking the same

Cabernet over and over? "We could open two bottles of red wine from neighboring wineries in Napa, and you and I could argue if they taste different or not," he said. "Isn't that the beauty of it?"

The Hood Canal is seventy-five miles long, and there are real differences in the oysters, he said, partly because the producers are trying to create distinctive oysters.

Some oysters are grown in the French style, in mesh bags set on racks anchored to the tidelands. Others are spread directly on the beach when it is exposed during low tide, with a net secured over the top to protect them from predators. Oysters grown in bags look different from oysters grown on the flats.

"In fact, I know of three growers who are sharing the same grounds and selling their oysters under three different trade names," Doctor said. There are 230 oyster growers in Washington State, and they are all trying to create something unique. The whole idea of a trade name is to get people to ask for your oysters—or your Napa Cabernet.

"Everybody says their oyster is the best. It's a little humorous. But the passion is a beautiful thing," said Doctor.

I asked him what he thought about banning oyster sales in the summer. "It kills me when I hear 'Don't eat oysters in months without an R,'" said Doctor. "At Taylor Shellfish, we don't sell any spawning oysters. We sell triploids in the summer—they are big, fat, and glycogen-filled."

Triploids are a sexless crossbreed of oyster. Just as a mule is a triploid cross between a horse and a donkey and can't reproduce, a triploid oyster is a cross that remains sterile; it doesn't produce any eggs like a normal (diploid) oyster.

So as the weather gets warm and regular (diploid) oysters start converting sweet-tasting glycogen to fishy-tasting reproductive material, the triploid just keeps making glycogen. Triploids are generally fatter and faster growing than their diploid cousins. Since oyster farmers in the

Pacific Northwest rely on seed oysters rather than natural reproduction, more and more of the oysters produced in hatcheries are triploids.

I have eaten my share of triploids, and I have to confess, they make a pretty convincing case for eating summer oysters. Any objections regarding the lack of glycogen are certainly set aside. These oysters are amazingly sweet in July and August.

But they aren't any less susceptible to *Vibrio parahaemolyticus*, the disease that has closed some oyster beds in Washington State for several summers in a row. Some people don't eat triploid oysters because they think they are the product of genetic engineering. But an oyster-bar owner in Toronto named Rodney Clark had the most unique objection to triploids I've ever heard. He asked me, "How can a sexless oyster be an aphrodisiac?"

"How do you get oysters horny?" I asked Ed Jones, the manager of Taylor Shellfish's Quilcene Hatchery. This was the space-age oyster hatchery that John Bayes, the Mad Max of Whitstable, had told me about. I had been dying to see it ever since. I had a trunk full of oysters in my car and I was due at Rowley's Christmas party in northern Washington in a few hours. But I couldn't resist the chance to tour a state-of-the-art oyster hatchery.

Jones walked me through the place, describing how the process works. It all starts with ten or twelve oysters. You put them in a sack, put the sack in a bucket, get them sexually excited, and, voila, you have enough sperm and eggs to create a whole lot of oyster larvae, he explained.

Of course, what I really wanted to know was: "What do oysters consider an aphrodisiac?" Jones said warm water, mainly. Of course, they have to be really fat and happy to begin with, he said. A big meal helps get them in the mood.

If the oysters are ripe—full of gonad and ready to spawn anyway—it's pretty easy. You feed them a lot of algae and raise the temperature of the water to simulate the onset of spring. If they came from very cold water and had ceased eating and lost weight, you have to feed them and warm them up slowly over the course of a couple of weeks.

Once they start to spawn, Jones will pull one oyster out of the bucket, shuck it, and stir the milky gametes (sexual material) back into the water. That will trigger the whole bucket of oysters to go into a frenzy. Oysters all have sex at the same time in the same place—they reproduce by orgy.

The spat, as the sperm and eggs that are secreted into the water are called, join to form larvae. Hundreds of millions of larvae are produced by ten or twelve oysters. The larvae are then placed into a twelve-thousand-gallon fiberglass tank that is ten feet tall and thirteen feet across. At this point, the larvae are swimming organisms that measure around fifty microns. Ed Young showed me one in the microscope. It looked like a mosquito larva.

They foul the water with lots of ammonia as they grow. The tanks are drained every two to three days, and the larvae are screened out and moved to clean saltwater in the next tank. This continues through a series of tanks and ever-larger screens. When the larvae get close to setting size, they're sent to another part of the hatchery.

In France, the spat are collected on mussel-shell-filled collectors such as plastic pipes. The pipes are emptied out at the oyster beds. As the oysters grow larger, the fragile mussel shells break into pieces, leaving the oyster farmer with individual oysters that can be placed in mesh bags.

In an American oyster hatchery, the larvae are put into a tank whose bottom is spread with "shell chips," this is the "oyster flour Billy Mariavelli told me about," pieces of oyster or scallop shell fragments no bigger than four hundred microns across.

The marriage of the shell chips and the oyster larvae is the magical part of the hatchery process. In nature, *C. gigas* oysters grow in clusters, attaching themselves to each other to form a reef. To create individual oysters, you have to fool the oyster into thinking it has joined the reef. To the three-hundred-micron oyster larvae, the four-hundred-micron pieces of shell seem plenty big. So they are convinced they are attached to something solid, and they begin the transformation into young oysters. The oyster larvae fall onto them and attach themselves. When they grow up, they become easy-to-handle individual half-shell oysters.

From there, the hatchery process becomes a nursery operation. The tiny oysters are transferred to a series of tanks called "downwellers" that keep a steady flow of saltwater moving through them. And they are fed copious amounts of algae. In fact, the main limitation on an oyster hatchery is how much algae it can produce.

They like a lot of variety in their diet. "We grow five or six different kinds of algae here," says Jones. The algae-growing tanks are the eeriest part of an oyster hatchery. The tall, round, transparent tanks glow in weird shades of yellow and green. They're lit by skylights and grow lights.

Oysters are most easily farmed in northern latitudes, where huge tidal variations make it easy to plant them on the intertidal flats so they are underwater at high tide and exposed at low tide. But the paucity of sunlight in the North makes it hard to grow algae for an oyster hatchery. Taylor Shellfish has come up with a unique solution to this problem. They send their oysters to Hawaii.

In Hawaii, where algae is easily grown, Taylor Shellfish raises the tiny oysters until they reach a larger size. Then they're shipped back to Washington and put in the FLUPSY (floating upweller system).

Oysters need to be of sufficient size to be set out on the beds. Until they reach that size, Taylor Shellfish keeps them in a FLUPSY, which is a raft equipped with a paddlewheel. It floats in a bay near the oyster beds, loaded with baby oysters. The paddlewheel draws water up and sends it flowing over the oysters.

I asked Ed Jones if using only ten or twelve oysters to produce millions of offspring constituted some kind of oyster inbreeding. Didn't it weaken the genetics?

That would be a concern if the oysters were actually reproducing, Jones told me. But since Washington oystermen buy seed oysters every year rather than relying on a natural set, it doesn't make any difference. A natural set is a nuisance in Washington; the ugly little spats look like barnacles on the nice smooth oyster shells.

Besides, a narrow genetic range makes for some interesting breeding experiments. He showed me some tanks that contained oysters with distinctive tiger-striped shells. Oysters with this unusual but attractive mutation were being set aside. Tiger-striped oysters are grown out in Totten Inlet, and are now appearing in oyster bars under the name "Totten Tigers."

After the Christmas party with Rowley, I was in no shape to drive to Seattle. So Rowley invited me to spend the night at his house in Port Angeles.

Rowley's wife Kate made us coffee in the morning and started baking an apple pie while Rowley put out smoked black cod and salmon a friend had given him on the ferryboat. We ate the smoked fish on buttered toast at a wooden dining table in the simply furnished front room of the little house.

"Tell me about the Great American Oyster Renaissance," I asked Rowley at the breakfast table. He hemmed and hawed for a while, playing the grumpy curmudgeon.

"It all got started with Billy Marinelli and Alice Waters in Berkeley in the 1970s, right?" I goaded. Rowley and Marinelli have been going at it for years.

"God created oysters—and Billy Marinelli created Royal Miyagis," Rowley quipped. "Royal Miyagi" is one of the more fanciful oyster names Marinelli has come up with. "Billy was very creative when it came to developing a selection of oysters for restaurants," Rowley said with a smirk.

I told Rowley that many varieties of oysters I had encountered in oyster bars, on both the East and West coasts, appeared to be exactly the same oysters with different names. That game, Rowley told me, has been going on for centuries.

Billy Marinelli told me that in the early days of the oyster business, distributors sat in a warehouse with lots of wooden cases full of *C. gigas* oysters. When an account called and ordered Fanny Bays, they got out the rubber stamp that said Fanny Bay. If the account asked for Hood Canal oysters, they got out the Hood Canal stamp. The oysters stayed the same, only the rubber stamps changed.

"That's still going on," Rowley said with a laugh. "Ask Billy!"

"So how did the oyster renaissance get started?" I pleaded with Rowley once he'd finished a cup of coffee. Kate suggested we move to some more comfortable chairs in the other room. She wanted us out of her way because she knew this lecture was going to go on for a while.

"Oysters went out of our consciousness, but there was once a culture of the oyster in this country. They were plentiful, inexpensive, and ubiquitous," Rowley began, delivering a speech that had obviously been well-honed.

From the 1860s through the 1920s, the oyster saloon became the epicenter of social life in America, not only in coastal regions, but also in Midwestern cities such as Chicago and St. Louis, Rowley said. Some of these establishments were huge three-story buildings. In Chicago, Rector's Oyster House was especially popular with artists, politicians, and socialites as a place to see and be seen.

The last golden era of oysters ended in the 1920s, Rowley said. During the Industrial Revolution, sewage pipes were built to serve a growing urban population without any thought about where the pollution would end up.

He paused for effect. Sewage and oysters don't go together well, he said.

Typhoid epidemics traced to contaminated oysters killed hundreds of people across the country and earned huge headlines. People stopped trusting oystermen and fishmongers. Chicago banned oysters.

Then matters grew even bleaker, Rowley said. Industrial development along the coasts added toxins to the water and destroyed the wetlands that fed the oyster's ecosystem. Then in 1929, Prohibition began. Oysters and alcohol were part of the same culture. You ate oysters with a drink, be it beer, wine, or spirits. When the alcohol was taken away, lots of oyster houses folded immediately.

Meanwhile, overfishing depleted the remaining oyster beds in areas with common fishing grounds. In places where oysters were harvested on public oyster reefs, there was no incentive to conserve the resource: You went to the oyster beds and got what you could before the other guy got it first. Long Island was one of the first places to privatize its oyster beds, and that's part of the reason it has lasted so long as an oyster region.

"The American oyster Dark Ages began in the 1930s," Rowley told me. Some old establishments across the country kept the flame from dying. The Grand Central Oyster Bar in New York, the oyster bar at the Drake Hotel in Chicago, and the Original Oyster House in Pittsburgh were among the oyster-eaters' museums. New Orleans and the Gulf Coast kept America's oyster culture on life support, and if you go there, you can still visit oyster saloons that date back to the original golden age of oysters.

The comeback began slowly, with many convergent strains, and, Rowley said, "Like the American Revolution, France played a role." French oyster culture was thriving while American oyster culture withered. "American expats in Paris, of which I was a Johnny-come-lately, had a passionate relationship with the oyster that wasn't happening in this country."

Expats such as Julia Child, M. F. K. Fisher, and Ernest Hemingway adopted the French enthusiasm for oysters during their years in France. They wrote about it, and they brought it back to the United States. Novelist Eleanor Clark, the wife of Robert Penn Warren, won the National Book Award in 1965 for her nonfiction work *The Oysters of Locmariaquer*, an account of the oyster culture of Brittany.

The Clean Water Act of 1972 was "The Great Facilitator," as Rowley tells the story. It was this law, which cleaned up American waters, that really brought the oyster back. When it was enacted, old family oyster companies like Taylor Shellfish were already poised to restart the cultivation of oysters on the tidelands they owned in Washington State, Rowley explained. And the state of Washington was ready to assist them.

I asked Rowley about his seminal oyster moment in Paris, an account of which I had read in a *New York Times* story by R. W. Apple Jr. Rowley suggested that we talk about it while we took the dog and the cat for a walk.

It was a chilly overcast day, and we hadn't gone far before Rowley pointed out a two-story house built in the 1920s that was much fancier than any of the others in the neighborhood. "That's Raymond Carver's house," he said.

I didn't remember Raymond Carver's short stories right away. But Rowley reminded me about Carver's bleak strain of fiction and the spiritual emptiness of the people who inhabited it. After a miserable alcoholic life, Carver spent his last ten years at the house in Port Angeles, staying sober and writing stories about the lives of hopeless middle-class families in a semi-rural landscape not unlike Port Angeles, Washington.

Rowley identified with Carver. When I asked him about his ethnicity, he told me he didn't have one. He grew up in Alaska and Oregon with two alcoholic parents, he said. When he left home, he became a commercial fisherman. For ten years, he spent summers fishing in Alaska and winters bumming around Europe, mostly France. He had bouts with depression and heavy drinking.

In the mid-1960s, Rowley's first daughter was hit by a drunk driver and died a slow death. He and his wife moved to Portugal and had another daughter. But the marriage didn't withstand the tragedy.

Rowley credits the passage about oysters from *A Moveable Feast*, Hemingway's posthumously published memoir of 1920s Paris, with changing his life. He was intrigued by the idea that something you ate could give you a positive outlook.

Rowley told R. W. Apple Jr. that after reading the passage in his shabby Paris hotel room, he resolved to "eat lots of oysters, as many as I could afford, and make it my quest to learn about oysters and how they are cultivated, distributed, and consumed."

> *"As I ate the oysters with their strong taste of the sea and their faint metallic taste that the cold white wine washed away, leaving only the sea taste and the succulent texture, and as I drank their liquid from each shell and washed it down with*

*the crisp taste of the wine, I lost the empty feeling and began
to be happy and to make plans."*

—*A Moveable Feast*, Ernest Hemingway

He started by getting on the Métro and spending the last of his money on a feast of oysters and wine at Le Dôme, he told me. When he returned in subsequent years, he educated himself, visiting oyster farms, oyster distributors, and oyster restaurants all over France. Oysters gave his life a purpose.

When he started working with oyster marketers, Rowley was a purist who wouldn't back down from his version of the gospel. When another Washington State oyster entrepreneur named Bill Webb started cultivating European flat *(O. edulis)* oysters and selling them as "Belons" in the early 1980s, Rowley was outraged. "I told him, you can't call them Belons, because the Belon River is in France."

The two men were asked to speak about oysters at various educational events, and their talks invariably ended up becoming debates. Eventually Webb started calling his American-raised European flat *(O. edulis)* oysters "Westcott Bay Flats," and the two became friends.

As a goodbye gift, Rowley gave me a copy of *Where I'm Calling From: Selected Stories* by Raymond Carver. Some time later, I picked up the book and read the story called "A Small Good Thing." In the story, a mother goes to a bakery and orders a birthday cake for her son. The little boy is hit by a car on the way to school and is taken to the hospital, where he goes into a coma. The baker keeps calling, angry that no one picked up the cake. In the end, the boy's mother and father go to the bakery in the middle of the night and confront the abusive baker. The man is chagrined and apologizes profusely. He sits the couple down and gives them hot cinnamon rolls and coffee.

"You probably need to eat something," the baker said. "I hope you'll eat some of my hot rolls. You have to eat and keep going. Eating is a small good thing in a time like this," he said. The resemblance to Rowley's tragedy was uncanny, and so was the small good thing of eating something as a way of coming back to life.

Just before I departed Port Angeles, Rowley took me for a ride in the car. We parked at Ocean View Cemetery, which is located on a grassy cliff high above the gray waters of the Strait of Juan de Fuca. We got out and walked around in the light drizzle. Over the cliff, I could see the shoreline of Vancouver Island in the distance.

In one of the rows of the cemetery, Rowley pointed out the low dark stone that marked Raymond Carver's grave. While we stood there, he produced two oysters and a small bottle of Jack Daniels with an inch left in the bottom from the pockets of his Gore-tex coat. He spilled a little oyster liquor on Carver's grave as he shucked. We toasted Carver with oysters and a warming slug of whiskey. Then we set the oyster shells and the empty bottle on the grave beside Carver's name and took a picture.

Rowley told me to put it in my collection of "Oyster Moments." And I did. (You can see the photos at www.robbwalsh.com.)

CARPETBAGGER STEAK

A "carpetbagger steak" is a beefsteak stuffed with whole oysters. At The Brooklyn in Seattle, several Pacific *(C. gigas)* oysters are stuffed inside a pocket cut into a large filet. In New Orleans, where the dish probably originated, one large Gulf *(C. virginica)* oyster is often stuffed in the steak, while another half dozen or so are simmered in butter and garlic and served alongside. You can customize your carpetbagger steak according to what kind of oysters you're using.

    4 eight-ounce filet steaks
    24 oysters, shucked
    Sea salt
    Freshly ground pepper
    2 tablespoons butter
    2 tablespoons olive oil
    4 cloves garlic, minced
    ½ cup white wine or Champagne

Preheat the oven to 450° F. With a sharp knife, cut a pocket into each steak. If the oysters are small, stuff each pocket with two or three oysters. If the oysters are large, stuff at least one into each pocket. Reserve the oyster liquor.

Salt and pepper the steaks. Heat the butter and olive oil in an ovenproof frying pan large enough to accommodate all four steaks. When the butter is hot, add the garlic and stir a few minutes until the garlic sizzles. Add the steaks to the pan and cook for five minutes until browned on one side. Flip the steaks and put the frying pan in the oven. Cook for about seven minutes for medium rare or to desired doneness.

Take the pan from the oven and remove the steaks to a platter. While the steaks rest for at least five minutes, deglaze the pan with the wine. Add the remaining oysters and oyster liquor to the pan juices and cook until the edges curl, about three minutes. Serve the steaks with the oysters and wine-butter sauce on the side.

TEN

Cajun Oyster Pirates

W E PULLED INTO A PARKING LOT at the Apache boat dock in Golden Meadows and waited for the fifty-seven-foot oyster lug named *Braud and Tracy* to pull in. The boat was named after captain Nick Collins's two kids. Jim Gossen and I jumped on board as soon as it pulled up to the dock. I was touring the Grand Isle region of Louisiana with Gossen, a Houston seafood dealer and oyster fanatic who grew up Cajun in Lafayette.

It was the week between Christmas of 2005 and New Year's 2006. After spending Christmas with Kelly and our six-month-old daughter, Ava Maeve, at Kelly's parents' house in Arkansas, I slipped away while everybody was doting on the new baby. Gossen had volunteered to take me down to his "camp" (beach house) on Grand Isle and introduce me to some of the old-time oystermen he knew.

It was a unique opportunity to get inside a secretive culture, so I jumped at the chance. I wanted to understand how the hurricanes had changed the oyster business in Louisiana. But I also wanted to ask the oystermen what they thought about *Vibrio* and how they would feel about more government regulation if it would improve the Gulf Coast oyster industry.

"How long have you been oystering?" I asked Collins.

"They used to chain my walker to that pipe when I was a baby," he said, pointing to a support pole in the middle of the deck. "I'm a fourth-generation oysterman, my cousin is fifth. I've been on these boats all my life."

We grabbed a couple of oysters off the pile on the deck and opened them with a shucking knife. The oysters had a good salt level, a little bit of glycogen, and a curiously strong mineral taste. It was an excellent flavor.

"They're from Chinaman Bayou, they're not bad," Collins said. "But they aren't as good as the Camanadas we got last week. Oysters from Camanada have a different flavor; they are not like the oysters over on the river side. Camanadas are the best."

"So how can somebody get Camanada oysters?" I asked him.

In Louisiana and Texas, oysters are sold as a commodity, like any other seafood. Collins said he had never heard of anybody selling Louisiana oysters by location. Sometimes the little local oyster shops that sell shucked oysters put "Grand Isle oysters" on their roadside signs, but that's about it.

I asked him if he has ever been in an oyster bar that sells lots of varieties of oysters.

"I have never been in an oyster bar," he said.

I explained that oyster farmers who sold oysters by brand name and location in other parts of the country were getting four and five times as much money as he was. And they badmouthed Gulf oysters as bland and tasteless.

"They are just saying that to promote their product," he scoffed. "We feel like we are farming oysters too. We filed a petition to get oyster cultivation in Louisiana recognized as farming, but they turned it down."

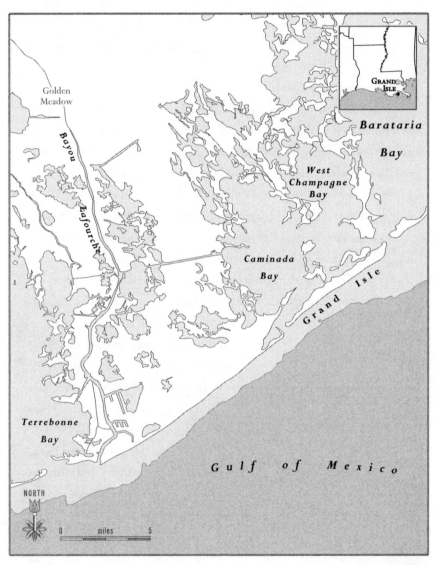

Grand Isle, Louisiana

Right now, oyster leases in Louisiana are in a state of flux. The hurricanes reshaped the underwater topography. You got hard ground where there used to be mud and mud where there used to be hard bottom, Collins said. And then there's the controversy over the canals. These new sources of fresh water will ultimately benefit oystermen, but right now they are upsetting the status quo.

One hundred years ago, the Mississippi River broke into a lot of little distributaries that flowed into the salt marshes of southern Louisiana. There were oyster reefs all along the coast in those days. But then a federal flood-control project built levees on the Mississippi River. The levees succeeded in controlling flooding, but they also cut off the flow of fresh water, which is why the wetlands are shrinking.

The decline in oyster production and the loss of a buffer zone to mitigate the force of hurricanes are two of the easily observed consequences of drying up the salt marshes. Much of the damage, such as the diminishing fish population due to the disturbance to the food chain, is less obvious.

A few years ago, the state of Louisiana launched an ambitious program to dig a series of canals that would reroute about half of the Mississippi River's flow back to the wetlands in order to restore the balance of freshwater. But, ironically, the completion of the big canals has damaged the leases of oyster fishermen.

In the long term, the oyster reefs will benefit, but some of the existing oyster leases at the mouth of the canals are being inundated with too much freshwater and silt. And the influx of freshwater has caused the oyster reefs to move. No one knows yet exactly where the new "sweet spots" will be.

In the interim, Louisiana oystermen are simply trying to find the oysters that the hurricanes left unharmed. In two days of dredging, the *Braud and Tracy* had filled only forty "boat bags," Collins complained.

While we were talking, a guy in a station wagon pulled up, gave Collins some folded money, and took a couple of sacks. Some more sacks were being loaded with a portable conveyor belt into the back of another buyer's truck.

"Let's buy some," I said to Jim Gossen. We paid $60 and took two half sacks. Oystermen buy used coffee sacks or cocoa sacks at the port in New Orleans to use for oysters. I got a clean one to put in my trunk to keep the oysters from stinking up the car too much.

When the oysters were loaded, I talked to Nick Collins about this year's harvest and the aftermath of the hurricanes. "The last of the good years was from 1985 to 1992. I don't know if we'll ever see oysters like that again," he said. "It's getting overfished. People don't move oysters around like they used to."

Louisiana maintains state oyster beds where tiny seed oysters can be harvested once a year and moved to private leases. Every oysterman I met had photos of his oyster boat loaded up to the windows with seed oysters.

It's a twenty-four-hour trip each way from Grand Isle to the state beds in Lake Borgne. The investment in fuel, labor, and time can run into the tens of thousands of dollars. It pays off as the oysters mature over a couple of years and the oystermen bring them to market. But the cycle was disrupted by the hurricanes. Oystermen lost not only their boats, they lost the investment they made in their leases.

"The oysters they seeded were lost in the storms," says Collins. "And now there aren't any seed oysters to harvest."

Louisiana is the nation's largest oyster-producing state, with four hundred thousand acres of underwater oyster leases. Before Katrina and Rita, Louisiana oystermen produced 40 percent of all the oysters in the United States, or around 750 million oysters a year. Most of the Louisiana oyster harvest was lost in the season of 2005–2006.

Not a single building was left standing in the town of Empire, the headquarters of the Croatian fishing fleet. This major oyster port, with all its docks, warehouses, ice-making equipment, and trucking facilities, was wiped off the map. Hundreds of boats sank, and the waterways became so cluttered with wreckage that navigation was impossible.

As for the oysters themselves, according to Mike Voisin, seventh-generation oysterman and head of the Louisiana Oyster Task Force, 50 to 70 percent of the oysters in the public beds of Louisiana east of the Mississippi River were dead. Barataria Pass and the Grand Isle region had a 60 percent mortality rate. The oysters that had been planted on leases in these areas were either dead or buried under so much debris they couldn't be dredged.

Fishermen's associations submitted Community Development Block Grant requests to the federal government for aid. The federal government allocated funds to restore the reefs, but gave nothing to fishermen who lost their boats, docks, and offices—an estimated loss of $500 million. Nevertheless, about 70 percent of the oyster fleet is back in operation.

"I believe that in 2006 we will produce 125 million oysters, or 50 percent of what we were producing in Louisiana before Katrina and Rita," said Voisin. "In 2007, we'll be producing 60 to 70 percent of what we were doing before. And maybe in four to five years time—when we've got our own hatchery and we are supplementing Mother Nature—we will be producing 120 percent."

Right after the hurricane, Collins says, the oysters put out the biggest spat set he has ever seen—triple the usual number of spats.

"So we could see a spectacular oyster season in 2008–2009, right?"

"Yeah, unless we get a drought. A saltwater intrusion would wipe us out again."

But regardless of the rebound of the oyster reefs, Voisin worries that negative perceptions about *Vibrio* and pollution in Louisiana waters will make it difficult for Gulf oysters ever to regain their former market share. American oyster-eaters and oyster-buyers are afraid of Gulf oysters.

I asked Collins how much it would hurt his business if the sale of raw half-shell oysters was banned in the summer.

"Not much," he said. "We sell only about ten bags of half shells a week in the summer."

So would he support some kind of regulation banning summer half-shell sales for the good of the oyster industry?

"No way. I would fight it," he said.

"But why, if it wouldn't cost you anything and it helped the reputation of Gulf oysters?" I asked.

"Because if you let them make one rule, then they are going to make another rule," the young man said.

Gossen shot me an angry glance. He had tried to explain to me that this kind of conversation wasn't going to make me any friends down here. "You have to understand these people," he told me in the car as we drove over here. "Grand Isle was Jean Lafitte's island. These people are descended from pirates. They hate the government."

"Let me ask you something," I questioned Collins as he continued to rant about the government. "Do you have any ancestors who were pirates?"

"Well it's funny that you ask, because somebody who did up a family tree said my grandmother Temise was a direct descendant of Jean Lafitte," Nick Collins said.

In the front yard of a ranch-style home in Golden Meadows, Louisiana, across the street from Bayou Lafourche, a stagnant canal that was once

a branch of the Mississippi River, there was a sign that read COLLINS
OYSTER CO., GRANDE ISLE SALTY OYSTERS FOR SALE, BY THE SACK ($50)
OR HALF SACK ($30). RING BUZZER.

"This is Captain Wilbert's house," Gossen told me. Wilbert Collins
was Nick Collins's father. I rang the buzzer and we went to the front door
and asked if we could speak with Captain Wilbert Collins. When Collins
came to the door, I asked if I could interview him. He let Gossen and me
come inside. But he didn't invite us to sit down.

We stood awkwardly in the dining room. Captain Wilbert had just
returned from a trip to New Orleans to pay the yearly fees on his oyster
leases. Covering two walls of his dining room were maps of the waters
of Barataria Bay and the Grand Isle region, with all the oyster leases out-
lined in red pencil. We looked at the maps on the wall for a while and
asked Captain Wilbert a few questions.

Things weren't going very well. When I asked him about how the
government might aid the oyster industry, Captain Wilbert launched
into an explanation of his pet conspiracy theory—he thought that the
lack of federal assistance for oystermen after Hurricane Katrina was a
plot to get rid of them. And the oilmen were in on it too.

I looked over at Gossen, who rolled his eyes and nodded his head
toward the door. He wanted to hit the road before I got old Captain
Wilbert riled up any more.

I tried to calm things down by asking Captain Wilbert some easy
questions. Like, how long had he been in the oyster business? He said he
had been oystering for fifty-six of his sixty-nine years, and he was third-
generation. "My grandfather tonged from a skiff. His hand was as hard
as a shell," he said. He talked about how much larger the oysters were in
the old days.

That gave me an idea. I sat down uninvited and opened my laptop
on his dining room table. I brought up a photo I had taken of two giant

oysters at the Taylor Shellfish plant in Shelton, Washington. "Talk about big oysters, take a look at these," I said to Captain Wilbert.

"Hey! That's Bill Taylor," he said, pointing to the guy holding the oysters. I showed Captain Wilbert a few more photos of oyster folks from around the world, many of whom he recognized. Then Captain Wilbert sat down and started holding forth. I felt like we were both members of an international secret society, and we had just given each other the secret handshake.

"I never did like the flavor of those Washington oysters," he confided. "They say they taste like watermelon and cucumbers and all kinds of vegetables. Me, I like oysters that taste like seafood. Connecticut oysters have the same taste as Louisiana oysters. I went to the Grand Central Oyster Bar one time; they had twenty kinds of oysters. They charged me $60 for two dozen!"

Captain Wilbert spoke English with a heavy Cajun accent, as do many people in this part of the country. "Fifty years ago, no one spoke English around here," he said. "Then when I went to school, the English-speaking teachers would hit your hand with a ruler if they heard you speak French." But the French culture is still strong in this isolated enclave in the Deep South.

I asked Captain Wilbert how the Cajun oystermen ate oysters in the old days and what they drank with them. They didn't drink any particular beverage, he said, because they ate oysters at every meal, in gumbo, in dressing, fried, and stewed.

"Everyone fished for a living. Oysters or crabs, or both. The French were on one side [of the peninsula], and the Croatians were on the other side. The Croatians were city people. They sold their oysters in New Orleans. They stayed away from the Cajuns. There used to be seventeen French oyster companies along Bayou Lafourche in the 1960s and 1970s. I am the only one left."

Did they eat only cooked oysters when he was growing up? "No. My parents loved raw oysters too," he said. "They served marinated oysters, raw oysters in hot sauce with onions and peppers. My mother, Temise, ate only the muscle. She threw the belly away. But in those days the oysters were too big for women. Just the muscle was the size of a scallop."

I wondered what they would think about that in Brittany. Temise ate the foot, all right, but she threw the rest of the oyster away. The majority of the French settlers of Acadia came from the Poitou region, just south of Brittany and north of Arcachon. I wondered if people from Brittany would recognize anything from the seafood-based Cajun cuisine.

Beyond the language, there were a lot of similarities between the oyster culture of Grand Isle and the oyster culture of France. In this part of Louisiana, as in Brittany, the entire population was savvy about oysters, and most had a relative in the business. And in both places, oysters were most often consumed at home. In Cajun Louisiana, as in France, oysters are a part of everyday life.

Before we left, I bought a half gallon of shucked oysters from Captain Wilbert for $40. They didn't look like any shucked oysters I had ever seen. They were bright and clear, not opaque. That's because Captain Wilbert doesn't wash the oysters, I was told.

The oysters were also incredibly salty, much saltier than most I'd encountered in southern Louisiana. "Last week I had some oysters that were too salty to eat," Captain Wilbert shrugged. "Every oyster bed is different."

Consistently salty oysters are hard to come by in Louisiana. So I asked him if he ever added saltwater to the plastic tub full of shucked oysters.

"Sometimes," he admitted sheepishly. "But you can't use too much because it makes the oysters shrink."

When my fried-oyster poor boy arrived, I asked fourth-generation oysterman Jules Melancon how his great grandfather, Duard Eymard, got
started in the oyster business.

"He was a bootlegger. Oysters were a front for smuggling liquor and
illegals," Melancon said as he bit into his hamburger. "Boats were built
for speed in the old days. Which made them good for smuggling too. My
great grandfather had liquor buried all over the backyard. When he died,
we found cigar boxes full of money in the attic."

We were eating lunch at the Leeville Seafood Restaurant on Louisiana
Route 1, across the bridge from Grand Isle and close to the dock where
Melancon kept his boat. We had stopped by the boat to pick up a DVD of
a two-hour interview with Melancon's father and grandfather. We chose
the restaurant because the fried oysters were big and plump and nearly
greaseless. The three of us split an order of twelve as an appetizer. I liked
them so much, I got the fried-oyster poor boy for lunch.

I asked Jules if his grandfather was a smuggler too.

"In the early days, probably. In the 1930s, my great grandfather used
to hide illegals, Chinese and Filipinos, in fifty-five-gallon drums right on
the deck. He had five oyster boats in Grand Isle. My grandfather worked
on the boats too, and he must have known what was in those barrels.

"My grandfather Louis Eymard was called 'Captain Beto.' He was a
millionaire at forty, but it wasn't from smuggling. He made it all from
the oyster business. He got paid partly in cash, and he hid a bunch of the
money in the walls of his house so he didn't have to pay tax on it.

"In 1969, on the night of the first oyster festival in Bayou Lafourche,
while my grandfather, Captain Beto, was being crowned the king of the
oyster festival, somebody broke into his house and stole all the money.
They knew where everything was. It was somebody in the family.

"He almost had a heart attack. He cried like a baby for weeks. Of course he owned property and had lots of money in the bank too, so he didn't starve. In fact, they found oil on some of the land he owned."

"He's ninety-four now. I bring him oysters sometimes, but he won't eat them. He says they don't taste the same anymore. I keep trying to tell him that it's him that doesn't taste the same anymore."

Jules Melancon and his wife Melanie ran the most popular oyster business on Grand Isle for many years. Jules ran the boat and harvested oysters on some of the best leases in the area. Melanie worked beside her husband on the boat during the busy seeding season. The rest of the year she supervised the shucking operation and ran the retail "oyster shop" on Grand Isle.

"My wife Melanie grew up in the oyster business too," said Jules. "She was a St. Pierre." Standing in the driveway of their home on Grand Isle, Melanie showed me the scars on her arms where the dredge chains pinched her while she worked on the boat alongside her husband. "I was the Oyster Queen," Melanie laughed.

During hurricane Katrina, Grand Isle was completely under water. When the flood subsided, the Melancon's oyster shop was gone. And so were their oyster beds. Melanie thinks the Louisiana oyster business is doomed, that there will never be another season like those of the good old days.

"I started driving the boat when I was eleven," Jules said, remembering his beginnings in the business. "My dad and my grandpa were partners. I tried college for two years, worked in the oil field for four years, but thirty years ago, an oil field worker didn't make as much as an oysterman. So I took over daddy's leases. He gave me the business for $60,000. I had some good years. I had a cooler in my front yard full of oysters and people would just stop by and leave their money in a cigar box. That was the best."

After lunch, we stuck the DVD into my laptop. The recording was an oral history of Jules's grandfather, Louis Eymard, and his father, Layman Melancon, talking about the way oysters were harvested in Louisiana in the days of the tongers. The interview was in French, so Jules translated for me.

The family's oyster business was headquartered on Independence Island, and their oyster leases adjoined it. The family operation had five steam-powered schooners that were later outfitted with diesel engines. The schooners hauled seed oysters from the beds at Lake Borgne. The seed oysters had to be kept in pens along the shore of the island to keep them away from the redfish until they were big enough. When they reached two inches or so, they were spread on the lease beds.

Crews of men worked from skiffs, tonging for oysters all day long, and lived at the camp on the island. "We lived on white beans and fried oysters and oyster soup," one of the oystermen recalled. A thousand sacks of oysters were delivered to the French Quarter twice a week by diesel schooner for the restaurant trade. But the big money was in steamed oysters.

The Southern Shellfish Company bought raw oysters, then steamed and canned them. "They shrink up tiny when you steam them, like those smoked oysters you get in the can now," Jules explained. Before refrigeration, canning was the most practical way to preserve oysters.

The oystermen were paid by the yield. But the cannery could handle all the oysters the oystermen could produce. "When Louisiana oysters were short, we went and worked in Texas or Mississippi," the oystermen on the DVD said. The oyster season was closed from Easter to Labor Day. In the summer they used the oyster boats to haul cattle to market.

"Independence Island is gone now," Jules told me. "It was lost to coastal erosion. We still own it—but it's underwater."

Louisiana State University is including Jules Melancon's leases in an experimental program to test the viability of growing oysters in the French rack-and-bag system, in which cultivated seed oysters are grown in mesh sacks suspended on poles that keep the oysters out of the mud, making them easy to harvest. LSU is also experimenting with triploid oysters in southern Louisiana.

"The tests began last year," said Jules. A limited number of racks had already been installed on his leases, and the first oyster sacks had been loaded.

"So how did the tests go?" I wanted to know.

"They didn't get any results," Jules said. "Somebody stole all the oysters."

My car was loaded with oysters when I left Grand Isle on Saturday morning, December 30, hoping to get back to Houston in time to watch the Texas Longhorns college bowl game on television that afternoon. I had half a boat bag of Nick Collins's Chinaman's Reef oysters in the shell, and what was left of the salty shucked oysters from his father, Captain Wilbert, in a plastic tub in a cooler in my trunk.

By the time I got to the first Avery Island exit on Highway 90, it was 10:30 AM and I was getting very hungry. I pulled off the highway and parked in front of the Pennywise Convenience Store in the Mobil Station.

I bought a single sleeve of saltines, a bottle of Tabasco sauce, and a cup of coffee at the convenience store. I also helped myself to a plastic fork. I took the tub of shucked oysters out of the cooler, opened it, and set it on top of the blue-and-white Igloo cooler. Standing in front of the open trunk of my car, I fished oysters out of the tub. I slid each one onto a cracker and doused it with Tabasco, and washed them all down with a cup of hot black Community Coffee.

When I told my friend Pableaux Johnson, who grew up Cajun in St. Martinsville, that I thought I had experienced the classic Cajun oyster breakfast, he objected. The appropriate beverage would have been beer, he argued.

"But it was in the morning, and I was driving," I said.

"Weenie," he heckled.

BAYOU LAFOURCHE HUÎTRES MARINÉES (MARINATED OYSTERS)

There aren't any oyster bars on Grand Isle or along Bayou Lafourche, although people eat lots of raw oysters. Rather than shuck them, locals go to their favorite "oyster shop" and buy a half gallon of unwashed, freshly shucked oysters. When company is coming, they often put out *huîtres marinées,* a big bowl of freshly shucked raw oysters marinated in a lemon juice sauce.

> 2 dozen freshly shucked Grand Isle oysters and their liquor
> 4 tablespoons lemon juice
> 1 teaspoon Tabasco sauce
> 1 teaspoon prepared horseradish
> 1 tablespoon catsup (optional)
> Salt to taste
> Freshly ground pepper to taste
> 2 tablespoons minced red onion
> 2 tablespoons minced green pepper

Combine the oysters and their liquor with the lemon juice, Tabasco sauce, horseradish, and catsup (if desired), plus salt and pepper to taste. Chill the mixture well, then transfer to a decorative bowl. Garnish with red onion and green peppers. Provide diners with cocktail forks or toothpicks and small plates so they can spear their own oysters. Serve with saltines and additional Tabasco sauce and lemon wedges.

Serves four to six.

ELEVEN

Rodney's Sand Dune

"Like a large breast in a small brassiere," said Rodney Clark as he held up the oyster he'd just shucked. The oyster meat was so fat, it bulged out of the cup of its bottom shell. "It doesn't get any better," Rodney said admiringly. "That, my friend, is a perfect oyster."

The perfect oyster was a *C. virginica* from an oyster farm on Prince Edward Island that called its oysters "Sand Dunes." It measured three and a half inches long and two and a half inches wide, and it was the climax of five years of traveling around the oyster-eating world not knowing exactly what I was looking for.

Now I know. And I owe it all to Rodney.

I had traveled to Rodney's Oyster House in Toronto in December of 2007. Jon Rowley was my traveling companion this time. Rowley insisted that I had to meet Rodney Clark if I wanted to understand North American oyster culture.

Rodney had established a middle ground in the oyster world. He bought oysters from both the new oyster farmers and the old oyster fishermen, but he wasn't drinking anybody's Kool-Aid.

When I arrived to visit him, the fifty-something oyster maven was dressed in blue jeans, a turquoise vest, and a flat cap. I sat down at his desk with my hat in my hand. "Rodney, what makes a great oyster?" I asked.

It sounds like a stupid question. But while I had eaten a lot of oysters and knew when they tasted good, I had yet to figure out exactly how to judge them. I'd heard a lot of varying opinions on the matter, but many of them were suspiciously self-serving.

"Here at the oyster bar, we had to develop our own grading system for oysters. The guys packing the boxes don't want to hear about grading systems," Rodney told me. "Right now you are lucky to get ten decent-sized oysters in a box of a hundred."

To decide on the price, Rodney's Oyster House rates the oysters it buys on a thirty-point scale. There's a one to ten rating for size, a one to ten rating for shell shape, and a one to ten rating for meat quality. "When it comes to oysters, size matters," Rodney said as he went at a Lamèque Island oyster with his customized "Chesapeake bugeye" shucking knife. "Big and fat is what you want."

Clark is an artist by training, which is probably why his colorful explanations of oyster attributes were so easy for me to understand.

If the oyster meat is sunken down into the shell, the oyster is "skinny." There's not much flavor in skinny oysters. They get skinny when there isn't enough food (plankton) in the water. (Makes sense, right?) When there's enough food in the water and the season is right, the oyster meat usually fills the bottom shell and you get an adequate oyster or even a very good oyster. And when the food in the water and the season and the temperature are all just right, you might be lucky enough to find one that's perfect.

The perfect oyster is not merely the result of geography; it's the product of a synergy of natural forces. The oyster has to mature in

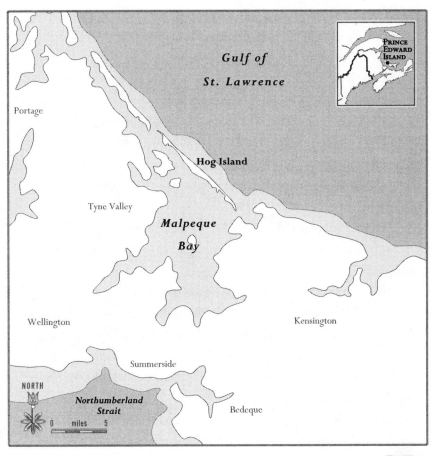

Gulf of
St. Lawrence

Portage

Hog Island

Tyne Valley

*Malpeque
Bay*

Wellington

Kensington

Summerside

NORTH

*Northumberland
Strait*

0   miles   5

Bedeque

Malpeque Bay, P.E.I., Canada

uncrowded conditions over months and years. The fresh water flowing into the oyster bed has to be loaded with plankton. A few months before harvest, the water has to be cold enough for long enough to cause the oyster to fatten. That's when you get spectacular oyster meat that looks like "large breasts in small brassieres," as Rodney so aptly put it. And then, like a vine-ripened tomato, the bulging ripe oyster has to be taken from its bed at just the right moment.

Rodney handed me the Lamèque oyster when he got it open. The meat filled the shell, but didn't bulge out like the Sand Dune on the plate in front of me. "You see the dark spot of the oyster's stomach?" he asked, pointing with the shucking knife. The flesh of the Lamèque oyster was partially transparent, so you could see some of its organs through the meat. "That transparency means the oyster hasn't fattened up enough," he explained.

"Now look at the color of the Sand Dune," he said. The meat of the fat Sand Dune was creamy beige and completely opaque. "That's the color of fat."

"Now look at these muscles," Rodney said, drawing a circle on top of the round white muscles in the middle of the two oyster meats with the tip of his shucking knife. The Sand Dune had a much larger abductor muscle than the Lamèque. The oyster uses the abductor muscle to hold the shell closed. It must be severed from the top shell by the oyster shucker to get the oyster open.

The scallop-shaped meat of the abductor muscle, which is also called the "eye," has a chewier texture and a nuttier taste than the softer surrounding tissue. "The scallop eye gets bigger as the oyster gets older," Rodney said. An oyster with a large "eye" has a more rounded flavor and a chewier texture than a younger oyster.

"Now look at the firmness. 'Benign' and 'flaccid' are two words dreaded in the bedroom and the oyster bar," Rodney joked as he poked the Sand Dune meat so that it moved around in the bottom shell. "You want your meat hard—it should be the texture of an artichoke bottom."

There should be plenty of oyster liquor; a good shucker doesn't spill much, he said. Rodney instructed me to pick up the Sand Dune specimen, and he picked up the Lamèque. "Now touch it to your lips," he said as he sipped a little of the oyster liquor. I followed his lead.

"What do you get?" Rodney closed his eyes and described the sensations. "First cold and then saltiness, with a touch of sweetness."

Then he opened his eyes and went on a rant. "People say oysters taste like the sea—rubbish," he said. "Have you ever tasted seawater? It's bitter. Oyster liquor is sweet," he said as he sipped a little and I did the same.

The oyster takes in seawater and runs it through its body, filtering out the food and minerals and giving it a little of its own flavor. "What you are tasting isn't seawater, it's oyster blood."

"Don't try to eat the oyster from the hinge side; eat it from the lip side, so it slides into your mouth easy," he said tilting back the half shell and chewing. I followed his example.

As I chewed, the taste of the perfect oyster exploded in my mouth. It wasn't that the flavors were different from those in other oysters I had eaten, there were just a lot more of them. Canadian oysters are always much saltier than the Gulf oysters I am used to. But the sweetness of the big Sand Dune was off the charts. It was as if I had stuffed my mouth full of butterscotch and sea salt. A vaguely mineral aftertaste lingered for quite a while after I swallowed, as if I'd licked the aluminum foil after removing the candy bar.

Rodney's called the largest ones Sand Dune No. 3s and sold them for $4.25 each—the highest price on the oyster menu. The little Sand Dunes that came in the same box averaged only two and a half inches; they were called Sand Dune No.1s and priced at \$2.59. The Lamèques sold for \$2. (Prices in this chapter are given in Canadian dollars.)

Rodney's Oyster House sells five species of oysters, but Rodney made no apologies for the fact that he likes *C. virginicas* the best. Eat them side by side with the other four species, and odds are you'll prefer the sweetness of the *C. virginica* yourself. And then there's the familiarity—they are the native oyster of Prince Edward Island, where Rodney grew up.

"These big Sand Dunes are the best oysters in Canada right now," Rodney said. It was one of the best I'd ever tasted. And now I was eager to look for one that was even better.

Malpeque Bay, the largest inlet on Prince Edward Island, is Canada's most famous appellation for oysters. The oyster reefs were overfished at the turn of the century when the federal government took control of the fishery. In 1915, 90 percent of the oysters were destroyed by disease. After a slow recovery, the oyster reefs eventually were repopulated through cultivation efforts.

Tonging is the only method of harvest allowed on the public oyster beds of Malpeque Bay. Rodney estimated that there are 450 active license holders and around a dozen plants that buy the wild harvested oysters. The oyster season on the public reefs of Price Edward Island opens on August 15 and closes in December, when the bays freeze over. Canadian oysters are at their best in late fall and early winter, just before the season ends.

Wild Malpeques are sorted into three grades—commercial, standard, and choice. Commercial oysters are the odd-shaped ones that end up in stews. Standard-grade oysters go to the retail sector, and choice oysters are the ones you see in American oyster bars.

The name Malpeque once meant a top-quality oyster, but today it's at the bottom of the totem pole. The oyster bars I visited in Toronto weren't even selling Malpeques, although I did find some in the seafood stalls at the St. Lawrence Market downtown. They were displayed in a big bin in a jumble of sizes, and they were selling for $7 a pound. I bought some and shucked a few at a table in the market. They were very disappointing. The meats were skinny and flavorless.

"The Canadian oyster industry mimics the Gulf oyster industry," Rodney said. "There is a little aquaculture, but mostly it's a fishery." Like Gulf oysters, Malpeques are cheap, but the good ones are mixed in with the mediocre ones. The best oysters from Prince Edward Island are fattened by leaseholders and then sold under trade names.

Some of the brand-name oysters in Canada are wild oysters gathered by tongers that are then relaid by farmers in private oyster beds, where they're grown to a larger size and fattened for the market.

In Europe, where oysters are graded by weight, you pay more for big No. 1s or No. 2s. If you want a small oyster, you can order a No. 4 or No. 5. But you always know exactly what you're getting. There's no official grading system in North America. That's why Toronto oyster bars started grading oysters themselves.

In the United States, when you order a Malpeque or a Fanny Bay, you might get one the size of a peanut or you might get one the size of a potato. You never know. But lately the oysters seem to be getting smaller and smaller.

One evening during my stay in Toronto, Rodney's Oyster House hosted an "oyster round table." Rodney, Seattle oyster expert Jon Rowley, and several other food writers and I got together to discuss the state of the bivalve. Rodney's son, twenty-three-year-old Eamon Clark, the current Canadian national oyster-shucking champion, opened the oysters. Rodney's lovely daughter, Bronwen Clark, the restaurant's front-of-house manager, orchestrated the event.

"This is a BeauSoleil," Rodney said, holding up a smallish oyster. Bronwen passed one of the small, freshly shucked oysters to each person at the table.

BeauSoleil means "beautiful sun" in French, but it was also the nickname of Joseph Broussard, one of the leaders of the Acadian resistance during the Great Expulsion. After Great Britain took sole possession of Nova Scotia in the early 1700s, French-speaking and English-speaking residents attempted to live together peacefully. The truce ended in 1755 when the English attacked a French fort and found three hundred Acadians among the French troops. In that year, French-speaking citizens began to be arrested and deported from the Maritimes. By 1763, ten thousand Acadians were arrested and deported by the British governor. The French Canadian oyster company, Maison BeauSoleil, is headquartered in Neguac, the village where BeauSoleil and his French Acadian rebels hid out between battles with the British in the summer of 1759.

It was Maison BeauSoleil that started the "cocktail oyster" craze, Rodney explained. Maison BeauSoleil operates three grow-out sites along the sparsely populated New Brunswick coast, close to the northern limit of the *C. virginica*'s range. At this latitude, oysters are extremely slow growing.

Although the BeauSoleil oyster we sampled was small, the meat was dense and very tasty. The company developed a floating bag system that allows oysters to be cultivated in warmer water near the surface during the summer months. The result is a clean oyster with a high density of meat in a small, attractive, rounded shell. "The BeauSoleil cocktail oyster is small, but it's a mature three-year-old oyster," Rodney said as we sampled the meaty little oysters.

"Little oysters can be good, and they are especially good for people who don't know if they like oysters," Rodney explained. "Much of the North American oyster-eating public is at the very beginning of a long learning curve, and we want to encourage them when they come to an oyster bar for the first time. Smaller oysters are less intimidating to the novice," Rodney said, hence their growing popularity.

I wondered if the owners of BeauSoleil were inspired by the popularity of Yvon Madec's boudeuses de Bretagne, the tiny "pouters" of Brittany I'd seen at Le Dôme. The founders of Maison BeauSoleil make no secret of the fact that their marketing is inspired by the French wine and oyster industries. Their oysters are packaged in little wooden boxes with gorgeous graphics.

"BeauSoleil has created a business model that allows growers to get oysters on the market fast," Rodney told those of us assembled at the table.

Oyster farmers often borrow money to buy tiny seed oysters. The loans get paid back when the oysters grow up and get sold. It often takes five years or more for an oyster to reach three inches in cold Canadian waters, and there's a lot of financial pressure to repay the loans as soon as possible.

So the idea of selling smaller oysters after fewer years of growing time is very appealing to oyster farmers and their financial backers. But the success of BeauSoleil spawned a host of imitators who weren't so scrupulous about quality.

"Other growers are taking oysters to the market that aren't ready," Rodney said. There's a huge difference between a meaty, mature oyster in a small shell and the tiny, immature oysters some growers are now bringing to the market.

"Pemaquid Oyster Company in Maine started selling immature oysters under the name Pemamotos," Rodney said. "It was an attempt to knock-off the Kumamoto."

The popularity of the tiny Kumamoto oyster has led a lot of North American oyster growers to try to come up with imitations. To illustrate his point, Rodney served us two more oysters. One was a Kumamoto and the other was an oyster that was sold under the trade name of "Kusshi." It looked just like a Kumamoto.

Kusshis are *C. gigas* oysters that are continuously rotated in a tumbler, Rodney explained. "It looks like a bingo machine." The rotating action prevents the oyster from developing a pointy end, or "beak." The Kusshi oyster is rounded with a deeper well, like a Kumamoto. Both oysters had well-developed meat.

Finally, Rodney served us two more oysters, one of them about the size of a loon, the Canadian one-dollar coin. It was an Olympia *(O. lurida)* oyster. Beside it was its much larger cousin, a Stellar Bay *(O. edulis)* flat. Ironically, it was the larger oyster that was immature in this case.

The European *(O. edulis)* oyster takes five to six years to reach maturity. But oyster diseases are killing off the *O. edulis* oysters in their third years, so producers are bringing immature oysters to market rather than lose their crop. The meat was pink in color and not nearly as flavorful as the little Olympia *(O. lurida)* oyster, which had the big, bold flavor I usually associate with European *(O. edulis)* flat oysters.

As Rodney's demonstration proved, you can't judge oysters by their size, but you can judge them by their maturity. Olympia oysters were once marketed as "cocktail oysters" because of their diminutive size. Lately, the name "cocktail oysters" has been revived as a marketing term for all kinds of smaller-sized oysters.

Cocktail oysters appeal to young oyster-eaters both because of their size and because they are less expensive. You pay an average of around

$25 for a dozen large, or "choice," oysters as they are often known, in a Toronto oyster bar, while a dozen tiny "cocktail" oysters can be had for $17. Lamèque cocktail oysters were the cheapest ones available at Rodney's Oyster House at $1.46 each.

At a hip oyster bar called Oyster Boy, on Queen Street, the grades of oysters offered on the menu included cocktail, medium, standard, choice, and large choice. I compared a couple of large-choice oysters from Colville Bay in New Brunswick, which sold for $3.25 apiece, with a couple of cocktail-sized La Mallet oysters from L'Étang Ruisseau Bar Ltd in New Brunswick, which sold for $1.65 each.

The Colville Bay large-choice oysters contained several tablespoons of oyster meat. The meats from the La Mallet cocktail oysters were so tiny, I slid one into my coffee spoon to measure it. The cocktail oyster yielded a tiny bit above a level teaspoon of meat.

Jon Rowley and I were sitting at Starfish, Patrick McMurray's Toronto oyster bar, sampling oysters. I'd met Patrick McMurray in Galway when he represented Canada at the world oyster-shucking championship.

There weren't any oyster bars in Toronto when Rodney Clark first opened his place in the 1980s. Rodney's enthusiasm proved contagious. Toronto now boasts some of the best oyster bars in North America. And nowhere will you find oysters that are more expertly shucked and beautifully presented. Along with the lemon wedges, fresh baked bread and butter, and oyster sauces, Toronto oyster shuckers grate a little pile of fresh horseradish to go with your oysters. It's a tradition Rodney Clark started.

Rodney also started the tradition of entering his shuckers in the Canadian national oyster-shucking competition. Rodney won the title himself in 1995. Fourteen of the last seventeen Canadian national oyster-shucking champions have worked at Rodney's Oyster House at one time or another. Patrick McMurray went on to become the world champion by winning the Guinness World Oyster Opening Championship in Galway in 2002.

While we were sitting there at the bar, McMurray showed us the custom oyster-shucking knife he used to win the competition. He calls it a pistol-grip knife, since the blade sticks out of the handle at an angle. The handle is made of plastic that has been molded to precisely fit McMurray's grip. McMurray told us that to win the championship, a shucker needed to open each oyster perfectly in two and a half seconds or less.

"This is the knife Ola Nilsson used to win the competition in 2004," McMurray said, handing me the double-bladed knife I'd seen in Galway. Evidently, champion oyster shuckers trade shucking knives with each other.

Starfish was serving the Totten Inlet *C. virginicas* that Rowley had helped develop. But Rowley was distraught to see that all of them weren't the designated size. He told McMurray that the three-and-a-quarter-inch Totten Inlet *C. virginica* had a much fuller flavor than the under-three-inch specimens. And since McMurray had both sizes in front of him, he did a taste test while we watched.

McMurray opened the little oyster first and slurped it down. He said he detected some melon flavors. Then he tasted the bigger one and agreed it had a much more developed flavor.

But I was surprised to hear a Canadian oyster shucker use the "melon" lingo. That's when I picked up a copy of McMurray's recently published book, *Consider the Oyster: A Shucker's Field Guide*, which was lying on the bar. Inside, I found McMurray's oyster flavor wheel.

I have never resolved the issue of how to describe oyster flavors. And it continues to puzzle me. The metaphorical language of wine writing is often emulated in oyster journalism. But if you put a string of evocative terms side by side, it's easy to get confused.

Consider, for example, these five descriptions of the flavor of Kumamoto oysters:

> "*The small Kumamotos grown in the wetlands of Washington have a gentle saltiness, with notes of cucumber and cold milk.*"
> —Matt and Ted Lee, "Oysters,"
> *Martha Stewart Living,* December 2006

> "*The Kumamoto oysters from the South Sound had a strong briny flavor that evolved right on the tongue, tasting of ocean, then shellfish, and then kelp.*"
> —Emily Hall, "Crappy Day; Cheap Luxury,"
> *The Stranger,* December 4, 2003

> "*Bite-size, fresh-smelling, and crunchy, [Kumamotos] have . . . a fresh, slightly nutty flavor.*"
> —R. W. Apple Jr., "The Oyster Is His World,"
> *New York Times,* April 26, 2006.

> "*Sweet, buttery, and moderately briny, the Kumamoto is a raw-bar favorite.*"
> —Jane Daniels Lear,
> *Gourmet,* November 2006

> "*The most delicate, diminutive oyster, a whisper of the sea on the tongue . . . slightly larger than Olympias, with a more assertive coppery flavor.*"
> —Product description on Amazon.com
> for Dean and Deluca's Kumamoto oysters

Wine writers once faced a similar adjective-overload problem, which was largely solved by the creation of the UC Davis Wine Aroma Wheel. The wheel standardized some of the descriptions of wine aromas and flavors so that wine-industry people could find a common language.

In the early 1980s, San Francisco oyster entrepreneur Billy Marinelli convened a panel of San Francisco food writers and tried to forge a standardized group of adjectives to describe oyster flavors. "Cucumber" and "melon" were among the words famously included on Marinelli's oyster adjective list. Marinelli's efforts got the ball rolling, but didn't yield any agreement.

McMurray's oyster-flavor wheel is the latest attempt I've seen to come up with some standard terms. Flavor wheels are evidently quite popular in Canada—the Canadian agricultural authority has even created one to describe the nuances of flavor found in maple syrup. (Standard terms include "marshmallow" and "cloves.")

McMurray's oyster flavor wheel is divided into three areas, for aromas, flavors, and aftertastes. Each of these is then subdivided. All in all, fifty-five words or phrases are proposed to describe oysters. (Yes, cucumber and melon are included.)

Personally, I found some of these terms very helpful. The wide differentiation between metallic flavors, including stainless steel, iron, tin, copper, bronze, and brass certainly expanded my vocabulary (though I am at a loss to tell the difference between bronze and brass).

But it seemed like there were an awful lot of words that described the same thing. What's the difference between "bland," "neutral," and "soft" in the aromas? Or "forest floor," "potting soil," and "silt" in the aftertastes? I'm not sure anyone cares about the subtle differences between "sulfury-egg," "sulfitic-match, rubber," and "sulfidic-sewage, gas" in the bad aftertaste department. And at least one of the floral aroma words, "alstroemeria," isn't all that helpful to horticultural illiterates such as myself.

I sympathize with McMurray's motivations and admire his courage, but I'm not quite ready to subscribe to the flavor wheel. Some of these words sound to me a little too much like they were coined by an over-zealous marketing executive.

I asked Rodney Clark where he stood on the matter, and he had a typically diplomatic stance. If such "garden words" as "cucumber" and "melon" help engage the first-time oyster-eater's imagination, then we shouldn't hesitate to use them, Rodney told me. You just have to be aware that the old salts will roll their eyes at these kinds of flowery adjectives. He said he preferred "ocean words" and more common terms like "sweetness," "minerality," and "saltiness" when talking about specific oysters.

Rodney maintains his neutrality in the riff between fishermen and farmers. He buys a lot of farm-raised oysters now. But he grew up around fishmongers. When his oyster bar first opened, he served oysters from the same supplier on Prince Edward Island that his father once traded with. "The wild Malpeque oysters used to be as good as that Sand Dune," Rodney lamented. "But not anymore."

"The wild oysters in Galveston Bay are good at the right time of year," I told Rodney. "But I have never had a Texas oyster as sweet as the Sand Dune you gave me."

Rodney surprised me by asking if I could put him in touch with an oyster dealer in Texas. He said he was looking for oysters to serve in January and February, when Canadian oysters went out of season. That's when Gulf oysters are the tastiest—and half the price of anything else on the market.

"Every oyster has a place at the table," Rodney said. And let that short sweet summation become the treaty that ends the silly war between American oyster cultures.

When I walked into the men's room of Rodney's Oyster House, I noticed three beautifully framed art photos on the far wall. All three depicted "bearded oysters," as that part of a woman's body has been euphemistically dubbed. On the surrounding walls, there was a wide variety of photos of amply endowed women. I wasn't thinking about sex when I walked into the men's room, but I certainly had it on my mind when I walked out.

Rodney explained that the photos in the men's room, as well as the Polaroids of people in various states of undress hanging on the walls of the dining room, were part of the ambiance that made Rodney's Oyster House famous.

The 1980s, when the oyster bar first opened, were boom years in Toronto, Rodney explained. The economy was soaring. But the bankers and financial types who worked downtown were a straight-laced bunch. The city needed somewhere to loosen up and get naughty, and Rodney's Oyster House filled that niche.

"The oyster provided the means to loosen up. A few oysters, a few drinks, and pretty soon the shirts came off and we had people dancing on the bar," Rodney recalled.

There was a book of photographs called *The Red Book* that used to be on display at the bar. "It started out with photos of people slurping oysters off of each other," Rodney said. "But it descended into pornography and I had to remove it." I asked if I could see it, but Rodney declined, saying, "It's in a museum now."

A working girl the employees called "The Cat Woman" frequented Rodney's Oyster House in the old days too. "She groped men at the bar. It was quite a floor show for some of the tables nearby. But we had to ask her to leave. She wrote us a very lovely letter apologizing for taking advantage of our hospitality."

When money tightened up and the 1980s financial boom came to an end, the wildness subsided at Rodney's Oyster House. The men's room photos are some of the last relics of that era. "These two photographer friends of mine got into a pissing parade to see who could get me the best shots of hot girls to hang in the restroom," Rodney said with a shrug.

The men's room photo gallery at Rodney's Oyster House drew the ire of a prominent Canadian feminist. "These are photos by famous photographers," Rodney protested. "But, you know, the difference between art and pornography is in the lighting."

I showed Rodney some of my own oyster photos on my laptop, confessing that oysters had become something of an obsession with me. I was supposed to have turned in this oyster book I was working on three years ago, but I kept thinking of new places I had to go to eat oysters.

He said he recognized the symptoms, and it didn't look good. "You're fucked. You'll be working on this book for the rest of your life."

I asked him if he had given any thought to the question of why it is, exactly, that people become so impassioned about oysters. He answered my question with a story.

"I broke my ankle once playing hockey," Rodney said. "I needed to go to the emergency room and get a cast. I was driving an '87 Toyota van with a refer [refrigerator] unit on top at the time. In the back, I had a load of oysters. Before I went to the hospital, I drove to my cold storage and unloaded two and a half tons of oysters on a broken ankle. Up and down steps. It hurt like hell, but I had to do it. I couldn't kill all those oysters.

"Oysters are alive. It's not like they are your pets or anything, but you do have a relationship with them, whether you realize it or not. It's the same reason that oysters are an aphrodisiac."

Rodney described the act with a flurry of gestures: You wrestle with this being and defeat its defenses to open its shell—and then, while it's lying there completely vulnerable and *tout ouvert*, as the French would say, you devour it. It's bound to have an effect on you. What a powerful thing—to eat this creature while it's still alive.

TWELVE

In My Bleeding Backyard

AT MY FEET WAS A BUCKET for empty shells. On the counter was a bowl full of freshly shucked oyster meats. My thumb was bleeding a little where an oyster shell had nicked it. Leaning over the sink, rinsing off another muddy oyster and prying it open with the big blunt "Galveston knife," I had a weird feeling—like my kitchen had been transported back in time. I expected to see the iceman come in the back door carrying a ten-pound block of ice in his tongs.

A few years ago, I would never have thought of shucking oysters at home. I wasn't set up for it. I didn't know where to store them. I didn't have an oyster knife—and wouldn't have known how to use one if I did. I was still in this mode when I visited Hog Island Oyster Company and failed to take advantage of the opportunity to bring some oysters back to my French host, Ray.

Ray gave me so much grief about coming back oysterless from Hog Island that I started thinking about eating oysters at home. I knew where to buy them. I knew how to shuck them. So why didn't I have any at my house?

When the 2005 oyster season started, I resolved to start buying bags of oysters right off the boats from Misho Ivic down in San Leon. The Texas season opens in November, so I bought my first sack for Thanksgiving. Since the oysters aren't very sweet at that time of year, I tested recipes for oysters Bienville and oysters Rockefeller and put a couple dozen in the turkey stuffing. My guests were impressed.

But that still left me with three dozen or more leftover oysters. As luck would have it, I have an extra refrigerator in my garage. It's an early 1970s model in an outdated shade of "harvest gold" and it leaks water on the floor. I keep beer in it. But it also proved to be an ideal place to store oysters.

If you keep oysters on ice, you have to drain the container constantly. If the oysters are covered with ice melt, they will take in this freshwater and discharge their salty oyster liquor—and then they will taste terrible. But if they are kept cold and dry, Gulf oysters *(C. virginicas)* are very good about keeping their shells closed, so you can store them for several weeks in a refrigerator.

For the week after Thanksgiving, I stood over the sink every morning, shucking a few oysters for breakfast. The perfect ones I ate with a drop of Tabasco, a cracker, and coffee. The rest I dumped into the shucked oyster bowl on the counter. These often ended up with bacon and eggs in a Hangtown Fry.

Suddenly, I started paying attention to the various styles of oyster knives. And I began noticing the old oyster plates and oyster cans that some of my friends collected. I felt like I was more in touch with Gulf Coast food culture than I ever had been before.

Oysters aren't such an expensive delicacy if you learn how to shuck them yourself. I paid $18 for a hundred-count bag of Galveston oysters. That's eighteen cents apiece. They are even cheaper if you buy them in boat sacks.

On the Friday before the Super Bowl in 2007, I stood in a refrigerated shed next to the truck dock at Misho's Oyster Company in San Leon, looking over a couple hundred sacks of oysters. According to the white tags attached to each bag, the oysters came from several different places. Some were from Galveston Bay; others were from Espiritu Santo Bay farther south.

With oyster knives in hand, my friend and fellow oyster lover Bernard Brunon and I selected samples from each lot. We'd driven down to Misho's Oyster Company in Bernard's pickup truck.

Bernard was born and raised in France. He had worked as an artist in Houston for more than eighteen years when I met him. We became close friends thanks in part to our mutual love of oysters. Bernard is not only an oyster connoisseur, he is a hell of a shucker.

The first time he volunteered to shuck at one of my backyard oyster feasts was Super Bowl 2006. I was very impressed when he showed me the three scars in his left palm where he'd stabbed himself with an oyster-shucking knife in his youth. I've come to think of such scars as the "shucker's stigmata." It seems like every veteran shucker has at least one.

For Super Bowl 2006, I bought a hundred-count bag of oysters from Galveston Bay and another of oysters from Houma Bay, Louisiana, and we compared them. Galveston Bay won hands down because the Houma Bay oysters were covered with mussels.

In 2007, we decided to raise the oyster count. I paid the lady in the office of Misho's Oyster Company $18 for the hundred-count sack and $35 for a boat sack. For my $53 dollars, I figured I had enough oysters for me and twenty of my closest friends—as long as nobody was going for the Wall of Fame.

The first oysters we tried in Misho's cooler were excellent—salty and sweet. The second ones we tried were even better—plump, very sweet, and very briny. After sampling four or five lots, we settled on the ones we wanted and hoisted them into the truck.

A boat sack holds a bushel, which is usually around 220 oysters. They are becoming less common because so many workers are injured trying to lift them. They can weigh more than eighty pounds. "I don't fool with them anymore," oyster dealer Jim Gossen told me. "Too many workman's comp claims. I stick with hundred-count sacks; they never weigh more than forty pounds."

The oysters in a boat sack are less processed than those in a hundred-count sack. Oystermen put their little oysters in the hundred-count sacks because that's what half-shell eaters want. In a boat sack, you see a wider variety of sizes. (If you buy one, don't try to lift it without help!) Sometimes you also see clusters of oysters still sticking together and odd specimens. We found a seven-inch-long oyster in the boat sack we carried back to Houston.

The party was a huge success, though everyone wanted to hang around the oyster bar and nobody really watched the game.

In 2008, Kelly and I moved our annual oyster party from Super Bowl Sunday to Valentine's Day. The lovers' holiday seemed like a more appropriate day to eat a lot of oysters anyway. The count went up again too. I bought four hundred oysters from Jim Gossen and asked him to find some big ones. He drove down to Grand Isle personally to pick up the oysters. There were quite a few five- and six-inchers. These giant sweet oysters were the hit of the party, and my personal favorites.

From the shell of one giant oyster, I pried off a tiny oyster that had attached itself. Inside the little shell, I found an oyster about as big around as a quarter. While Kelly wasn't looking, I fed my nineteen-month-old daughter, Ava Maeve, her first oyster. She ate it without comment, but didn't want another.

I had more than a hundred oysters left over. They kept very well in the garage fridge, but then again, they were harvested only a day or so before I got them. Some of them were still perfect three weeks later, though most of them began to lose water and look a little shriveled after a week and a half. I ate most of them cooked in stews or with eggs and bacon after the first week.

Kelly didn't eat any of those Valentine's Day oysters. She was pregnant again and feeling nauseous.

Learning to shuck is the home-oyster-club's initiation ceremony. It's not as hard as most people think.

In fact, opening oysters is easy—if you do it with a hammer. And that's what many commercial shuckers do. Early oyster knives had heavy hammer-like handles to break open the oyster before cutting the shell apart.

The thin, pointy side of an oyster, where the upper and lower shells come together, is called the bill, as it resembles a duck's bill. The thick side where the shells are joined is called the hinge. The easy way to shuck oysters is to break the bill and slip a knife inside. Commercial shuckers in Apalachicola use a grinding wheel to cut a notch in the bill of the oyster. If you are shucking to save the oyster meats and you're throwing the shells away, it doesn't matter how you do it.

Shucking oysters for presentation on the half shell is the real challenge, and unless you are seeking employment in an oyster plant, that's probably the kind of shucking you need to learn. I wish that written descriptions could make the chore effortless, but it just doesn't work that way. Be careful, but don't be too intimidated; it's not rocket science.

Ten Tips for Learning How to Shuck

1. Watch an oyster shucker at work. Seeing how it's done is the best way to start. If you can't find an oyster shucker to watch, take a look at the oyster-shucking videos on YouTube or elsewhere on the Internet.

2. Make sure the oysters are good and cold. Cold oysters have less resistance.

3. Use an oyster-shucking knife—don't try to shuck with a butter knife or a screwdriver. For Gulf oysters, you will need a big "Galveston knife"; for little Pacific oysters, you will want a smaller, more delicate oyster knife. Try to avoid the sharp-pointed French oyster knives until you get some experience.

4. Wear a glove on your non-knife-wielding hand or wrap a towel around your hand while you work to cut down on the bloodshed. There's a new metallic "chain mail" oyster-shucking glove on the market that even world champions like Patrick McMurray use sometimes.

5. Start with some small Pacific or Kumamoto oysters if possible; their thin fragile shells are easier to open. *C. virginicas* have thicker shells and require stronger knife blades and more pressure.

6. Lay it down on the table, cup side down. Someday when you have a lot of experience, you can hold the oyster in one hand and the knife in the other. But the easiest way to shuck when you are just starting out is to hold the oyster steady on a table.

7. Screw it open. Don't try to shove the knife into the shell with brute force—that's how people end up stabbing themselves. Insert the knife firmly into a leverage point at the back of the hinge and rotate the knife as if you were turning a screwdriver, first one way, then the other until you get the oyster open a crack. Then insert the knife into the crack and leverage the oyster shells apart.

8. Find the abductor muscle. Cup-side down, draw an imaginary cross on top of the oyster. The abductor muscle is in the top right quadrant.

9. Cut the abductor muscle without scrambling the meat. Once you get the shells apart slightly, you need to insert the knife blade to scrape the muscle away from the top shell while avoiding the meat.

10. Bottoms up. Cut the other abductor muscle away from the bottom shell and flip the oyster meat over for a perfect presentation. (This will also cover up the mess if you cut into the top part of the oyster meat.)

It will take you a long time to shuck the first couple dozen, but you will gain speed with practice.

The traditional Texas accompaniments to half-shell oysters are saltines, lemons, Tabasco sauce, and beer. And I still eat oysters that way on Saturday afternoons while watching football. But now that I've learned how they eat oysters in Paris, Galway, London, and Seattle, I like to mix it up.

For an elegant winter dinner party, I like to serve martinis and oysters as an appetizer. Oysters and stout make a great lunch for company.

For oyster parties, I serve the oysters French-style with lemon wedges and fresh caraway rye from an excellent Jewish bakery. I like to eat the chewy slices of rye with sweet, unsalted French butter sprinkled with large-grain finishing salt on top. The salt crunches when you chew the bread. My oyster party guests are instructed to bring a bottle of their favorite oyster wine.

I usually have a few oysters left over. I look forward to eating oysters by myself while leaning over the sink for the next few days after a party. That's when they really feel like a part of my everyday life.

Eating oysters at home completely changes your point of view about them.

As much as I love oyster bars, I've realized that they are pursuing their own agendas. Except for a few enlightened examples, like Cassamento's in New Orleans, oyster bars are open all year long, so they have a vested interest in convincing you that it's okay to eat oysters in the summer. And that's making it harder to solve the *Vibrio* problem.

And then there's the provincialism. Whether the oyster bar is located in Washington State, New York, or Louisiana, the shucker is going to tell you that his oysters are the best, and that oysters from elsewhere are either too small, too flavorless, too expensive, or they are going to kill you. And a lot of people are taking this jive seriously.

When you hear this stuff, remember Rodney Clark's adage: "Every oyster has a place at the table."

In March of 2008, I put Rodney Clark in touch with Houston seafood dealer Jim Gossen. The first Gulf oysters ever sold at a Toronto oyster bar were from Galveston Bay, Texas. Gossen asked the Jeri's Seafood folks to set aside some select large oysters. Since it was March, the Texas oysters were bulging out of their shells, just like Rodney likes them. The oysters started out at a cost of around twelve cents apiece. With packaging and airfreight, they ended up costing Rodney close to $1 each. After Rodney's processing and a retail markup, they sold for more than $3 each at Rodney's Oyster House.

"They may be the first Gulf oysters ever sold in Canada," Jon Rowley speculated.

The Galveston Bay oysters weren't as salty or full-flavored as Canadian oysters, and some of Rodney's employees didn't approve of them. But they sold out quickly and Rodney ordered more. He also began ordering Apalachicola Bay oysters from Thirteen Mile Oyster Company through Jim Gossen that spring. The Gulf oysters filled a hole in Rodney's schedule. They are at their fattest when northern oysters are hard to harvest due to the cold.

These days, I try to emulate Rodney Clark in my oyster shopping habits. I buy Canadian oysters in the early fall, but I pay more than $1 apiece for them wholesale. (They come a hundred to a box, so I split the box with a friend or have a party.) And I eat Connecticut oysters on the half shell when they are at their peak; they run about $1 each. But I really look forward to mid-winter when Gulf oysters are the sweetest.

Oysters seem like an exotic luxury item when you pay $3 apiece for them at an oyster bar. But when you buy the same oysters by the sack and serve them at home, they lose their mystique and become a part of the way you eat.

The American oyster culture will experience a true revival when a lot more of us start eating oysters at home.

In the summer of 2008, Hurricane Ike hit Galveston Bay. Oystermen suffered extensive damage to their boats, their docks, and their buildings. A lot of oysters were covered up with silt and debris when the storm surge receded. Some Texas oyster fisherman told reporters that the Galveston Bay oyster population was a total loss.

After sonar studies of the reefs and test dredgings by Texas Parks and Wildlife, the oyster mortality rate following Hurricane Ike was estimated at around 40 percent for the public oyster reefs in West Galveston Bay and 80 percent for the East Bay area between Smith Point and the Bolivar Peninsula, Lance Robinson told me. Leaseholders were allowed to dredge their oysters up out of the silt and many leases were in good shape. Overall, the oyster harvest will likely be only about 50 percent of normal in from 2008 until 2010.

Texas Parks and Wildlife will seek Federal funds to restore some of 8,000 acres of lost habitat by filling it in with cultch material likes limestone and broken concrete. But marine biologists and naturalists are optimistic about the long-term health of the oyster population. "A hurricane is like a wildfire," one wildlife specialist observed. "It damages the habitat, but it also cleanses it and encourages new, healthier growth."

It's a mistake to think of Katrina, Rita, Gustav, and Ike as isolated natural disasters. Hurricanes have smashed the islands and bays of the Gulf coastline for all of recorded history. And oysters have done just fine.

Sex is their survival mechanism.

Misho Ivic told me about an experiment he witnessed at Texas A&M Galveston some years ago. Gulf oysters were submerged in warm seawater in a shallow plastic pool. Then a sudden influx of cold fresh water was introduced, simulating a storm. The oysters responded by going into a reproductive frenzy. The experiment demonstrates what happens when an oyster population in the wild senses sudden changes in salinity, water temperature or atmospheric pressure.

Huge spat sets are generally observed after a hurricane. If the offspring can survive the maturation period without interference from drought or another storm, oysterman can expect to see record harvests three years later.

"Oysters are uniquely adapted to respond to hurricanes," Robinson pointed out. "Oysters will change their sex from male to female or female to male—whatever it takes to increase the population. Short term, Hurricane Ike will have a detrimental effect on the Galveston Bay oyster industry," he speculated. "Long term, it will probably be positive."

Oysters don't have lobbyists, and they don't vote. And even oyster lovers are unlikely to put the protection of shellfish at the top of their political agenda. But the national interest in protecting wetlands has been brought back into focus by the hurricanes. The wetlands and barrier islands that should have dissipated the force of these storms are gone. After billions upon billions of dollars in damage, restoring our coastline suddenly seems like a real good idea. Hopefully, we'll improve the oyster habitat in the process.

We may envy the oyster utopia that the French have created, but to expect "collective oyster farms" to replace private property in the United States isn't very realistic. But hopefully we can learn a little from the French about how oysters and development can coexist.

We lost our nation's greatest oyster fisheries when pollution and the destruction of wetlands turned New York Harbor, Chesapeake Bay, and San Francisco Bay into industrial-waste dumps, just as the English lost their oysters when the Industrial Revolution contaminated the Thames Estuary. These were once the greatest oyster centers of the world, and they will never come back to their former glory.

But thanks to the Clean Water Act, a lot of American oyster-growing areas—in Washington State, California, Oregon, New England, and the Gulf of Mexico—have recovered. What a shame it would be to lose them yet again.

This is not a blue-state/red-state issue. Cleaning up the waterways of America was a bipartisan effort. It was Ronald Reagan, a Republican president, who signed the Clean Water Act of 1972 into law. George

Bush Sr. and Bill Clinton's administrations both adopted a "no net loss of wetlands" policy that was once vigorously enforced.

Oyster lovers of all political persuasions can only hope that the protection of wetlands and the enforcement of strict clean-water laws return to the top of the American agenda. And maybe, if the Great American Oyster Renaissance really takes off, oyster-eaters can hope for even more.

Perhaps there is an American way, in between the French way and the English way, that could spark a major expansion of the U.S. oyster fishery.

We have a "drug czar" to run the "war on drugs"; how about an "oyster czar" to referee between the many overlapping agencies that regulate the oyster-cultivation business and the oyster fishery? How about creating an "oystermen's guild" to come up with some ideas for cooperative management of wild oyster reefs? And what if we had a little government incentive to build more hatcheries and expand the leases?

Given the fact that the United States has 95,000 miles of coastline, compared to France's 2,100 miles, it's easy to imagine the emergence of an American oyster industry that is bigger and better than the French one—and if bigger and better isn't the American way, then what is?

JON ROWLEY'S WASHTUB OYSTER BAR

Jon Rowley came up with this excellent setup for a portable oyster bar. The shaved ice isn't absolutely necessary, but it sure looks good. Your local grocery store probably uses shaved ice in their seafood display. Ask them in advance to set some aside for the appointed day.

    1 small galvanized washtub
    1 soup pot
    3 ten-pound bags of regular ice
    1 ten-pound bag of shaved ice
    100 oysters, fresh and unshucked
    6 lemons
    2 loaves of fresh caraway rye bread, sliced thin
    1 pound expensive butter
    Fleur de sel (French sea salt of the highest quality)

Wash out the tub and drain it. Turn the soup pot upside down in the bottom of the galvanized tub to cut down on the amount of ice required and the overall weight. Set the tub up so the top is at counter-surface height so that you can display the oysters where people can see them. Fill the tub at least halfway up with the big ice cubes, then cover the top with a layer of finely crushed ice. Shuck as people eat the oysters so they are always freshly opened—don't try to shuck too far in advance.

To serve the oysters:
Provide your guests with plates, oyster forks or toothpicks, napkins, and a place to dump the shells. Beyond that, you can make your oyster party as casual or as elegant as you like.

I like to set up my oyster bar outside. Oysters taste great outdoors in cool weather.

Accompaniments:

French-style

In the middle of the table, place a bowl of lemon wedges, a plate of rye bread, premium quality butter, and sea salt or fleur de sel. Each diner should spread rye bread with butter and sprinkle it with salt as an accompaniment to their oysters. Serve with your favorite oyster wine.

London-style

Substitute martinis, stirred, not shaken (see recipe on page 141), for the wine.

Galway-style

Substitute Irish brown bread (see recipe on page 85) for the rye and Guinness stout for the wine.

Gulf-style

Substitute saltines for the rye bread, Tabasco for the butter, cocktail sauce for the fleur de sel, and cold beer for the wine.

appendix

The Oyster Bars

HERE IS A LIST, in order of appearance, of the oyster bars in this book, accurate at the time of publication.

Gilhooley's Raw Bar
222 9th Street, San Leon, Texas
(281) 339-3813

> Gilhooley's, which has been described by its detractors as a biker bar, has an admittedly rough-hewn ambiance. But when Galveston Bay oysters are sweet and plump, the ones at Gilhooley's are always just a little sweeter and just a little plumper. And during the rest of the year, when smart consumers eat their oysters cooked, there's "oysters Gilhooley," a magnificent plate of barbecued oysters grilled over pecan wood, dusted with Parmesan, and dripping with garlic butter.

Gibson Inn
51 Avenue C, Apalachicola, Florida
(850) 653-2191

The bar at the Gibson Inn is a magnificent place to eat oysters in old Southern splendor. Sit in a captain's chair at the wooden bar, or at one of the half dozen white-linen-covered tables. The bar and restaurant are located on the ground floor of a Victorian mansion overlooking expansive wraparound porches. Founded in 1907 and listed in the National Register of Historic Places, the inn was restored in the mid-1980s.

Drago's Seafood Restaurant and Oyster Bar
3232 N. Arnoult Road, Metairie, Louisiana
(504) 888-9254

Croatian immigrant Drago Cvitanovich worked for two years as a shucker at Acme Oyster House before opening his own oyster bar and restaurant in 1970. The main attraction is a dish that Drago's son Tommy invented: "charbroiled oysters," made by grilling oysters drizzled with garlic butter over a gas flame. Today, 90 percent of Drago's customers order charbroiled oysters.

Acme Oyster House
724 Iberville Street, New Orleans, Louisiana
(504) 522-5973

The Acme Café was founded in 1910 at 117 Royal Street, around the corner from the current location. The café burned down in 1924. It was renamed the Acme Oyster House and opened at its current location in the same year as the fire. The restaurant has won a long list of awards recognizing its status as one of America's favorite oyster bars. Additonal locations: 3000 Veterans Memorial Blvd., Metairie, (504) 309-4056; 1202 N. U.S. 190, Covington, (985) 246-6155.

Cassamento's
4330 Magazine Street, New Orleans, Louisiana
(504) 895-9761

> The sign on the window reads CASSAMENTO's, and then, in smaller letters underneath, OYSTERS. The ambiance of the brightly lit, all-tile interior has been compared to that of a restroom. The restaurant is closed in months without an R. The half-shell oysters are the best in town because they're kept in a metal cold box rather than on melting ice. The fried oysters are cooked in pure lard, and they melt in your mouth.

Moran's Oyster Cottage
The Weir, Kilcolgan, Ireland
353-91-796113

> Considered by some to be the finest oyster bar in the world, Moran's on the Weir serves oysters from the family oyster beds located at the mouth of a stream on Dunbulcaun Bay. The old cottage has been the home to seven generations of Morans. The family has also produced several champion oyster shuckers. Freshly shucked Irish natives, house-baked Irish brown bread with butter, and Guinness stout are the specialties of the house.

Paddy Burke's Oyster Inn
Clarenbridge, Galway, Ireland
353-91-796226

> This legendary pub has served the village of Clarenbridge since 1650. Under the ownership of the late Paddy Burke, it was the site of the first Clarenbridge Oyster Festival in 1954. The oysters are supplied by Kelly's Oysters.

Grand Central Oyster Bar
Grand Central Terminal
89 E. 42nd Street, New York, New York
(212) 490-6650

> Opened in 1913, the Grand Central Oyster Bar is a museum of American oyster eating. Since the renovation of Grand Central Station in 1997, the old oyster bar has once again become a popular eatery. There are regularly more than thirty varieties of half-shell oysters available. Grand Central Oyster Bar currently sells around two million oysters a year.

SoNo Seaport Seafood
100 Water Street, South Norwalk, Connecticut
(203) 854-9483

> This is the company oyster bar of the Hilliard Bloom Shellfish, Inc., and it's just down the street from the historic South Norwalk oyster docks. It's a pretty good bet that you will find the freshest Blue Point oysters in Connecticut here.

The Company Shed
129 Coast Road, West Mersea, Essex, England
01206-382700

> The floors are wet and there's always some shiny fish and raw eels on display. You bring your own bread and beverages, and sit at picnic tables alongside the fresh-fish counter. Yes, it's weird, but it's also the only eatery in the environs of the Colchester oyster beds that serves the local oysters. *Fruits de mer* platters, with an assortment of cold seafood, are excellent. On weekends, Japanese tourists sometimes line up hours in advance to eat here.

J. Sheekey
28–32 St. Martin's Court, London, England
0871-2238016

J. Sheekey got started over a hundred years ago when Lord Salisbury commissioned his favorite fishmonger, Josef Sheekey, to set up an oyster bar in his building. It evolved and expanded into a famous no-frills seafood restaurant. It was acquired by a conglomerate and went bankrupt in 1993. Five years later, J. Sheekey's was restored and reopened by a fashionable restaurant group.

Rules
35 Maiden Lane, London, England
020-7836-5314

Rules opened as an oyster bar in Covent Garden in 1798. The interior is crammed with curiosities, cartoons, and antiques, and the comfortable upholstered chairs and banquettes make you want to stay all night. Oysters on the half shell are still a specialty. So are old-fashioned oyster dishes like steak, kidney, and oyster pie.

Bentley's
11–15 Swallow Street, London, England
020-7734-4756

In 1916, with their oyster business booming, the Bentley family decided to open their own oyster bar in a Victorian building in London's fashionable West End. The interior was inspired by the arts and crafts movement—the oyster bar is a magnificent slab of marble.

Green's Restaurant and Oyster Bar

36 Duke Street, London, England

020-7930-4566

Founded in 1982 by Simon Parker Bowles, Green's of Duke Street, St. James, is a clubby hideout in a fashionable neighborhood for proper gentlemen of excellent taste. Which means: Don't show up in blue jeans and sneakers—and bring a wad of cash.

Wheelers Oyster Bar

8 High Street, Whitstable, Kent, England

01227-273311

If you just want oysters, you can stand in line for a stool at the four-seat counter. Don't forget to bring your own wine. If you want to eat dinner, you better book in advance; there are only a couple of tables in the back dining room and they are always full. You can find a history of this eccentric restaurant, as well as signature recipes, in a 2003 cookbook by author Mandy Bruce called *The Oyster Seekers: Recipes and Stories from Britain's Most Special Seafood Restaurant*, from Metro Publishing of London.

Le Dôme

108 boulevard de Montparnasse, Paris, France

01-43-35-25-81

One of the most magnificent brasseries in Paris, Le Dôme's interior features an art deco–style decor with portraits of famous patrons lining the walls. Le Dôme, which is owned by the same group as Le Zeyer, is considered one of the foremost seafood restaurants in Paris—their oyster selection is the best in the city.

Le Zeyer
234, avenue du Maine, Paris, France
01-45-40-43-88

> At the well-stocked *fruits de mer* display outside under the
> bright yellow awning, you can check out the oyster selections
> of the day. Order the "oyster shucker's choice" and you'll get
> a mixed platter of whatever's freshest. When Henry Miller
> was writing *Tropic of Cancer* in the 1930s, he went to Le Zeyer
> nearly every day.

Huîtrerie Régis
3 rue de Montfaucon (just off boulevard Saint-Germain), Paris, France
01-44-41-10-07

> A tiny, spotless dining room serving a degustation (tasting)
> of Marennes oysters from a premium producer and little else
> besides rye bread, white wine, and coffee, this is a highly recom-
> mended stop for oyster aficionados. If you have ever wondered
> what Marennes oysters are supposed to taste like, this is the
> place to try them.

Brasserie Flo
7, cour des Petites Ecuries, Paris, France
01-47-70-13-59

> It's a real challenge to find this place, which is hidden in a series
> of alleyways in the tenth arrondissement. The sign above the
> door reads BRASSERIE ALSACIENNE FLO. The most old-fashioned
> of the Alsatian brasseries in Paris, Flo is an experience not to
> be missed. The oysters are displayed on the sidewalk outside in
> the winter.

Xinh's Clam and Oyster House
221 W. Railroad Avenue, Shelton, Washington
(360) 427-8709

> Thanks to its association with Taylor Shellfish, the Vietnamese
> seafood restaurant called Xinh's, in tiny Shelton, Washington, is
> one of the best-stocked oyster restaurants in the world. You will
> regularly see four species, including the rare Olympia *(O. lurida)*
> oyster, on the menu. And when they have European *(O. edulis)*
> oysters on hand, you can sample five species.

Elliott's Oyster House
1201 Alaskan Way, Pier 56, Seattle, Washington
(206) 623-4340

> With its spectacular view of the waterfront, Elliott's is a favor-
> ite tourist attraction. In the late 1990s, the restaurant installed
> its showcase oyster bar. Progressive oyster happy hour offers
> great deals on half-shell oysters.

The Brooklyn Seafood, Steak, and Oyster House
1212 Second Avenue, Seattle, Washington
(206) 224-7000

> The appetizer menu offers various tastings of oysters and wines
> and oysters and microbrewery beers. Among the entrées is an
> excellent carpetbagger steak (steak stuffed with oysters). The
> historic restaurant is located in the Brooklyn Building across
> from the Seattle Art Museum.

Rodney's Oyster House
469 King Street West, Toronto, Canada
(416) 363-8105

An old-fashioned oyster house where a broad spectrum of society sits shoulder to shoulder enjoying the best oysters available, expertly shucked, and served in a wildly convivial atmosphere. Former Canadian oyster-shucking champion Rodney Clark has educated a new generation of oyster lovers and set the high standards of service that have turned Toronto into one of the world's top oyster-eating cities.

Oyster Boy
872 Queen Street West, Toronto, Canada
(416) 534-3432

Oyster Boy's slogan is "mollusks for the masses." Located in the grungy Queen Street district, the hip little vest-pocket restaurant features pub-style, chest-height bar tables and a long bar. Six or seven kinds of oysters in a variety of sizes are regularly on hand. Oyster Boy is named for Adam Colquhoun, former Ontario oyster-shucking champion.

Starfish
100 Adelaide Street East, Toronto, Canada
(416) 366-7827

World champion oyster shucker Patrick McMurray's oyster bar is an elegant place for oysters and dinner. The shucking is world-class. Entrées like *steak frites* and grilled fish are also excellent.

Recipe Index

about the author

© Will van Overbeek

ROBB WALSH has been a food writer for twenty years. He has been the restaurant critic for the *Houston Press* since 2000 and was formerly the food columnist for *Natural History* magazine and the editor in chief of *Chile Pepper* magazine. He currently writes for *Gourmet, Saveur,* and other publications. He has been nominated for the James Beard Award thirteen times and won twice. He has also won the Bert Greene Award for Newspaper Food Journalism as well as several awards from the Association of Food Journalists.

Walsh's newspaper and magazine articles appear in several anthologies including *Best Food Writing 2001-2008* and *Cornbread Nation, Best Southern Food Writing I, II & IV,* from the Southern Foodways Alliance and University of North Carolina Press. His books include *The Texas Cowboy Cookbook, Legends of Texas Barbecue Cookbook, The Tex-Mex Cookbook,* and *Are You Really Going to Eat That?*

Visit www.robbwalsh.com for more details and the "Oyster Moments" slideshow.